PEASANTS
VERSUS
CITY-DWELLERS

PEASANTS
VERSUS
CITY-DWELLERS

Taxation and the Burden
of Economic Development

RAAJ K. SAH

JOSEPH E. STIGLITZ

CLARENDON PRESS · OXFORD
1992

Oxford University Press, Walton Street, Oxford OX2 6DP
Oxford New York Toronto
Delhi Bombay Calcutta Madras Karachi
Petaling Jaya Singapore Hong Kong Tokyo
Nairobi Dar es Salaam Cape Town
Melbourne Auckland
and associated companies in
Berlin Ibadan

Oxford is a trade mark of Oxford University Press

Published in the United States
by Oxford University Press, New York

© R. K. Sah and J. E. Stiglitz 1992

British Library Cataloguing in Publication Data
Data available

Library of Congress Cataloging in Publication Data
Sah, Raaj Kumar.
Peasants versus city-dwellers : taxation and the burden of
economic development / Raaj K. Sah, Joseph E. Stiglitz.
p. cm.
Includes bibliographical references and index.
1. Developing countries—Economic policy. 2. Developing
countries—Economic conditions. 3. Rural development—Developing
countries. 4. Rural poor—Taxation—Developing countries.
5. Income distribution—Developing countries. 6. Taxation—
Developing countries. I. Stiglitz, Joseph E. II. Title.
338. 9'009172'4—dc20 HC59.7.S256 1992 91–33923
ISBN 0–19–828581–7

Typeset by Alliance Phototypesetters
Printed and bound in
Great Britain by Biddles Ltd,
Guildford and King's Lynn

PREFACE

This book is written with three audiences in mind: development economists, public finance economists, and economic historians. One objective of this book is to address certain central questions facing today's LDCs (less developed countries) such as: Who should bear the costs of development? How should the investment funds required for modernization be mobilized? Associated with such broad questions are a host of specific policy questions, such as: Should the urban sector be taxed? If taxes are imposed on the urban sector, should they be imposed at a uniform rate or at different rates across different goods and individuals? If differential tax rates should be imposed, on what principles should the rates be differentiated? Should the government provide food subsidies to the urban poor? Should the government tax or subsidize fertilizer and other modern inputs in the rural sector? To what extent should the relative prices of industrial and agricultural goods be moved against or in favour of the agricultural sector? That is, what should the 'size of the scissors' be, to use the terminology employed in the Soviet industrialization debate following the October Revolution and more recently in the People's Republic of China? Alternatively stated in the terminology of modern public finance: What should the appropriate level of taxation or subsidy be on the rural sector?

We believe that the policy issues of the type described above can be addressed only by developing and using models that adequately capture the central features of LDCs. One cannot simply apply the results of the standard neoclassical model to LDCs even if one thinks this model is appropriate for developed countries. Thus, one of the contributions of this book is to construct a range of simple but comprehensive general-equilibrium models of LDCs. These models are simple enough to yield qualitative results and to identify the central parameters relevant for policy analysis, but comprehensive enough to allow us to deal with the great diversity of institutions and behaviour observed in different LDCs.

The issues of development policy that this book addresses are those which LDC governments and their advisers are required to face. For this reason, we have attempted to make the conclusions, and the intuitions and assumptions which lie behind them, accessible to those outside the circle of academic economists. Each chapter contains a statement of the problems at hand and a summary of the analysis.

Another audience this book addresses is that of public finance economists. The past three decades have seen rapid advances in the theory of public finance, for example the analysis of tax incidence within general-equilibrium models, and developments of the Ramsey–Pigou analysis of optimal taxation. But these two strands of the public finance literature have, for the most part, remained apart. We combine some central elements of these two approaches within the context of LDCs. At the same time, we emphasize a more recent development in public finance, namely, the identification of Pareto-improving tax reforms.

A third audience to whom we address this book is that of economic historians. A central concern in the process of economic development is the effect of different policies on the distribution of welfare between the urban and rural sectors. The conflict between these two broadly defined groups constitutes a longstanding controversy. It was at the root of the Ricardo–Malthus debates on the Corn Laws and it lay behind the discussions of industrial tariffs in the United States prior to the Civil War. Some of the models we develop in this book also allow us to look at the Soviet industrialization debate that followed the October Revolution. Our interpretation of these debates is an alternative to the conventional Marxist interpretation in terms of the class struggle or in terms of inevitable historical processes. Similar debates have occurred, with a different terminology and emphasis, in most of today's non-socialist LDCs. This is because the conflict between the town and the country represents a fundamental trade-off in the initial phases of development.

The approach and the models that we have developed are potentially useful outside development economics. Two features of our approach in particular should be noted. First, we represent the economy through a set of reduced-form relationships, which are shown to encompass a variety of microeconomic structural assumptions. This approach provides our analysis with not only a greater generality and compactness, but also with a way of dealing with many of those instances in which there are insufficient data (as is usually the case in LDCs as well as in developed countries) to identify which of several alternative structural hypotheses is correct. Thus, although this book is primarily concerned with issues of taxation, the general methodology which we develop has other applications as well. As an illustration of this, we provide an analysis of the determination of the social cost of labour for the cost–benefit analysis of investment projects.

Second, we have attempted to *derive* many central institutional features of the economy under consideration, based on underlying assumptions such as those concerning technology and preferences. One should not simply take institutions as given. A good theory should attempt to explain why institutions take the form they do, why they differ from country to country, and why they change over a period of time. These issues are not just of academic concern because the same policies interact differently with different institutions. Moreover, policies have consequences for institutional change. For instance, development economics has often taken the urban wage (and often the rural wage too) as institutionally determined. But wages that are above market-clearing levels may well change when government policies change. We develop a general theory of urban and rural wage-determination in which government tax policies may indeed affect wage levels.

Both authors have been interested in the issues addressed in this book for many years. Sah began dealing with these issues in 1975–6 while working for the Government of India. At that time political pressure had already begun to be felt from farmers' organizations for higher prices for their outputs and lower prices for their inputs, and from vocal groups of city-dwellers for lower food prices and for highly subsidized consumption goods distributed through government-controlled shops. By the end of the 1980s these phenomena had already become an institutionalized part of the national agenda, the subject of demagoguery and a source of electoral battles. The situation is essentially similar in many other mixed-economy LDCs though the institutional details vary. Stiglitz's interest was stimulated by an extensive discussion on 'price scissors' with a delegation from the People's Republic of China at a conference at Wingspread, Wisconsin in 1980. This was followed by a reciprocal visit to Beijing sponsored by the US National Academy of Sciences in 1981.

Many individuals have given us their comments on this book and on our joint papers which serve as a basis for this book. We would like to thank Jere Behrman, David Cass, Jacques Cremer, Partha Dasgupta, the late L. K. Jha, Herbert Levine, Michael Lipton, Michael Montias, Lawrence Summers, Gordon Tullock, and Martin Weitzman. Parts of the book have been presented at seminars at the University of California at Berkeley, the University of Chicago, the University of Pennsylvania, Stanford University, and at the World Congress of the International Economic Association in New Delhi in 1986. We have benefited from the comments of the participants. Research assistance was provided by Tetsushi Honda. The typing was done by Glena Ames. Support for the research was provided by the International Center for Economic Growth, the Olin Foundation, the National Science Foundation, and the Hoover Institution. To all of them, we are most grateful.

University of Chicago   R.K.S.
Stanford University   J.E.S.

CONTENTS

PART I

An Introduction to Issues and
Methodology

1

INTRODUCTION

The last three decades have witnessed, in numerous LDCs (less developed countries), riots, protests, demonstrations, and other forms of civil unrest through which city-dwellers have attempted to persuade the government to lower or maintain food prices. At the same time food producers have attempted to put pressure on the government to raise food prices. The list of countries which have faced such civil unrest includes Argentina, Bolivia, India, Israel, and Zaïre. These events continue to focus attention on a basic but unresolved question: Who should bear how much of the burden of the cost of development? The process of growth requires investments; it requires that the present generation make sacrifices, in the hope that future generations may be better off. But who among the current generation should bear how much of this burden?

There is a simple rhetorical answer: the rich. However, an unfortunate fact of life for most LDCs is that there are not enough rich people. Even if the entire wealth of the richest 5 per cent of the population were confiscated and used to finance investment, there might still be insufficient investment funds. Thus, part of the burden must be borne by the workers in the urban sector and by the peasants in the rural sector. But how should this burden be divided between them?

This question has a long history. It was at the heart of the controversies over the Corn Laws in Britain in the early nineteenth century; it was implicit in the debates over industrial tariffs in the United States in the period prior to the Civil War; and it was at the centre of the great debate on industrialization in the Soviet Union in the days following the October Revolution. The question that Ricardo had called the town versus the country controversy was relabelled by the Soviet revolutionaries as the question of the 'size of the scissors'. And it is with this vocabulary that the post-Mao leaders of the People's Republic of China have discussed whether they should reduce the implicit tax burden imposed on their peasants for the past thirty-five years. No matter what the vocabulary, the same question is confronted by most of today's non-socialist LDCs.

Given its importance, it is not surprising that economists have had much to say on the matter. But what they have said has been dictated more by ideology than by economic analysis. Those whose primary concern is efficiency argue that the commonly observed food subsidies to those in the urban sector in LDCs are inherently bad. By the same token they oppose trade taxes (which in many LDCs take the form of export levies and tariffs on industrial goods, both of which work to the detriment of those in the

rural sector) on the grounds that they interfere with the production efficiency of the economy. This argument fails to take into account the many
inefficiencies present in most LDCs, as well as the second-best welfare the-
orems which cast doubt on economists' ability to make unambiguous statements under such circumstances.

By contrast, those whose primary concern is with inequality insist that the
government must subsidize the urban poor, and possibly the rural poor as
well. This perspective fails to take into account not only the country's budget
constraint, which implies that not every individual can be subsidized, but
also the fact that increases in consumption by the poor of today are partly
at the expense of consumption by the poor of the future, because a reduction
in the supply of investible funds today reduces future incomes.

Economic realities have a way of rudely intruding upon those who ignore
current and inter-temporal budget constraints. In the world of the 1980s the
spoilsport has usually been the IMF, imposing harsh terms—frequently including the elimination of food subsidies—on those who wish to obtain
credit. Whether the IMF is simply the bearer of the bad news about budget
constraints, as its supporters contend, or whether it is the enforcer of a particular kind of orthodoxy, as its critics claim, has been widely debated.

The aim of this book is to provide a rigorous framework within which
the fundamental question of who should bear the burden of development
can be addressed in a systematic way. Aspects of this analysis include:

(a) Identifying the critical institutional features of the economy, and the
critical parameters (for instance, the magnitudes of demand and supply responses) which determine the consequences of changes in taxes,
prices, and other policies.

(b) Ascertaining conditions under which certain reforms in pricing and
taxation would increase welfare, while showing explicitly the role played
by value-judgements about how the welfare of various groups, both
today and in the future, should be weighed.

1.1 NORMATIVE VERSUS POSITIVE ANALYSIS

A central contention of our analysis is that too often economists have been
lax in separating the description of the incidence of a tax or subsidy from
normative judgements concerning the desirability of particular changes. It
is imperative that the participants in policy debates distinguish which disputes
arise from differences in values, and which disputes arise from differences
in judgements concerning the structure of the economy and the concomitant
differences in judgements concerning the consequences of the policy.

Judgements concerning appropriate welfare weights (how much society
should value an increase in consumption by a poor individual in the rural

sector versus an equal increase in consumption by a poor individual in the urban sector; how much society should value an increase in consumption by those in either sector today versus an equal increase in consumption by those in future generations; how much society should value an increase in consumption by the landowners in the rural sector versus an equal increase in consumption by the landless rural workers) are likely to differ. Therefore we ask: What statements can we make about desirable pricing and taxation policies which are valid regardless of these welfare judgements? As we point out later, this is the same as asking: What can we say about the nature of Pareto-efficient tax and price structures?

We also ask: What statements can we make on the basis of relatively weak hypotheses concerning the nature of the welfare weights? An example of such a hypothesis is that societies' attitudes towards an increase of a dollar's income for an individual depends only on that individual's income, not on whether he happens to reside in the rural or urban sector. Naturally, conclusions obtained under such a weak hypothesis will be more widely acceptable than those obtained, for instance, by assigning particular numerical values to the social worth of a dollar's income gain to different individuals.

1.2 ANALYSIS UNDER LIMITED DATA AVAILABILITY

Disagreements about desirable tax and pricing policies arise not only from differences in values (welfare weights), but also from differences in beliefs about the structure of the economy (for instance, concerning the degree of rigidity in the labour-market), and the size of critical parameters. The data that are required to provide a complete answer to the questions which we have posed are seldom available in LDCs, or, for that matter, in any country. Hence, just as we seek to identify the kinds of statement upon which there can be agreement, given relatively weak welfare judgements, we also seek to identify the kinds of conclusions upon which there can be agreement, given relatively weak assumptions concerning the sizes of certain parameters.

For instance, a critical parameter in determining the structure of optimal commodity taxes is the compensated elasticity of labour supply. If the compensated elasticity of labour supply is zero, and if all goods can be taxed, then uniform commodity taxes (taxing all goods at the same percentage tax-rate) are desirable; these taxes are equivalent to a tax on labour, which is, by assumption, non-distortionary. Unfortunately, after hundreds of studies and millions of dollars spent in conducting experiments (mostly in North America), there is no consensus on the magnitude of the compensated elasticity of labour supply. Most economists believe that it is small, but some claim that it is large. If it is small, we do not have to enquire into the value of the cross elasticity of demand between different pairs of commodities. If it is not small, the optimal tax structure depends critically on the value of cross-elasticities of demand. Disagreements about the values of parameters that are difficult to estimate, such as cross-elasticities of demand, will translate into marked disagreements about appropriate policies.[1]

Recent work, in both economic theory and econometrics, has stressed the importance of knowing the structural parameters of the economy. Unfortunately, the data are frequently insufficient to distinguish clearly among alternative structural specifications of the economy. Economists may, however, be able to agree about certain reduced-form relationships. For example, they might agree about the approximate magnitude of the elasticity of supply of the agricultural surplus but not about why the price response takes this magnitude. Therefore, in this book we have attempted to ascertain how much can be said on the basis of such reduced-form relationships.

1.3 POLICY AND POLITICAL ECONOMY

An analysis of the type outlined above can be of use to those LDC governments that wish to follow a more clearly articulated or 'rational' policy, by helping them to think through the full consequences of their actions. Identifying the full efficiency and distributive consequences of alternative pricing and taxation policies may help to clarify debates within these countries about the appropriate policies to follow.

This suggests an alternative use of the analysis in this book. In many Third World countries, existing policies are often justified on the basis of egalitarian objectives. Our analysis provides a framework within which we can ascertain whether these policies are consistent with the stated objectives. Are these countries subsidizing the poor, or are they in fact simply subsidizing those living in urban areas, who, though poor by Western standards, are in fact the rich within these countries? Do these subsidies reflect a systematic bias in favour of those living in urban areas? To what extent can the confused patterns of subsidies and taxes that are observed in so many LDCs simply be explained by a failure of governments to take full account of the consequences of their actions and of the budget constraints which they face? (They may really believe that they can subsidize both those in the urban sector and those in the rural sector.) Exposing the discrepancies and inconsistencies in existing policies is an important part of the democratic process, even if it does not immediately lead to changed policies.

[1] The importance of these econometric problems cannot be overstressed (see Deaton 1981). Many common specifications of the demand systems used for econometric specification, such as the linear expenditure system, have strong implications which follow from the assumed parametric specifications rather than from the parameter values which have been estimated. For instance, Atkinson and Stiglitz (1976) show that, with the linear expenditure system and an optimal linear income tax, there should always be uniform commodity taxation.

For most of this book we focus on questions such as: If a country can impose differential tax burdens on those in the rural and urban sectors, how should it do it? If a country can impose subsidies or taxes on various commodities, how should it do it? Clearly, the ability to tax different commodities differentially may be abused (for example, by one group exploiting another), as well as used for beneficial purposes. We do not address the question of how likely abuses are, given the nature of the political process.

These questions of political economy are, however, fundamental. Though economic theorists may have little to say about them, the past two centuries have provided a wealth of experience on the basis of which certain judgements can be made: the benevolent leader, so beloved of those who engage in traditional welfare analysis, seems more marked by his absence than by his presence. One might therefore conclude, perhaps reluctantly, that a responsible economist's best advice to many developing countries may be to forswear the possibility of using differential taxation and pricing policies. This conclusion is not the product of concern solely for efficiency (we show that, in principle, there are government interventions which would improve efficiency), but rather of concern for the efficacy of government interventions. Such judgements also rest on views concerning the magnitudes of the gains that might be attained through differential taxation. We present, for instance, certain central cases in which uniform commodity taxation or no commodity taxation is optimal. Even if the conditions assumed in these results are not precisely satisfied, the results suggest that, if the economy is even approximately described by the underlying models, there are at best only limited gains to be had from non-uniform taxation.

1.4 GENERAL-EQUILIBRIUM ANALYSIS

A central feature of our analysis is the construction and use of simple general-equilibrium models of the economy. This is important for several reasons. First, many governments have imposed a vast array of subsidies and taxes on both the agricultural and urban sectors. In many cases the government attempts to persuade all groups that they are the beneficiaries of its largess. We noted earlier the unhappy role that budget constraints play in forcing governments to come to terms with reality. These budget constraints also imply that not all groups in a society can be net beneficiaries of transfer and subsidy programmes (although all can be net losers from the inefficiencies associated with some transfer programmes).[2] It requires a general-equilibrium model to identify the true net gainers and the true net losers.[3]

---

[2] By the same token, to the extent that government programmes lead to productive public goods, all can be net beneficiaries.

[3] In many cases governments deliberately try to obfuscate the real issue. There are some taxes for which it is difficult to tell who really pays. This is true, for instance, of the corporation

Second, actions taken in one sector often have spill-over effects in other sectors, and one needs a general-equilibrium model to take these interactions into account. The description of the total set of repercussions resulting from a policy change is referred to as the incidence of the policy. Although incidence analysis has played a central role in public finance literature, it has been slow in making inroads into the analysis of development policies. We show that tax policies in one sector may have important and often interrelated sets of repercussions that have been ignored in the earlier literature. For example:

(a) they may affect tax revenues derived from taxes and tariffs imposed elsewhere in the economy;

(b) they may affect wages, with direct effects on the welfare of workers and indirect effects on profits and productivity;

(c) they may affect prices of non-taxed goods, with a host of indirect repercussions on welfare;

(d) they may affect urban–rural migration, again with indirect effects on wages and income in both sectors of the economy, and thus on the welfare of residents in both sectors;

(e) they may affect employment, with important implications for the welfare of workers.

Third, in general the government often does not alter one policy alone. If, for instance, a certain tax is increased, either government expenditure is increased or some other tax is decreased, or government borrowing is reduced. Again, it requires a general-equilibrium model to keep track of all the consequences of these actions.

1.5 THE STRUCTURE OF THE BOOK

This book is divided into four parts. Part I presents an introduction to the issues and to our methodological approach. A central contention of this book is that the desirability of particular policies is dependent on the structure of the economy in question and on the set of instruments available to the government. In Chapter 2 we present an outline of what we view as the essential features of a less developed economy which must be captured in any model purporting to provide policy prescriptions. This book can be viewed as an exercise in applied welfare economics, an examination of what

---

income tax. Individuals may believe that corporations pay the tax, and politicians may try to persuade taxpayers that this is the case. We know, however, that in the end some individuals must bear the brunt of the tax, although it may not be obvious whether these individuals are the corporation's workers, shareholders, or customers. Governments also often claim that it is the rich who do or should pay the taxes to finance the government's activities. However, since there are too few rich individuals, some of the middle- and lower-income individuals must necessarily be net contributors to the public treasury.

economics has to say about an important set of issues facing less developed countries. It makes use of many of the tools and perspectives which have been developed in recent years. Chapter 3 presents a critical survey of those aspects of the theory which are relevant to our concerns.

Part II presents some basic models and analyses pricing and taxation in these models. It turns out that the analysis is simplest in the case of an open economy in which the government has the ability to tax goods in the urban sector at a different rate than in the rural sector (that is, the government can introduce a tax border between the two sectors). We thus present this case first. We then show how the analysis can easily be modified if the government must impose the same prices in the urban and rural sectors. Such a constraint is present in those LDCs that have highly limited administrative capabilities. This is also the model that best describes the issue of tariffs in pre-Civil War USA and the debate over the Corn Laws in Britain. Similar issues are addressed in the context of a closed economy in Chapter 6. This is an appropriate model for understanding the debate in the Soviet Union concerning the size of the scissors during the period following the October Revolution. Variants of this model have recently been employed (including by Osband (1985) and Li and Tsui (1987) for the USSR and China respectively) for studies of the price scissors.

Parts III and IV extend the basic framework by generalizing the models of the rural and urban sectors respectively. In Chapter 8 we allow for the heterogeneity of individuals within the rural sector, and address the question of the effects of alternative policies on the distribution of welfare within the rural sector. We also deal with alternative forms of rural organization (e.g. the extended family and share-cropping) as well as the presence of rural unemployment. In Chapter 9 we ask: Given that there are a variety of inputs and outputs within the rural sector, how should they be subsidized or taxed?

Part IV focuses on the urban sector. In Chapter 10, we present a model of the determination of urban wages and employment. This general model allows us to identify the key elements of the induced effects of tax policy changes on urban wages and employment. Chapter 11 presents a brief discussion of some aspects of the wage–productivity hypothesis which are relevant for taxation analysis. We then ask, in Chapter 12, what the detailed structure of taxes and subsidies in the urban sector should be when the endogeneity of urban wages and employment is taken into account. Chapter 13 deals with urban–rural migration (which is of central importance in many LDCs), and shows how the preceding analysis can be modified to incorporate the migration effects of taxation policies. In Chapter 14 we highlight some of the central features of the model of the urban sector we have developed, among them the endogenous determination of urban wages, migration, and unemployment. This model is then used to summarize briefly the general approach adopted here for taxation analysis.

Chapter 15 illustrates how this framework can be used to enhance understanding of policy issues other than taxation, by providing a general formulation of cost–benefit analysis and project appraisal. We focus on the determination of the social cost of labour, taking into account taxation and pricing interventions (which are widely present in most LDCs) as well as other important features of the economy. This analysis is considerably more general than the analysis of the social cost of labour hitherto available; in fact, almost all the existing results on the social cost of labour turn out to be special cases of our analysis.

1.6 THE NATURE OF THE RESULTS

This book is primarily concerned with providing a conceptual framework within which one can think about the central problem of how to raise revenues efficiently and equitably within LDCs. It provides, as we have said, a formulation within which most earlier studies can be viewed as special cases. The formulation highlights both the features of the economy and the value-judgements that are central to arriving at informed policy decisions. Several of the features which distinguish LDCs from more developed countries have received insufficient attention in the literature on the design of taxation and other policies in LDCs. Our analysis is thus also useful in pointing to the limitations of that literature.

Among the policy prescriptions often associated with the modern theory of public finance are the following: taxes should not be imposed on imported goods because such taxes interfere with production efficiency; different goods should be taxed at different rates in the urban sector to reflect differences in elasticities of demand (in accordance with the principles of efficient taxation set out by Ramsey 1927); in particular, food in the urban sector should not be subsidized, except possibly as a second-best way of redistributing money to the urban poor (in which case the food subsidies should be focused on those foods consumed by the very poor, for example, millet rather than rice); and shadow wages should be considerably below market wages to reflect the pervasiveness of unemployment, but above zero to reflect the fact that investment is more valuable than consumption, and to reflect that increasing the wage bill diverts resources away from investment.

Each of these conclusions is suspect.

(*a*) Because of the limitations on the government's ability to impose taxes, trade taxes may be desirable.

(*b*) The structure of taxes in the urban sector has little to do with the considerations upon which the literature based on Ramsey analysis has focused. This literature has focused on effects which are of second-order importance in LDCs, such as the labour–leisure trade-off, while ignoring the effects which are of first-order importance. For example, it has failed to take into account the effects of tax and pricing policies on wage-setting in the urban sector, on urban–rural migration and urban unemployment, and on workers' productivity.[4]

(*c*) Earlier cost–benefit literature was deficient, not only in omitting an analysis of the effects of hiring additional urban workers on urban wages and unemployment, but also in failing to incorporate the effects of the often large distortions associated with existing taxation policies.[5]

The results presented in this book consist of a series of 'if . . . then . . .' statements, that is, 'if the economy has such-and-such features, then given certain value-judgements, the following policies are desirable.' It becomes a matter of judgement whether the 'if' statements apply in any particular context, and therefore whether the 'then' statements are relevant. This book emphasizes not only elements of the economy which LDCs have in common, but also the differences among them. One of the advantages of our general approach is that it easily accommodates these differences; for example, slight variations in the model allow it to be used to analyse tax policies in an economy in which trade unions are important in the urban sector, or one in which they are not. Similarly, slight variations of our model can deal with an economy in which extended families are predominant in agriculture, or one in which share-cropping is significant.

While many policy recommendations may, accordingly, vary from country to country, there are certain common elements of sufficient importance to merit special attention. In understanding policy design certain bench-mark models play a critical role. For instance, while the general analysis focuses on the dependence of productivity on the consumption of various goods, we pay particular attention to the special case in which productivity depends on the individual's utility: that is, the consumption of a particular good affects productivity in exactly the same way that it affects the individual's welfare. Similarly, the bench-mark models for analysing migration assume that migration continues to the point where expected utilities in the urban and rural sectors are equalized (taking into account the differences in prices and earnings in the two sectors). For these bench-mark models some of our findings are as follows:

(*a*) In the absence of migration, and urban wage and productivity effects, and given egalitarian values which give no special weight to those living in the urban sector, the rural sector should be taxed only if taxes

---

[4] These effects have also been ignored in the development planning literature and in the related literature on traditional growth theory. These literatures have had the additional weakness of focusing on the investible surplus alone; when workers' welfare was included, attention was focused exclusively on the workers in the urban sector. Whether these assumptions were introduced in order to simplify the analysis, or whether they reflected an ideological bias against the rural sector, a bias shared by Marx (see e.g. Marx and Engels (1848)), need not concern us. What is needed is a more balanced perspective of the kind we attempt to present here.

[5] Indeed, as discussed in ch. 15, it turns out that the effects of hiring additional workers in the urban sector, on which the earlier cost–benefit literature focused, are dominated by the effects which it ignored.

are also imposed on urban workers. This conclusion is reinforced in the presence of migration, with urban wages set at levels in excess of market clearing.

(b) If wages adjust to keep urban utility levels fixed, then, in the absence of productivity effects, or if productivity depends only on utility levels, there should be no differential taxation of commodities in the urban sector. If food consumption has a particularly strong effect on the productivity of urban workers, then food consumption should be subsidized.

(c) For cash-crops (such as cotton, fruits, and plantation crops) and manufactured inputs used in agriculture (such as fertilizer, pesticides, tractors, and other machine inputs), we show that the case for taxing or subsidizing these outputs and inputs is weak, on either equality or efficiency grounds. The case is even weaker for taxing some of these inputs and outputs while subsidizing others. These results hold regardless of which outputs in addition to the cash-crops farmers produce and which inputs in addition to the manufactured inputs farmers use. These results also hold for a variety of ways in which the rural wage might be determined.

1.7 SOME REMARKS ON THE ROLE OF THEORY

The relationship between politicians and bureaucrats (those who are in a position to make decisions on policy matters) and economic theorists has always been a difficult one. The former often dismiss the recommendations of the latter as irrelevant or utopian; the latter denigrate the policies of the former as inconsistent and, if not self-serving, at least dictated by unnecessarily myopic and narrow concerns. There may be a grain of truth in both positions. Everyone, including politicians and bureaucrats, employs a theory when making any policy recommendation. When we predict the consequences of a particular policy, we usually have only limited experience on which to base our prediction. Even when a policy has been tried in the past, one cannot be sure that the consequences will be the same in the future: the world is always changing. So the essential question is whether the central features of the economy that determined the policy's past success or failure have changed. This is almost invariably a matter of judgement. Empirical data, whether analysed in an unsophisticated or sophisticated manner (using modern econometric techniques) may shed light on the range of likely outcomes, but even here, a judgement must be made as to whether the environment from which the data were drawn sufficiently resembles the present circumstances in order to make the results currently applicable. Thus, even if a host of other common controversies are ignored (for example, the accuracy of the data, the suitability of the model, and the appropriateness of the statistical techniques), our judgements in each case are based on our worldview—our theory.

A key issue is the extent to which one makes the assumptions underlying one's analyses explicit. Good theory attempts to identify its fundamental assumptions clearly and to derive its propositions from a well-articulated set of premises. Of course, there is a price to pay for everything, including consistency: the theorist's assumptions often represent a gross oversimplification of reality.

To policy-makers the price is too high. As has often been said, consistency is the hobgoblin of little minds. Their objections are often well founded: their suspicions about one theorist's policy recommendations are invariably reinforced when another theorist, using a somewhat different model, comes up with different recommendations. Unable to judge among the seemingly irrelevant assumptions that enter into each theorist's model, the policy-maker throws up his hands and resorts to his own half-articulated 'theory' of the world.

The fact that a theory represents a significant over-simplification of the world is not to be treated as criticism. The objective of theory is to ascertain the features of the world that are central to determining the consequences of, say, a particular policy change. But how does a theorist know what is essential? In the construction of all theory, the theorist makes a guess concerning what is and what is not essential. Though a theory may begin with little more than such a guess, the hallmark of good theory (whether pure or applied) is an attempt to test its robustness. In the experimental sciences, theories can be tested by constructing controlled experiments in which the predictions of the theory can be isolated, identified, and then verified or disproved. This cannot be done in economics (or for that matter in astronomy), though there have been a few instances of social experiments, with limited success.

The tool of modern economic theory is instead the thought-experiment: the economist constructs a variety of idealized models to ascertain whether slight but plausible changes in the assumptions do or do not lead to significant changes in the conclusions. In some cases (such as the standard theory of Walrasian competition which was developed under the hypothesis that there is perfect information) it turns out that the theory is not robust, and a more general or alternative theory needs to be constructed. In other cases (such as the theory presented in this book) the results appear to be robust.[6] This technique of analysis—experimenting with the consequences of a wide variety of alterations of the assumptions underlying the model—provides the methodological underpinning of this study. This kind of thought-experimentation, while essential to the theorist who wishes to have confidence in his analysis,

---

[6] Even here one needs to be cautious: although we experimented with the consequences of changing what appeared to be all the significant assumptions, it is possible that an implicit or incompletely articulated assumption underlying the analysis may play a significant role in determining the results of the theory.

can often be demanding to all but the most assiduous students of the subject. Journals discourage the publication of the thought-experiments which confirm the robustness of models, leaving the reader simply to trust that the theorist has in fact carried out exhaustive thought-experiments.

Fortunately, in the present context, matters are better: in various LDCs there is a variety of institutions and economic systems, so that the set of assumptions which are appropriate for each is likely to differ, in at least some important ways. Thus, there are real-life counterparts to the theorist's thought-experiments. We show that the theoretical framework which we develop, and its basic qualitative results, apply across a wide variety of institutional arrangements. They apply, for instance, to share-cropping economies, plantation economies, and economies dominated by peasants who own their own farms; they apply to economies in which urban wages are rigid, as well as to economies in which wages change in response to certain changes in the economic environment; they apply to economies characterized by different levels of rural–urban migration. Indeed, in most instances we are able to derive expressions which hold regardless of the institutional setting. Of course, in each setting the interpretation of the derived expressions may differ and, more importantly, the value of the relevant parameters may be quite sensitive to the institutional setting.

2

THE OBJECTIVES AND INSTRUMENTS OF GOVERNMENT POLICY AND THE STRUCTURE OF THE ECONOMY IN LDCs

One of the concerns of this book is with government policies towards food and other agricultural goods, and with how a government treats producers in the rural sector and consumers in the urban sector. Governments—both in LDCs and in several developed countries—play an active role in setting the food prices received by farmers and the food prices paid by city-dwellers. Therefore, it is important to identify what are the salient characteristics of LDCs relevant to such policies, what are the stated objectives of these policies, and what are the alternative instruments at a government's disposal for attaining these objectives.

2.1 STATED OBJECTIVES OF FOOD-RELATED POLICIES

The stated objectives of a government attempting to alter prices which would emerge in the absence of government intervention are several:

- to increase the income of peasants, who are often among the poorest in the economy.
- to subsidize the poorer city-dwellers. In most LDCs direct income subsidies are generally thought to be infeasible, and food subsidies may be an effective way to help the poor.
- to tax the agricultural sector, in order to capture resources for investment and the creation of public goods. A long tradition of thought and practice has viewed this method of surplus creation to be crucial for development. Among the recent prominent advocates of this method has been Lee Kuan Yew (see *The Economist* 1991, for example.)
- to attain some level of self-sufficiency in specific goods, and to avoid excessive dependence on the international market.[1]
- to counteract the effects of rigidities in the economy, such as price and

[1] We do not address in this book the question of why governments pursue this set of objectives, or the extent to which their objectives can be derived from more fundamental criteria. We suspect, for instance, that the goal of food self-sufficiency may be misguided. It might be justified in terms of a concern for the consequences of a cut-off of food imports. However, given

wage rigidities in domestic markets or the lack of access to a free
international trade and borrowing environment.
- to stabilize prices faced by consumers and producers.[2]
- to redistribute income away from middlemen towards consumers and
producers, or from one region to another.[3]

In some cases, the stated objectives seem at variance with the policies
adopted. Though the government may claim that food subsidies are meant
to help the urban poor, it may not subsidize the grain consumed by the poor
(millet, for example), but rather the grain consumed by those who are relatively
better off (rice, for example). In other cases, the government may fail to
achieve its objectives due to incompetence. Though the intended objective
of a marketing board may be to help producers and consumers, in some
cases it may actually harm both groups by running excessively costly operations.

In other cases, the stated objectives appear inconsistent or confused.[4] The
government attempts to subsidize everyone, to increase the prices received
by farmers and to lower those paid by city-dwellers, without making explicit
who is to pay for the subsidies and, indeed, without a clear view of the full
incidence of the complicated set of taxes and subsidies. This confusion is
further compounded when many different agencies set prices for different
goods. Often these agencies act independently of one another, under contradictory assumptions about society's objectives and the constraints facing
the economy.

Though there is a wide range of objectives, we shall focus here primarily
on the implications of various policies for (*a*) government revenue, (*b*) the
welfare of those in the rural sector, and (*c*) the welfare of those in the urban
sector. Following standard convention, we shall refer to government revenue
as the investible surplus. It is, however, important to remember that public
funds, important as they are for investment, are not the only source of
investment. Private savings, within both the urban and rural sectors, are not
only potentially important, but have in fact played a critical role in economic
development. Moreover, not all increments of funds at the disposal of the
government will go into investment.

---

the cost of such a policy, given reasonable assumptions concerning the likelihood of a food
cut-off and the ability of the economy to respond to such an event, and given the typical extent
of risk aversion, the goal of food self-sufficiency is hard to justify for most countries.

[2] See Newbery and Stiglitz (1981). We do not deal with price stabilization policies in this
book.

[3] This goal is often associated with other political objectives: in many LDCs middlemen are
of a different ethnic group than those controlling the government.

[4] Similar inconsistencies appear in the agricultural policies of some developed countries.
While these policies are often justified in terms of the help they provide to small and
medium-sized family farms, the policies are designed such that rich farmers receive most of the
benefits.

2.2 PUTTING AGRICULTURAL POLICIES
IN PERSPECTIVE

It is important to keep in mind the range of instruments through which the government imposes the burden of development costs on some groups, or by which it subsidizes other groups. One of the contributions which economists can make is to point out that things are often not what they seem to be: the government can claim that it is subsidizing urban workers by providing food subsidies, that it is subsidizing agricultural workers by providing fertilizer subsidies, and that it is subsidizing manufacturing by providing credit subsidies; but the basic fact is that not everyone can be subsidized.[5] The issue can be viewed in the following way: national income can be thought of as a pie. The government can alter the share of the pie going to each group in the population and it can alter the size of the pie. If the size of the pie remains unchanged, then if one group gets more, some other group must get less. However, it is often a complicated matter to ascertain, in the end, whose share has increased and whose share has decreased as a result of government action.

Most government policies affect not only how the pie is divided, but also its size. Thus, policies which lead to inefficient resource allocation inevitably shrink the size of the pie. In this book we are interested in identifying both situations in which everyone's slice can be increased, and situations in which a slightly smaller pie might be acceptable, provided that those who are particularly needy get a sufficiently large increase in the size of their slice.

Other Policy Instruments

Governments affect the size and the distribution of national income not only by tax and subsidy policies (which commodities are taxed, which commodities are subsidized, at what rates, whether individual and corporate incomes are taxed, and if they are, what allowances are provided, etc.) but also by a variety of other policies. In many LDCs, governments (through quasi-governmental agencies such as marketing boards) take an active role in purchasing crops from farmers and then selling them to consumers; the difference between the buying price and the selling price, taking into account the necessary transaction and transportation costs, is equivalent to a tax or subsidy. Governments also provide price floors, and supplement the difference between the market price and the guaranteed price, or purchase crops from the market to the extent required to ensure that the market price is equal to the price floor.

---

[5] For those countries receiving significant amounts of foreign aid, all groups in the population can receive more than they would in the absence of such aid. The question of how such foreign largess is divided among the population is qualitatively similar to the question of who should pay for the costs of development.

Governments intervene in still other ways: they may set prices (such as for foreign exchange) at levels which do not clear the market, and then deal with the resulting disequilibrium by rationing the demanders according to certain rules. One particularly important market in which rationing occurs is the credit market. In most LDCs the government plays a central role in allocating credit, not only among government agencies, but also to the private sector. Providing credit at below market interest rates (often at negative real rates of interest) is one of the ways in which governments can confer favours on particular groups or individuals and thereby redistribute income.[6]

Some governments provide a certain number of basic necessities at below market-clearing prices, rationing the supply. If individuals can resell their rations, these systems are equivalent to providing each individual with a subsidy equal to the difference between the market price and the price charged for the ration, times the quantity of the ration. If resale is restricted, then the gains to individuals vary. Another instrument that has been used on a widespread basis is the provision of subsidized goods (food, in particular) through queues in which individuals must wait in order to obtain these goods. Queues have often been justified as improving equality, on the basis that only the poor will make use of them because the value of their time is low. On the other hand, restrictions on the resale of rations have often been criticized as Pareto-inferior because no one would be made worse off by an opportunity to trade. Such views are incorrect because they are not based on an explicit comparison of alternative instruments.[7]

Limitations on Government Policy

In order to discuss and evaluate alternative government policies, it is necessary to know the nature of all instruments the government has at its disposal, not only those related to agricultural pricing. One of the important ways in which developed and less developed economies differ is in the set of feasible instruments. For instance, if one of the primary objectives of government policy is equality, then taxes and subsidies on commodities may, in general, be an inefficient method, provided the government can use income taxes to redistribute income.[8] But in most LDCs the government cannot impose

[6] Note, however, that there may be credit rationing even in competitive capital markets, as long as information is imperfect (see Hoff and Stiglitz 1990, Stiglitz 1990, and Stiglitz and Weiss 1981; 1986).

[7] Sah (1987) compares the outcomes, on the welfare of the poor and the rich, of non-tradable rations, tradable rations, queues, and the unhindered market, as means to distribute a limited quantity of a good. He shows that, for the poor, the ranking of instruments is: tradable rations, non-tradable rations, queues, and the market. In contrast, for the rich, the market is the most beneficial. These comparisons hold in the presence of administrative costs as well as of certain types of pre-existing taxes.

[8] See Atkinson and Stiglitz (1980). Their argument is not based on the fallacious argument, used by Friedman (1952) among others, that to do so introduces additional distortions to the economy. As long as there are some distortions, removing one distortion may or may not

comprehensive income taxes; attempts to do so would involve large administrative and compliance costs (e.g. record-keeping).[9] There is likely to be significant tax avoidance, resulting in large inequities and inefficiencies. It may also be undesirable to impose an income tax because income (as reported or reportable under tax statutes) may rather badly reflect the 'desired' tax basis, e.g. ability to pay. These limitations on the instruments of government policy will play a central role in the ensuing analysis.

There are other limitations which apply to most LDCs. For instance, the government cannot easily monitor transactions within the rural sector; this makes taxes on trade within the rural sector infeasible or at least very costly to administer. If imposed, there will generally be extensive tax evasion. Thus, taxes on wage income in the rural sector are usually infeasible.[10] For similar reasons, taxes on wage income received by workers in the urban sector are typically practical only for government employees and the employees of the corporate sector. Such individuals constitute only a fraction of the urban population in a typical LDC. In some cases, the government may even find it costly to administer taxes on purchases and sales within the urban sector. The only easily administered taxes are those on trade between the country and the rest of the world. Even then, there may be considerable smuggling and tax evasion (e.g. through under-invoicing).

In many cases, the government would like to charge rich individuals a higher price, say, for food, than poorer individuals; but again, this is generally infeasible.[11] Thus, in most of the subsequent analysis, we shall assume that the government can only impose uniform rate taxes within a sector.

In some of the subsequent analysis, we shall assume that the government can tax the trade between the urban and rural sectors. Thus, prices in the rural sector can differ from those in the urban sector.[12] In some countries,

---

represent a welfare improvement. This is the central lesson of the theory of the second-best (see Meade 1955; Lipsey and Lancaster 1956–7). Though one cannot simply count distortions, it turns out that in at least some central cases, no commodity taxation is desirable.

[9] A distinction between developed and less developed countries should be noted here: in developed countries, most firms keep records for a variety of other reasons (monitoring and controlling sub-units within large organizations). Hence, the incremental cost associated with the record-keeping required to implement an income tax may be relatively small (see Stiglitz 1987*b*).

[10] In most of the recent literature on taxation in developed countries, it is assumed that the government can impose taxes on all transactions, including the purchases and sales of all types of labour services (see Diamond and Mirrlees 1971). For a critique of this assumption, see Stiglitz and Dasgupta (1971).

[11] This should be contrasted with a strand in the recent literature on taxation in developed countries, in which non-linear tax schedules are employed. The imposition of such taxes presupposes that it is difficult to set up secondary markets for tax arbitrage (see Katz 1984). For most commodities, such non-linear schedules are not feasible. In fact, recent discussions of tax reform in the United States have emphasized a simplification of the tax code, such as that which would result from a flat-rate income tax schedule. Many of the complexities of the tax code and much of the administrative cost arises from differences in marginal tax-rates faced by different individuals.

[12] Again, this assumption should be contrasted with that conventionally made in the theory

such policies are implemented through a sales tax. In others, they are implemented through public marketing boards which control the sale of particular goods in the urban sector and control the purchase of certain agricultural commodities in the rural sector. This assumption may or may not be reasonable, depending on the country. Even under the best circumstances, some inter-sectoral trade will escape the tax collector's net. The question is: How widespread will the evasion and avoidance of taxes on inter-sectoral trade be?

Limitations on Wage Policies.   In many LDCs urban wages appear to be much higher than rural wages. Economists from developed countries frequently recommend that the country lower wages paid to urban workers. The LDC governments say that this is beyond their control. In Part IV of this book (for example, in Chapters 10 and 11) we discuss many possible economic reasons (not limited to the presence of trade unions) why this may be so. Furthermore, we discuss why it is inappropriate to assume for many modern-day LDCs that the government can impose urban wage taxes or subsidies. If the government cannot lower the real wage directly, then it is reasonable to assume that it cannot do so indirectly, through the imposition of taxes.

Inability to Control Migration.   One of the consequences of high urban wages is that, workers are induced to migrate from the rural to the urban sector, resulting in urban unemployment. In this context, an important limitation on the government is that it cannot control this migration directly. In some instances governments have tried to do this: they have passed laws against people migrating to the city unless they already have a job offer, and they have attempted to repatriate the unemployed to their rural homes (as in Tanzania). These programmes have, for the most part, met with only limited success, as workers re-enter the urban sector almost as quickly as they are removed. Only by using repressive measures of the kind usually associated with totalitarian regimes can such migration be kept under control.

Equivalence of Different Policies

An important result in tax theory is the equivalence between taxes which appear to be quite different. For instance, under a set of assumptions, a sales tax is equivalent to, and therefore has the same effect as a value-added tax, and a consumption tax is equivalent to a wage tax.[13] In such cases, the

---

of taxation for developed countries. There it is usually assumed that all consumers must face the same prices.

[13] Assuming that individuals make no bequests and receive no inheritances, the present discounted value of an individual's lifetime tax payments under a flat-rate consumption tax will be the same as his payments under a wage tax at that rate.

alternative taxes would be equivalent only in the absence of administrative costs associated with implementing the tax. However, administrative costs (and the extent of compliance) are quite different for different taxes; they differ markedly, for instance, for a value-added tax and a sales tax.

Likewise, in LDCs it is important to recognize the possible equivalence between what may appear to be quite different policies. A marketing board which controls consumer and producer prices for food has some consequences similar to those of taxes and subsidies levied on consumers and producers. This enables us to state some of our results either in terms of taxes to be imposed on the two sectors, or in terms of the pricing policies to be followed by a marketing board.

Similarly, it has long been recognized that an export tax on the agricultural sector hurts that sector in exactly the same way as an import tariff on manufactured goods; it turns the terms of trade against them. The framers of the US Constitution failed to recognize this equivalence. Concerned that the industrial North might use such taxes to benefit itself at the expense of the agricultural South, they prohibited the imposition of export levies. However, a similar effect was later achieved through import tariffs on industrial goods.

The point which so many governments fail to recognize is that it is relative prices, and only relative prices, which are important. Governments have typically developed a confusing array of taxes and subsidies, making it difficult to ascertain who is really being subsidized, and who is really being taxed. By the same token, the confusion may also have an advantage: all groups may believe that they are being subsidized.

2.3 THE ECONOMIC STRUCTURE OF LDCs

There is enormous variation among LDCs in resources, institutions, and economic systems. Within the past two decades, a general view has emerged concerning at least some of the critical features which LDCs have in common. Any model purporting to analyse the consequences of tax and pricing policies for LDCs and to evaluate these policies must reflect these features.

The Importance of Agriculture and the Dual Economy

A critical feature that distinguishes most LDCs from the more developed economies is the important role played by agriculture. In the United States agriculture accounts for less than 5 per cent of output and employment; in a typical LDC it accounts for in excess of 60 per cent of output and in excess of 70 per cent of employment. During the past two decades increasing attention has been directed at improving productivity in agriculture, in contrast to the earlier view in which the process of development was almost synonymous with the process of industrialization and increased urbanization.

Life in the urban and rural sectors is often markedly different. Those in the urban sector enjoy services (and possibly amusements) which may not be available in the rural sector. On the other hand, urban squalor may make living conditions far worse than in the rural area. Yet, in spite of this squalor, the rural poor have continued to pour into the urban centres. They perhaps believe that the long-run prospects in urban areas are sufficiently great to warrant bearing some significant temporary costs. This migration has resulted in high urban unemployment rates in many LDCs, which have posed both economic and political problems for governments throughout the Third World.

For an economic theory to capture these essential concerns of developing countries, it must be based on at least a two-sector model (with an urban and rural sector).[14] It should also allow for the possibility of migration from the rural sector to the urban sector, and thus incorporate the effects of any policy change on the level of this migration.[15]

Market Imperfections

The persistence of urban unemployment is but one piece of evidence showing that the 'perfect market' assumptions that theorists concerned with developed economies commonly employ may be inapplicable in LDCs. Any model whose assumptions lead to the conclusion that there will not be any unemployment cannot provide a basis for relevant policy prescriptions for a country where the level of unemployment is one of the central concerns.[16] Also, while there may be only one way in which an economy is 'perfect', there are many ways in which it can be imperfect. There may be many rigidities which give rise not only to unemployment, but also to other resource misallocations.

The rigidity with which development economists have been most concerned is the rigidity of real wages in the urban sector. It may, however, not be enough simply to note the rigidity and its consequences: we need to explain why wages are rigid. Is it because of government wage restrictions? Is it because of trade unions? Or is it because firms find that the productivity of their workers increases if they increase their wages above the market-clearing

---

[14] This is not to say that a full description of the economy would entail only two sectors. The art of economic theorizing is finding the simplest possible model which captures the essence of the problem at hand. Adding additional sectors would, for most of our analysis, complicate without clarifying. Note also that, in some instances, it has been argued that both sectors may be rural, but one a 'primitive' rural sector and the other a more developed (industrial or plantation) rural sector. For some purposes, the distinction is not important, but for others it is. In later discussion we will consider the possibility of imposing different tax-rates in the urban and rural sectors. This is usually feasible only if the two sectors are geographically separated.

[15] The failure to consider the effects on migration is a major criticism of the approach to cost–benefit analysis advocated in the Little and Mirrlees (1968) OECD manual (see ch. 15).

[16] Whether these perfect market assumptions have much applicability to developed countries is also a matter of debate.

level, that their labour turnover decreases, and that they obtain a higher quality labour-force? The hypothesis that the productivity of workers depends on the wage they receive, through any of these or other mechanisms, is referred to as the efficiency–wage hypothesis, or more generally, the wage–productivity hypothesis. In this book we make several contributions to the formulation of this hypothesis. The aspects of this hypothesis that are highly relevant for taxation analysis are described in Chapter 11.

The question of why wages are rigid is not just a matter of idle intellectual curiosity, but may have profound policy implications. If the reason for wage rigidity is minimum-wage legislation, then the the economist's first policy recommendation is likely to be to remove this restriction: this will decrease inequality and increase economic efficiency. The fact that governments seem loath to do this puts those who believe in optimal government policies in an awkward position. Is it plausible that the government is likely to follow the economist's complicated and refined strictures about how to set different tax-rates, when it turns down what would seem to be an obvious welfare-enhancing recommendation, a recommendation whose consequences can be understood without much sophistication? And if there are political constraints which dictate that wages cannot be lowered, is it not plausible that the government may claim that there are other political constraints which dictate that certain taxes cannot be raised or certain prices cannot be lowered? These constraints thus need to be built into taxation analysis.

On the other hand, when firms set the real wage at a level above the market-clearing level, because workers' productivity is thereby increased, tax policies will need to take into account both their effects on firms' wage-setting behaviour, and the indirect effect that this has on workers' productivity and on unemployment.

The Rural Sector

The rural sector in most LDCs has several distinguishing characteristics which need to be incorporated into any plausible model. In many countries, farms are run by extended families in which there is considerable sharing among family members; they each receive their average output, rather than their marginal contribution, and this may result in a distortion which policy analysis needs to take into account. In addition, share-cropping is prevalent to some degree in several LDCs. Share-cropping means that workers do not receive the full marginal value of their extra effort, and this may lead to an undersupply of labour. If this is correct, then government policies will need to take it into account. The welfare loss from a policy which reduces the marginal return to effort may be much more serious in this case, because it exacerbates an existing inefficiency, than it would be in an economy in which workers own their farms.[17]

---

[17] That is, one can view the landlords' share as a tax on the workers' output. Since the welfare

Just as it is important to understand the explanation of wage rigidities in order to grasp the full consequences of any change in government policy, it is also important to understand the explanation of alternative forms of rural organizations. We deal with these issues in Chapter 8.

Investible Surplus, Private Investment, and Government Consumption

In this book we follow a long tradition of using a shorthand in describing government revenues as the 'investible surplus', funds that are available for increasing the economy's capital stock. We trade off the consumption of the current generation for the investible surplus—the consumption of future generations. We should emphasize, however, that not all government revenues are spent on investment, and not all income of workers in the rural and urban sectors is spent on consumption. For instance, a tax on the rural sector reduces private rural investment. The gain for future generations from the tax is smaller on two accounts: first, private investment is reduced, and secondly, some of the government revenue is used for current consumption. As long as the marginal propensity to consume for the government is less than that for workers in the rural and urban sectors, the qualitative properties we describe remain valid. In the absence of any dead-weight loss associated with the tax, it can also be shown that the trade-offs remain unaffected, and accordingly the optimal tax-rates remain unchanged.

This can be seen as follows. In the analysis below, we relate the optimal tax-rates to social weights on current consumption in the urban and rural sectors (denoted by β^u and β^r respectively) and also to the shadow price on investment (denoted by δ). Assume the government transferred a dollar of income from urban workers to itself, and that urban workers save a fraction s^u of their income. Then the social value of the loss in current utility of urban workers is $(1 - s^u)\beta^u$, and the social value of the gain in the investible surplus is $\delta(1 - s^u)$. In the analysis below it will be apparent that what is relevant is the relative social weight. This relative social weight is $(1 - s^u)\beta^u/(1 - s^u)\delta = \beta^u/\delta$. This remains unaffected by private saving.

With distortionary taxation, however, the gain in inter-generational redistribution (future consumption for current consumption) associated with any tax-rate is lower, and hence there is a presumption that the optimal tax-rates will be lower. This conclusion is reinforced if the government is less efficient in investing than the private sector. The same reasons that explain why it is difficult for the government to control the rural sector directly suggest that the government is likely to be even less effective than farmers in making rural investments—other than the provision of basic infrastructure,

---

loss increases with the square of the effective tax-rate, the welfare loss from a 5% tax in a peasant economy in which farmers own their own land is much less than from a 5% tax in a share-cropping economy, in which the worker already gives the landlord 50% of his output.

such as roads and irrigation. This may even be true if the government provides the funds to the rural sector in the form of loans. The government
must still make a decision about which farmers are most likely to make productive use of the loans, and it must still monitor that the loans are used in
the ways intended. These problems are exacerbated if there are no strong
penalties for default.

Furthermore, the ideological view that industrialization is the only path
to true development has often created an urban bias on the part of government officials, leading many governments to concentrate their investments
in the urban sector, even when the country's comparative advantage may lie
elsewhere. There is, accordingly, a concern that the value of investment dollars in the hands of the government may be considerably less than that of
investment dollars in the hands of rural workers. In that case, even if there
were no dead-weight loss associated with taxation, the level of taxation that
should be imposed on the rural sector may be considerably less than the
analysis in the ensuing chapters suggests. It is even possible that urban
workers should be taxed in order to subsidize rural workers.

To see this, suppose s^r is the saving-rate of rural individuals. Recalling the
notation used earlier, a transfer of a dollar from rural workers to the government reduces the social value of current rural consumption by $\beta^r(1 - s^r)$,
while it increases the social value of investment by $\kappa\delta - s^r\delta$, where κ is the
efficiency coefficient of government investment expenditure, relative to pri-
vate investment expenditure. (κ is assumed to be less than unity.) Next, consider a transfer of a dollar from urban workers to rural workers. Assume
that urban workers do not save. Then this transfer reduces the social value
of current consumption by $\beta^u - (1 - s^r)\beta^r$, and increases the value of investment by $s^r\delta$. Such a transfer is desirable if $\delta > [\beta^u - (1 - s^r)\beta^r]/s^r$. If, as is
commonly assumed, investment is more valuable than consumption from a
social view-point (i.e. $\delta > \beta^u$), then for large enough s^r, such a transfer is
desirable.

It should be apparent that a slight modification of the formulae that we
derive in the ensuing chapters allows us to take account of both private
investment and government consumption. To repeat, the use of the term
'investible surplus' does not mean either that we believe government expenditures are the only, or even the best, source of investment funds, or that government revenues are spent, particularly at the margin, on investment.

Openness of the Economy

Still another characteristic of the economy which must be built into any
plausible model is the extent to which it is open to trade. While many LDCs
are small and very dependent on trade, a large fraction of the Third World
population lives in its two largest countries—China and India. Whether it
is appropriate to model these countries as open or not is a matter of some

debate. Still other countries, such as Brazil, have chosen to limit their imports severely. An economist must thus consider the consequences of alternative policies under the hypothesis that some LDCs may continue their existing trade policies. Finally, even those countries which are small often find the market for their exports severely limited. They would look askance at any economist who informed them that they should be able to sell as much of any commodity as they liked at the world price. These 'facts of life' also need to be incorporated into the model.

More generally, the question is: At the margin, what is the elasticity of demand for the country's exports? While it may not be zero, in many cases it may be small enough so that the model of a small economy closed at the margin may be more appropriate than that of an open economy facing an infinite elasticity of demand.

2.4 CONCLUDING REMARKS

This list of the essential ingredients in any model of an LDC is not meant to be exhaustive. We present it here both to indicate the range of issues which will be covered in this book and to suggest why the standard neoclassical models, which have been constructed for developed economies, are likely to be of limited use in examining public-finance policies in LDCs. This discussion should also make clear that any model that one constructs should be adaptable to a variety of settings. The models presented in this book have this property.

3

AN APPROACH TO APPLIED
WELFARE ECONOMICS

3.1 INTRODUCTION

One of the contributions of this book is to use and develop the principles of modern public finance for the analysis of LDCs. We thus borrow heavily from two intellectual traditions: that relating to public finance, and that relating to development economics. It may be useful at this juncture to review briefly the four major strands in public finance literature which form the background to this study.

3.2 THEORETICAL BACKGROUND

General-Equilibrium Analysis

The central theoretical contribution in this area is Harberger's classic 1962 paper, analysing the effects of a tax on capital in the corporate sector. In that paper, he traced these effects on the movement of capital from the corporate to the unincorporated sector, and the resulting changes in wages and relative prices. Having ascertained these effects, it was then possible to determine how workers and owners of capital were affected by the tax.

The parallels between our problem and his are clear: this book considers two sectors (urban and rural) and analyses the effects of a variety of policies imposed on one or the other sector. But there are some important differences. Harberger assumed that factors were perfectly mobile; we assume that capital is largely immobile,[1] and that labour may be only partially and imperfectly mobile. He assumed full employment with wages and prices adjusting to clear markets; we consider both exogenous and endogenous wage rigidities. He assumed that firms in both sectors were profit-maximizing, and that there was a separation between households (consumption) and production; by contrast most households in the LDC rural sector both produce and consume. Harberger assumed, of course, a closed economy;[2] we shall be concerned with closed as well as open economies. For our purposes, however, the

---

[1] Subsequent work (e.g. by McLure 1971; 1974) has extended the Harberger model to consider cases in which factors are imperfectly mobile.

[2] Since then, variants of his model have been extended to open economies (see, for instance, Stiglitz 1988).

central contribution of Harberger was his emphasis on a clear articulation of a simple general-equilibrium model within which the effects of any policy on each of the major groups in the economy can be assessed.

We noted earlier that, in general, the government cannot and does not alter one action alone. Economists engaged in the analysis of the incidence of taxes have recognized this and, in response, have developed a variety of alternative incidence concepts. An example is what is called balanced-budget incidence analysis, which assumes that when the government increases taxes, it increases expenditures accordingly. Our analysis uses a variety of concepts. In some cases it is assumed that government revenue is fixed, and one tax is substituted for another.[3] In other cases, we assume that an increase or decrease in government revenue simply increases or decreases the investible surplus. In interpreting the results based on this approach, one should keep in mind the broad interpretation of the investible surplus described in the previous chapter.

Pigouvian Welfare Economics and Optimal Taxation

The second strand of thought is Pigouvian welfare economics, which can be viewed as an attempt to continue the nineteenth century's utilitarian idea of designing social institutions that maximize the sum of individuals' utilities. This research programme has extended over more than a century. Edgeworth (1897) showed that utilitarianism had strong implications for tax design, in particular for the progressivity of the tax system. While Edgeworth had assumed that the government could impose lump-sum taxes, subsequent researchers employed more realistic assumptions. In this vein, Pigou posed the following question to his student Frank Ramsey: 'What set of commodity taxes would minimize the inefficiencies resulting from those taxes?'[4] Mirrlees (1971), who subsequently analysed the optimal income-tax schedule when the government can levy only income taxes, was concerned with the incentive effects (i.e. the income–leisure trade-off). Atkinson and Stiglitz (1976) provided a synthesis of the analyses of commodity and income taxes. They showed that the absence of an income tax has an important effect on the nature of desirable commodity-tax policies.

The Pigou–Ramsey results were accordingly not of much relevance for

---

[3] Since in our model we assume that marginal additions to or subtractions from government revenue go to the investible surplus, an analysis which keeps investment unchanged corresponds to what has been called balanced-growth incidence analysis.

[4] Although the Ramsey analysis was discussed in Pigou's classic textbook on public economics, it did not become a focus of attention until the work of Meade (1955), Boiteux (1956), Baumol and Bradford (1970), and Diamond and Mirrlees (1971). Diamond and Mirrlees made an important contribution by extending the Ramsey analysis to an explicitly general-equilibrium context. In doing so, however, they made a number of other assumptions, some of which are discussed below, which led them to obtain somewhat different results from those obtained earlier by Ramsey. There have been several surveys of optimal taxation in recent years, including one by Atkinson and Stiglitz (1980).

those countries which employ income taxes extensively. On the other hand, they could, in principle, be relevant to LDCs, where income taxes are of little importance. However, as we will show, the structure of an LDC economy is so different from that assumed by Ramsey and Pigou (and their followers) that their results are largely vitiated.

The New Welfare Economics

The third major strand that provides the intellectual background to this work is the New Welfare Economics, which was in part a response to the Pigouvian Welfare Economics described above. The New Welfare Economics began with the observation that inter-personal utility comparisons were not meaningful. From that, it was concluded that the utilitarian approach of adding up utilities was nonsense. Economics, in this view, could describe the results of various policies, but could not, in general, make value-judgements. The only case in which economists could say that one allocation was better than another was when some individuals were better off in one situation than in another, and no one was worse off: that is, when the first allocation was a Pareto-improvement over the second.[5]

New New Welfare Economics

The fourth strand could be referred to as the New New Welfare Economics. This emerging strand borrows elements from the three preceding approaches. It continues, for instance, the Harberger tradition of emphasizing the general-equilibrium effects of taxation. It differs from the New Welfare Economics and from the more recent optimal tax approach in several important ways:

(a) it seeks to analyse, rather than take for granted, the scope of tax instruments available to the government; and

(b) it takes into account market imperfections (such as wage rigidities) and the alternative organizations that exist in the economy. It seeks not only to take them into account but also to explain them.

Like the recent literature on optimal taxation, but unlike the New Welfare Economics, this strand recognizes that non-uniform lump-sum taxes are not, in general, feasible. Like the New Welfare Economics, but unlike the literature on optimal taxation, it looks for Pareto-improvements. Tax structures which are such that—given the limitations on the feasible tax instruments—no one can be made better off without making someone else worse off are called Pareto-efficient tax structures (see Stiglitz 1987a).

Like the literature on optimal taxation, but unlike the New Welfare

---

[5] The classic works in the New Welfare Economics include books by Little (1950) and Van de Graaff (1957).

Economics, this strand of theory recognizes that in many contexts, choices among policies require making inter-personal welfare judgements. Economists can be helpful in providing systematic ways of making such judgements.

3.3 APPLIED WELFARE ECONOMICS FOR LDCs

This book is very much in the spirit of the New New Welfare Economics. In the paragraphs below, we discuss how various aspects of this approach are particularly germane to the problems with which we are concerned in this book.

Limited Taxation

Unlike much of the public finance literature, this book tries to avoid making arbitrary assumptions about the available set of instruments.[6] We argue why particular sets of taxes may or may not be feasible under particular LDC circumstances. Having established the constraints on the set of feasible policies which the government can implement, the New New Welfare Economics then asks: What are the possible Pareto-efficient allocations, and what are the corresponding Pareto-efficient policies?

The analysis of tax policies can change rather dramatically depending on the assumptions concerning available tax instruments. For instance, we already noted that as long as both income and commodity taxes can be imposed, the Pareto-efficient set of commodity taxes looks markedly different from that which Ramsey analysed (where he assumed that only commodity taxes were feasible) (see Atkinson and Stiglitz 1980). In one central case there should be no commodity taxation at all. More generally, the Pareto-efficient commodity tax structures depend on how the marginal rate of substitution between any commodity and the numeraire commodity changes with changes in leisure, and not on the elasticities of demand and supply, as Ramsey had argued. Of course, Ramsey was correct, given his assumption of the absence of lump-sum taxes and of an income tax.[7]

Information-Related Constraints on Feasible Taxes. Costs and unavailability of information are undoubtedly central sources of constraints on the set of available policy instruments. This explains why governments cannot impose lump-sum taxes differentiated on the basis of ability, and accordingly why

---

[6] For instance, the reason why lump-sum taxes are not feasible is quite simple: the government cannot observe endowments (e.g. abilities) of individuals and, thus, it cannot impose lump-sum taxes on individuals' endowments.

[7] In Ramsey's model, where there is a 'representative individual', there is no compelling reason why a lump-sum tax could not be imposed.

governments must resort to distortionary taxation if they wish to redistribute income.

In unincorporated enterprises, there is no way that any tax authority can identify whether a particular dollar is a return to labour or to capital. While the notion of the marginal return to capital or the marginal return to labour may be conceptually well defined, the distinction is operationally meaningless. Hence there must be a uniform tax on the two kinds of returns. This is not so in the corporate sector, where the firm must label whether a particular dollar is a return to capital to be distributed as dividends or interest, or a return to labour to be paid as wages; these labels have consequences beyond the mere determination of tax liabilities.

Most governments provide simple rules for depreciation (the decrease in the value of a machine as it becomes older); these rules frequently do not correspond to true economic depreciation, that is, to the true decrease in the value of an asset. The failure to use true economic depreciation is known to cause economic distortions. But this failure is at least partly attributable to the inability to measure true economic depreciation with any accuracy. Rather than engage in a costly process of assessing the value of each machine, tax authorities resort to simple rules of thumb.

An important restriction on the set of feasible taxes in the design of tax structures is the absence of 100 per cent profits taxes. One explanation for this restriction is that government cannot distinguish between pure profits and quasi-rents (returns to capital, returns to entrepreneurship, etc.) A 100 per cent pure profits tax would, in principle, have no distortions, but in practice would undoubtedly have significant distortions. The consequences of the absence of 100 per cent pure profits taxes are important. Ramsey assumed that there were no pure profits taxes, and found that the optimal tax structure depended critically on the supply elasticities. In contrast, Diamond and Mirrlees (1971) assumed that there were constant returns to scale in the private sector, so that there were no profits to be taxed, and found that the optimal tax structure depended only on the elasticities of demand. When their model was extended to decreasing returns industries, the conclusion that the optimal tax structure depended only on the properties of the demand curves was shown to hold only if there were 100 per cent profits taxes. Stiglitz and Dasgupta (1971) were able to derive a formula for the optimal tax structure which reduced to the Diamond–Mirrlees results with 100 per cent profits taxation, and to the Ramsey results with no profits taxation.

Administrative Costs as an Explanation of Tax Bases. The examples just given are of situations where information costs provide an important set of constraints on the set of feasible taxes. There are other cases where it might be feasible to impose taxes on a variety of bases, but then the costs of administering one set of taxes might be sufficiently less than for another set.

For all practical purposes, it is as if there were a constraint on the set of feasible taxes. Thus, most countries monitor trade into and out of the country. Since there are usually only a few ports capable of handling large shipments, it is less costly to monitor and, thus, taxes on foreign trade are imposed. On the other hand, the costs associated with monitoring, and thus imposing taxes on domestic production and consumption may be high. The reason that many LDCs resort to foreign trade taxes may not be because they wish to discourage international trade, but because it provides a method of raising revenue with low transactions costs.

Political Constraints.   As noted above, it is desirable that a constraint on the set of admissible taxes be derived from more basic considerations (information costs, transactions costs, tax arbitrage, etc.). Many governments may claim that they must, in addition, deal with political constraints. Thus, many LDCs have urban wages (including those of government employees) at above market-clearing levels. A reduction in these wages would increase both equity and efficiency.[8] However, a government may say that it is politically impossible for them to effect this. What are we to make of such claims? How should these constraints be treated in our analysis? We discuss these issues at greater length in Chapters 10 and 12. For now we simply note that a policy analysis which assumes that the government will, upon the recommendation of the adviser, eliminate these distortions is not likely to be treated seriously. The approach taken here is to ask: What should government policies be with respect to taxation, given that wages are not reduced to their market-clearing level? What should government policies be in the unlikely possibility that wages are reduced?

The fact that we cannot fully explain some observed constraint does not mean that the constraint is not there. A seemingly persistent anomaly, such as the persistence of wages at above market-clearing levels, should at least suggest that there is something wrong with a model which claims that wages could be at non-market-clearing levels only temporarily. It is better to construct a model which at least incorporates the constraint rather than ignores it. While, in the former case, policy recommendations may sometimes go astray (since the nature of the constraint may be affected by the policy changes under consideration), the policy recommendations in the latter case are almost surely subject to question because they are based on a counterfactual model. The fact that we do not fully understand why a giraffe has a long neck or how blood is pumped all the way to its head does not mean that the giraffe does not have a long neck; and any analysis of giraffes and their behaviour must take this fact of life into account.

---

[8] Those who advocate high urban wages often use equity arguments, ignoring the fact that such wages may reduce employment. Depending on whether the wage elasticity of demand for labour is equal to or greater than unity, total wage payments are unchanged or increased when wages are reduced, but are divided more equitably among potential workers.

Changes in Feasible Tax Instruments in LDCs. As is repeatedly emphasized in this book, the structure of LDCs imposes a number of constraints on the set of admissible taxes. At the same time, some taxes which would not be feasible in a developed country may be possible in a less developed country. In developed countries, it is frequently impossible to impose differential tax-rates on different groups and regions because the market will effectively undo any attempt at discriminatory taxation. In many less developed countries it has been feasible to impose different tax-rates in the urban and rural sectors. We consider this possibility in Chapter 4. Thus, the absence of well-functioning markets may enable the imposition of taxes which would otherwise not be feasible. Accordingly, changes in the economy may necessitate changes in the tax structure.[9]

General-Equilibrium Effects

We share with the earlier Harbergerian approach a concern for general-equilibrium price effects—a concern which was explored only under very special assumptions in the recent literature on optimal taxation. By assuming a complete set of commodity taxes and by assuming 100 per cent profits taxes, this literature was able virtually to divorce the determination of production prices from consumer prices. Such a separation, however, is not possible unless every transaction can be taxed. General-equilibrium effects are extremely important in the design of the optimal tax system whenever there does not exist a complete set of commodity and factor taxes. For instance, when wages in the rural sector cannot be taxed, then any change in government policy which affects the demand and supply of rural labour will affect the rural wage. In turn, this has important distributional effects which need to be taken into account. By contrast, in a world with a complete set of factor taxes, any such effect could be offset by a change in the tax imposed on rural wages; thus the conditions for optimality can be expressed in a way which ignores the effect on wages.[10]

Institutions

It is now widely recognized that LDCs exhibit wide diversity in their economic institutions. A rural economy with extended families can be quite different from an economy with share-cropping. It is, of course, better to explain these institutional features, for example to relate the presence of share-cropping to the absence of certain risk markets and to the difficulties

[9] For instance, improvements in the functioning of capital markets in the United States have reduced the government's ability to tax capital income and, in particular, to tax different kinds of capital income at different rates.

[10] General-equilibrium effects have also been shown to be extremely important in the analysis of the design of the optimal income tax (see Allen 1982; Stern 1982; and Stiglitz 1982*b*).

of monitoring inputs (Stiglitz 1974*b*). But even if one cannot explain the institution, it is better to recognize its existence than to assume that a share-cropping economy behaves in the same way as an economy of family farms or plantation farms.

Similarly, it has been shown that the social cost of labour (the net opportunity cost resulting from increased employment in the urban sector) depends critically on the nature of migration from the rural to the urban sector and on how wages in the urban sector are determined.[11] This book repeatedly emphasizes that in assessing the consequences of changes in prices in LDCs it is important to take these economic relations and institutions into account.

Inter-Personal Welfare Comparisons

The first stage in our analysis entails determining the effects of any policy change on each individual or group of individuals. This analysis entails no welfare judgements, other than to say that any government policy which results in a Pareto-improvement is desirable. Unfortunately, few policy changes are Pareto-improvements, although the scope for such improvements in those LDCs which have pursued policies that result in significant resource misallocations is perhaps greater than that in other LDCs. More generally, however, it becomes necessary in the evaluation of policies that the gains of one group be set off against the losses to other groups. As Hugh Dalton, Chancellor of the Exchequer in Britain in the period following World War II, put it: 'This is a difficult calculus, but . . . statesmen must handle it as best they can, since there is no practical alternative' (1954, p. 142).

Some method of making welfare judgements in such situations is required. This book seeks ways of doing this systematically, and it seeks to delineate the kinds of normative statements that can be made by making increasingly stronger normative judgements. Thus, it may ask: What kinds of policy changes would be agreed upon by all individuals who believe that a change which increases inequality without increasing the mean income is undesirable? There are many policy reforms which require only such a weak kind of welfare comparison. There are other changes about which different individuals, all of whom are egalitarian, would disagree. There may still be systematic ways of making welfare comparisons in such situations by using a social welfare function.

At this last point, our approach becomes similar to that of optimal tax theory. A social welfare function is viewed as a convenient way of summarizing into a single statistic all the myriad effects on different groups in the economy. We recognize that no single statistic provides an adequate description of the economy, but the complexity of the effects is such that some summary measures are required, and a social welfare function provides one way

---

[11] See Harberger (1971) and Stiglitz (1974a; 1982c).

of doing this. At the same time, our view (reflected in those parts of the book in which the analysis is based on a social welfare function) is that such an analysis is more useful if it is based on relatively weak restrictions on the social welfare function. An example of a strong assumption, often employed in optimal tax theory, is that the social marginal utility of income is a constant elasticity function of the level of income and independent of prices. This assumption represents a value-judgement about which there is far less agreement than, say, about an individualistic Bergson–Samuelson social welfare function. This function hypothesizes that social welfare depends only on the level of utility attained by each individual, and that it is an increasing and concave function of individuals' utilities (i.e. social welfare is higher if an individual's utility is higher, and society has some aversion to inequality).

An altogether different, and we believe innovative, use of this normative analysis is to find out whether actual policies pursued in an LDC are consistent with the accompanying egalitarian political rhetoric. We provide many examples of how such inconsistencies can be detected. It will also become apparent that the same methodology can be employed to study potential inconsistencies in a variety of policies (for example, income taxation) in the context of developed countries as well as LDCs.

PART II

Inter-Sectoral Taxation Policies

4

RURAL–URBAN PRICES IN
OPEN ECONOMIES

4.1 INTRODUCTION

In this chapter, we begin analysing the basic question: How should the burden of financing economic development be shared between those in the urban and rural sectors? We consider here an economy which can trade at fixed international prices with the rest of the world, and in which there is a tax border between the urban and rural sectors. The latter assumption indicates that the government can impose different sets of taxes in the two sectors and, as a result, market prices in the two sectors can differ. In such an economy, the question posed above turns out to be equivalent to asking: What should be the relationship among prices received by farmers, prices paid by city-dwellers, and international prices?

The analysis in this chapter is based on the simplest model which can highlight the central trade-offs involved in taxing or subsidizing the rural and urban sectors. We enlarge and modify this model in subsequent chapters to take into account a number of considerations deliberately left out at present. The present model abstracts from intra-sectoral heterogeneity of individuals and goods, and from inter-sectoral flows of factors such as labour and capital. Also, to keep matters simple, we assume at present that the urban wage is fixed in terms of the industrial good, which we take to be the numeraire.[1] Further, the present analysis abstracts from the effects of prices and wages on productivity (that is, the effects that changes in prices and wages have on the net output of workers); these effects are incorporated towards the end of the chapter.

The basic model has rural peasants selling their agricultural surplus in order to buy the industrial good. Taxing the rural sector lowers peasants' welfare; the revenue raised by the government from a tax on a peasant's surplus, denoted by Q, is just the tax times Q. As the tax increases, the surplus sold normally decreases. If it decreases enough, total revenue decreases. We establish that if the tax is currently higher than a critical positive level, then by lowering the tax-rate the government can make peasants better off and increase government revenue. In other words tax-rates in excess of a certain critical level are Pareto-inefficient.

---

[1] The effects of tax policy on urban workers and on the investible surplus depend, in part, on the mechanism which determines the urban wage; for instance, how the urban wage adjusts to changes in prices. These aspects are discussed extensively in part. IV of the book.

With fixed international prices, the price received by peasants is just the international price of food minus the tax on food. Hence, the result that taxes above a critical level are Pareto-inefficient is equivalent to the result that there exists a critical rural price, $\bar{p}^r$, such that prices below $\bar{p}^r$ are Pareto-inefficient. We show that this critical price is lower than the international price. In other words, there is a limit on the extent to which the rural sector can be squeezed (see Fig. 4.1).

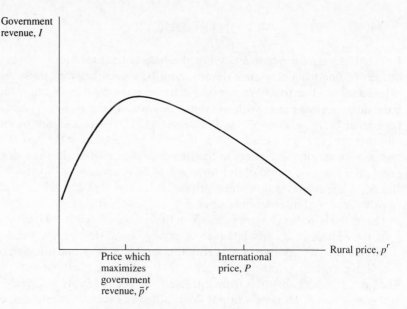

Fig. 4.1 Pareto-inefficient regimes.

There is a critical rural price, $\bar{p}^r$, which is lower than the international price, P, such that prices below $\bar{p}^r$ are Pareto-inefficient.

Similarly, by imposing a tax on food purchases in the urban sector, the government raises revenue but lowers the welfare of those in this sector. The revenue received from this tax is just the quantity purchased times the tax, where the tax is the food price paid by city-dwellers minus the international food price. As the tax paid by urban consumers increases, they reduce their demand.[2] Again, it is easily shown that there is a critical level of tax such

[2] The reduction in tax revenues may be large in LDCs since, in general, not all commodities can be taxed or can be taxed equally heavily. For instance, if the tax-rate on an expensive (high-grade) cereal is increased then some individuals who could previously afford this cereal will switch to lower-grade cereals and to foods which can be brought into the urban sector from the rural sector without paying taxes. The deleterious effects on government revenue may be exacerbated by changes in migration: the tax may reduce the pressure of migration to the urban sector, since the welfare of those in the urban sector is reduced by urban taxation, and this may reduce the aggregate consumption of the urban sector. An opposite migration effect arises if the tax on the rural output is increased. These migration effects are studied in later chapters.

that, if the existing taxes exceed that critical level, both city-dwellers and the government may be made better-off by a reduction in the tax-rate. Urban taxes above such a critical level are Pareto-inefficient. Equivalently, urban food prices above some critical level are Pareto-inefficient.

For urban prices lower than the critical level there is a trade-off: a price reduction makes urban workers better off but reduces government revenues (and hence reduces investment and the potential welfare of future generations). Similarly, for rural prices higher than the critical level, $\bar{p}^r$, there is a trade-off: a price increase makes peasants better off but reduces government revenues. How the government should set the urban and rural prices will then depend on value-judgements concerning the social desirability of future consumption (investment) relative to that of current consumption in each of the two sectors. Our subsequent analysis shows the following. First, if the government, at the margin, values consumption in the urban sector as much as it values investment or other public expenditures, then it should neither tax nor subsidize food in the urban sector. Second, if the government, at the margin, values consumption in the rural sector as much as it values investment, then it should neither tax nor subsidize the rural sector.

In the early stages of development it is presumed that investment is, at the margin, more valuable than current consumption.[3] For these cases we establish that there should be a tax on both the urban and the rural sectors, that is, the price paid to farmers should be below the international price, and the price paid by consumers in the urban sector should be above the international price. This conclusion seems to contradict the policies pursued by many LDCs, where there are food subsidies in the urban sector but taxes in the rural sector.[4]

Further, in many LDCs real incomes in the rural sector are substantially below those in the urban sector. In these cases the apparent inconsistency of typically observed policies is even deeper. We show that if peasants are worse off than urban workers, then with an egalitarian social welfare function (i.e. one which displays some aversion to inequality), the urban sector should be subsidized only if the rural sector is subsidized. However, the converse is not true: it may be desirable to tax the urban sector while subsidizing the rural sector.

The optimal magnitude of the taxes or subsidies depends, of course, not only on the marginal valuation of investment relative to consumption in the two sectors, but also on certain behavioural responses, in particular on the price response of demand in the urban sector and the price response of the agricultural surplus sold by the rural sector.

---

[3] For simplicity, the present analysis focuses only on public savings as the 'investible surplus'. In the introductory chapters, we discussed how this analysis can be interpreted and enlarged to take account of private savings and investment in the rural and urban sectors.

[4] In later chapters, we shall attempt to assess whether this observed pattern can be accounted for by some feature not included in the present simple model.

In the following section we set up a simple model and derive these results. We are able to describe the effects of price changes in the rural or urban sector. We are also able to describe the optimal set of prices and taxes in terms of two sets of parameters which respectively capture certain behavioural responses of consumers and producers, and the social marginal valuation of investment versus consumption.

4.2 A SIMPLE MODEL

We begin by considering an economy in which there are two aggregate commodities and two aggregate sectors. Food and food-related products are produced in the agricultural or rural sector (represented by the superscript r). A generalized industrial good, which can be used either for consumption or for investment, is produced in the industrial or urban sector (represented by the superscript u). Both goods can be freely traded with the rest of the world. The international price of the agricultural good in terms of the industrial good (which is the numeraire) is denoted by P.

Agricultural Sector

The agricultural sector consists of homogeneous farm households whose members decide how much labour to supply, given the prices at which they can sell their surplus. We denote this price by p^r. Clearly, the level of utility which peasants can attain is a function of this price. We write the utility level of a representative peasant as $V^r(p^r)$.[5] Some of the agricultural output is consumed within the agricultural sector and the surplus is sold to the industrial sector or abroad. This surplus per peasant is denoted by Q. Since the agricultural producers are assumed, at present, to be homogeneous, we assume that Q is positive; this assumption is relaxed in Chapters 8 and beyond where we incorporate rural heterogeneity. The surplus Q is a function of the price which peasants receive. We denote the price elasticity of the surplus by

$$\varepsilon^r_{Qp} = \partial\ln Q/\partial\ln p^r .$$

Economic theory puts no constraints on the sign of ε^r_{Qp}. In particular, one cannot rule out the case of a backward-bending supply schedule of surplus where the substitution effect (that is, the effect of higher prices inducing individuals to produce more for sale) is dominated by the income effect (that is, the effect of higher prices making individuals better off, inducing them to work less and to consume more of what they do produce). We focus attention on the empirically supported case in which an increase in price increases

[5] The derivation of the indirect utility function, $V^r(p^r)$, as well as of other key expressions in this chapter, is summarized in the Appendix to this chapter.

the marketed surplus (see the Appendix to this chapter). That is, $\varepsilon^r_{Qp} > 0$. The formulae below can, however, be reinterpreted for the case in which $\varepsilon^r_{Qp} < 0$.

We assume that the government has very few policy instruments to influence peasants' behaviour; it cannot directly control their output or their consumption. This, we believe, is the correct representation for most LDCs, since much of the farming in these economies is done on numerous small plots, and the ability of the government to monitor and control the actions of peasants seems sufficiently limited so that only indirect incentives are administratively feasible.[6] We also assume that complex pricing schemes are infeasible. Non-linear pricing schemes, for example, in which the unit price paid to a peasant depends on the amount he sells, not only entail large administrative costs but also typically induce underground (unaccounted) transactions. Accordingly, we restrict ourselves to schemes which pay a common price to all peasants regardless of the quantities they transact.[7]

Industrial Sector

In contrast to the agricultural sector, we assume that there are many policy instruments feasible in the industrial sector. In fact, the polar assumption is made that the government has sufficient instruments so that the distinction between direct and indirect control of production can be virtually ignored. In many LDCs the government not only is the largest industrial producer and employer, but also taxes private producers' profits and can sometimes control their prices and quantities. Yet the above assumption of direct control is not completely satisfactory; though the government can tax profits, for instance, it cannot impose a 100 per cent profits tax.[8] In fact, questions have rightly been raised as to whether the government can control its own

[6] In any event, our present analysis does not deal with a collectivist agriculture or with an agriculture based on government-managed parastatals. In these cases it might be feasible to control rural consumption, but to assume that output can be directly controlled (as has been frequently done in the planning literature) is, in our view, inaccurate.

[7] It should be obvious that non-linear tax–subsidy pricing schemes are better in the Pareto sense than standard linear pricing, provided such schemes are feasible and they are costless (for instance, they do not entail additional administrative costs). This is simply because in such cases a non-linear scheme provides more instruments to the government than does a linear pricing scheme, and the government cannot do worse by having more instruments. By the same logic, restricted non-linear schemes, such as those implemented by quotas and rations, are desirable additions to standard pricing provided these schemes are costless. In more realistic circumstances, the case for such policies is much weaker. For instance, for non-linear schemes to be effective, they have to be accompanied by regulations which restrict resale. Such regulations not only serve as an invitation to corruption, but also, if rigorously enforced, give rise to a variety of bureaucratic inefficiencies. Yet governments do make some limited use of non-linear schemes, in particular for food rationing in the urban sector. See Sah (1987) for an analysis and comparison of several such non-price instruments including queues. See Sah and Srinivasan (1988) for an analysis of the distributional consequences of subsidized urban food rations, which takes into account the economy-wide general-equilibrium effects.

[8] There are good reasons for this. For instance, it is difficult to isolate pure profits from the return to capital, on the one hand, and from the return to entrepreneurial effort and risk-taking, on the other.

nationalized industries, let alone the multinationals.[9] Our assumption that the government can control the industrial sector is made partly to simplify the analysis and partly in order to dramatize the difference between the urban and rural sectors. As we discuss later, this analysis can be modified for those cases in which the government's control over the industrial sector is limited and indirect.[10]

The factory system enables workers to be monitored more effectively than they can be in agriculture. At least hours on the job, if not effort, can easily be monitored in factories. It has sometimes been argued that one of the main reasons why the assembly-line system increased productivity was that it facilitated the monitoring of workers.

In the simple model analysed below, the government takes the urban wage-rate, denoted by w^u, as given, but it can control the price, p^u, at which food is sold in the urban sector. Thus, we write the welfare of an industrial worker as $V^u(p^u, w^u)$. For expositional brevity, we assume that the number of hours worked by an industrial worker, L^u, is fixed for technological reasons.[11] An industrial worker takes his income, $w^u L^u$, and the price, p^u, as given and decides how much food to consume. This quantity is represented as $x^u(p^u, w^u)$. The price elasticity of urban food consumption is $\varepsilon_{xp}^u = -\partial\ln x^u/\partial\ln p^u$, which is positive since consumption goods are assumed to be normal.

Investible Surplus

The revenue currently available to the government for investment is the difference between the value of industrial output and industrial wage payments,[12] plus the net tax revenue from the quantity of food supplied by farmers and the quantity of food purchased by urban consumers:

$$I = N^u(Y - w^u L^u) + (P - p^r)N^r Q(p^r) + (p^u - P)\, N^u x^u(p^u, w^u) \qquad (4.1)$$

| Profits of industry | Rural Tax revenue | Urban Tax revenue |

[9] For an analysis of the limited ability of governments to discipline public enterprises in LDCs, see Sah and Weitzman (1991).

[10] We often anthropomorphize the government, speaking of it as if it were a single individual. In fact, it is a complex set of institutions, with individuals in different positions delegated certain rights and responsibilities, with certain interests which they pursue that may not coincide with someone else's conception of the public interest. For instance, nationalized industries often pay their workers above market wages. Whether this increases inequality (by increasing the disparity between such workers and comparably skilled workers in private industries) or decreases inequality (by reducing the disparity between such workers and more skilled workers in private industries) depends on one's point of view.

[11] The analysis corresponding to variable labour hours of workers in the urban sector can be easily worked out, by specifying that workers can work the number of hours they wish, and that a worker's labour supply is given by $L^u(w^u, p^u)$. An analogous formulation can be used if workers are rationed concerning the maximum number of hours they can work.

[12] An assumption here is that the government has sufficient power to appropriate all non-economic industrial profits.

where N^r is the number of peasants, N^u is the number of industrial workers, and Y is output per industrial worker. (For a derivation of (4.1) see the Appendix to this chapter.) Though we use the symbol I throughout this book to denote the investible surplus, as we have explained in the introductory chapters, it is not assumed that the entire surplus is necessarily spent on productive investments.

4.3 ANALYSIS OF CHANGES IN AGRICULTURAL AND INDUSTRIAL PRICES

Pareto-Improving Price Reforms

There are three groups in our model: peasants, industrial workers, and the government, which represents future generations through its control of the investible surplus. For each value of p^r and p^u, one can calculate feasible combinations of V^r, V^u, and I (see Fig. 4.2). We first show that certain price changes can make all groups in society better off.

Note that an increase in rural food prices makes the peasants better off. It does not affect industrial workers since the price they pay for food can be set independently.[13] Thus, a change in the rural price affects investment only through the tax revenue from rural surplus. Specifically, a higher rural price lowers the tax revenue on the existing rural surplus, but it increases the tax revenue because, given a positive price response of the rural surplus, the rural surplus becomes larger. The condition under which a higher rural price leads to a larger investible surplus (that is, $\partial I / \partial p^r > 0$) can be obtained by differentiating (4.1) with respect to p^r.[14] The condition is

$$p^r < P/(1 + 1/\varepsilon^r_{Qp}) \equiv \bar{p}^r. \tag{4.2}$$

Thus, if the food price in the agricultural sector is less than $\bar{p}^r$, then a price increase is desirable, since it will not only improve the welfare of peasants but will also increase government revenue, without affecting the welfare of industrial workers (see Fig. 4.1). This is an example of what is referred to as a Pareto-improving reform.

[13] This independence occurs because the economy is open to external trade. If the economy is closed at the margin, a Pareto-improving price reform involves simultaneous changes in rural and urban prices, unless the government has additional instruments of control (see ch. 6 below).

[14]
$$\frac{\partial I}{\partial p^r} = N^r \left[(P - p^r) \frac{\partial Q}{\partial p^r} - Q \right] = N^r Q \left[\frac{(P - p^r)}{p^r} \frac{p^r}{Q} \frac{\partial Q}{\partial p^r} - 1 \right]$$

$$= N^r Q \left[\frac{P - p^r}{p^r} \varepsilon^r_{Qp} - 1 \right]$$

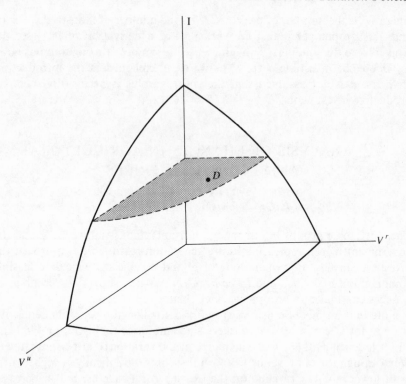

FIG. 4.2 UTILITY POSSIBILITIES SCHEDULE
If current prices are such that the society is at a point such as D, then a Pareto-improving price reform is possible.

It is also clear from (4.2) that

$$\bar{p}^r < P.$$

That is, the critical price level, $\bar{p}^r$, is lower than the international food price.

A simpler statement of the above reform rule is possible in terms of taxes. Let $t^r = (P - p^r)/p^r$ denote the tax-rate on food in the rural sector. Then, an increase in the rural food price is Pareto-improving if

$$t^r > 1/\varepsilon_{Qp}^r . \tag{4.2a}$$

That is, if the current rural food tax-rate exceeds the inverse of the price elasticity of the rural surplus, then an increase in the rural food price is Pareto-improving.

Similarly, a decrease in the urban food price makes the industrial workers better off without affecting the peasants. It increases government revenue if $\partial I/\partial p^u < 0$. From (4.1) the corresponding conditions are:

(a) the urban demand elasticity of food is larger than unity, and (b)

$$p^u > P/(1 - 1/\varepsilon^u_{xp}) \equiv \bar{p}^u. \tag{4.3}$$

That is, if the demand elasticity is larger than unity and if the urban food price is above $\bar{p}^u$, then a decrease in the urban food price is desirable for society.[15] Lowering p^u in this case raises investible surplus and improves the welfare of urban workers, while leaving the rural sector unaffected. Note, however, that if the urban demand elasticity of food is less than unity, then raising p^u lowers the welfare of urban workers and increases the investible surplus. In this case, there is always a trade-off between the welfare of urban workers and the size of the investible surplus.[16] The statement of the above reform rule is, once again, simpler in terms of taxes. If $t^u = (p^u - P)/p^u$ denotes the tax on food in the urban sector, then a decrease in the urban food price is Pareto-improving if

$$t^u > 1/\varepsilon^u_{xp} . \tag{4.3a}$$

That is, if the urban food tax exceeds the inverse of the price elasticity of urban consumption, then a decrease in the urban food price is Pareto-improving.

We have thus derived two rules for price or tax reform, which are Pareto-improving:

1. If the price of food in the rural sector is less than $\bar{p}^r$, then the price should be increased, at least to the level $\bar{p}^r$.
2. If the price of food in the urban sector is higher than $\bar{p}^u$, and the price elasticity of demand is greater than unity, then the price should be lowered to at least $\bar{p}^u$.

These rules of price reform have several virtues. First, they identify a lower limit for the rural food price and an upper limit for the urban food price. Second, they allow the questions of reform in the rural and the urban prices to be addressed independently of one another. Third, the use of these rules requires very little information. Apart from the world price, only demand and supply elasticities are needed. The rules do not require social weights on different individuals' gains and losses, which will be needed to implement optimal prices. Moreover, the value of the behavioural parameters (that is, the elasticities of demand and supply) which are needed to use these rules

---

[15] Expression (4.3) is derived from the following derivative:

$$\frac{\partial I}{\partial p^u} = N^u \left[(p^u - P) \frac{\partial x^u}{\partial p^u} + x^u \right] = N^u x^u \left(\frac{p^u - P}{p^u} \frac{p^u}{x^u} \frac{\partial x^u}{\partial p^u} + 1 \right)$$

$$= N^u x^u \left(\frac{P - p^u}{p^u} \varepsilon^u_{xp} + 1 \right) = N^u x^u \left(\frac{P}{p^u} \varepsilon^u_{xp} - \varepsilon^u_{xp} + 1 \right).$$

[16] See, however, the modifications of this conclusion described below, which arise due to productivity effects of price changes.

of reform (as well as other rules for Pareto-improvement which we will derive later) are those associated with the current equilibrium, which can be calculated from the local properties of the demand and supply functions. This should be contrasted with the optimal pricing rules discussed below in which the relevant elasticities are evaluated at the social optimum. To do this, one needs to know the global properties of the demand and supply functions.

In addition, these rules hold in models more general than the one considered above. The main conditions required are

$$\frac{dV^r}{dp^r} > 0 \quad \text{and} \quad \frac{dV^u}{dp^u} < 0. \tag{4.4}$$

Interpret, for instance, V^r and V^u as representing the aggregate welfare of the entire group of peasants and industrial workers, respectively. Then (4.4) implies that the aggregate welfare of peasants increases if the price of their output is increased, and that the welfare of industrial workers decreases if the food price they face is increased. So long as these conditions are satisfied, the above rules of price reform continue to hold.

For instance, the rule for reform of the urban food price holds regardless of the distribution of income among industrial workers. Similarly, the rule for reform of the rural food price holds no matter how agricultural land is distributed among peasants, provided there are no peasants who are significant net buyers of food. Of course, when there is inequality in, say, land ownership, labour services will be bought and sold. Then, a change in p^r affects the rural wage. We show that even in such a disaggregated model of the rural sector, our present conclusion holds under plausible circumstances (see chapter 8). Moreover, as we shall see later, these rules of reform can be extended in a straightforward manner when prices affect individuals' productivity, and when there is migration between the two sectors.

The main point we wish to establish in this section, however, is not that the rules of price reform derived above are valid in every circumstance (of course, they are not if the economy is very different from the present model), but that one can often determine a set of rules to identify those price reforms which improve the welfare of all groups in society.

Welfare-Enhancing Price Reforms

We showed above how only the knowledge of the elasticities of rural surplus and urban demand is sufficient to weed out inefficient pricing policies. However, the above rules do not distinguish between numerous pricing policies which are efficient. A choice among these policies necessarily entails trade-offs between the interests of peasants, industrial workers, and future generations. In this section, we show how to analyse these trade-offs. To do this, we employ the following Bergson–Samuelson welfare function to aggregate individuals' utilities:

$$\psi = N^r W(V^r) + N^u W(V^u) , \tag{4.5}$$

in which $W(V)$ is the social welfare function defined over an individual's utility level, and this function is increasing and concave in V.[17] Aggregate social welfare is the social welfare of the representative peasant times the number of peasants plus the social welfare of the representative urban worker times the number of urban workers. This social welfare for all periods from now up to the relevant future is discounted to the present, using some discount rate. The maximization of this discounted aggregate social welfare is the same as the maximization of

$$H = \psi + \delta I, \tag{4.6}$$

where δ is the social value of marginal investment.[18] Using derivatives of H with respect to p^r and p^u,[19] it is easy to show that

---

[17] If social welfare is not anonymous between rural and urban individuals (that is, the social welfare imputed for an individual depends not only on his utility level but also his location), then the function W will be different in each of the two sectors.

[18] Expression (4.6) represents current national income in utility terms. See Arrow and Kurz (1970) for a standard exposition of this Hamiltonian formulation. The results presented in this chapter hold at every point in time. The same formulation can also be employed to trace the path of optimal prices and other variables over time. We assume here that investment is employed to increase the capital stock in the industrial sector. Alternative specifications of the investment allocation can, however, be easily examined. For instance, our pricing rules remain unchanged if government revenue is partly invested in technological innovation or in creating rural infrastructure, but the government cannot directly levy user fees.

[19] The derivatives are obtained, using nn. 14 and 15, as follows:

$$\frac{\partial H}{\partial p^r} = N^r \frac{\partial W}{\partial V^r} \frac{\partial V^r}{\partial p^r} + \delta \frac{\partial I}{\partial p^r} = N^r Q \left[\frac{\partial W}{\partial V^r} \lambda^r + \delta \left(\frac{P - p^r}{p^r} \varepsilon^r_{Qp} - 1 \right) \right]$$

$$= N^r Q \beta^r \left\{ 1 + \frac{\delta}{\beta^r} \left[\frac{P - p^r}{p^r} \varepsilon^r_{Qp} - 1 \right] \right\} .$$

$$\frac{\partial H}{\partial p^u} = N^u \frac{\partial W}{\partial V^u} \frac{\partial V^u}{\partial p^u} + \delta \frac{\partial I}{\partial p^u} = N^u x^u \beta^u \left[-1 + \frac{\delta}{\beta^u} \left(1 - \varepsilon^u_{xp} + \frac{P}{p^u} \varepsilon^u_{xp} \right) \right] .$$

In the above derivations, we have used the fact that $\partial V^r / \partial p^r = \lambda^r Q$ and $\partial V^u / \partial p^u = - \lambda^u x^u$. For details, see the Appendix to this chapter. We assume that μ^r and μ^u are positive. From (4.9), μ^r is positive if $\varepsilon^r_{Qp} > \beta^r / \delta - 1$. We expect this condition to be met in LDCs at early stages of development since the social weight on investment is likely to be higher than that on rural income. From (4.10), $\mu^u > 0$ if $\varepsilon^u_{xp} > 1 - \beta^u / \delta$. This condition may not always be met, especially if the urban demand elasticity of food (with respect to price) is very small and if the government does not care about the industrial workers (that is, if β^u / δ is close to zero). If $\mu^u < 0$, then the urban price should be increased. Note, however, that the present model abstracts from effects of prices on workers' productivity. As we shall see, increasing the urban price beyond some level would not be desirable when these productivity effects are taken into account, even if the government does not care about the welfare of industrial workers.

$$\frac{\partial H}{\partial p^r} \gtrless 0, \quad \text{if} \quad p^r \lesseqgtr P\mu^r \tag{4.7}$$

$$\frac{\partial H}{\partial p^u} \gtrless 0, \quad \text{if} \quad p^u \lesseqgtr P\mu^u, \tag{4.8}$$

where

$$\mu^r = 1 \left/ \left(1 + (1 - \frac{\beta^r}{\delta}) \frac{1}{\varepsilon^r_{Qp}} \right) \right., \tag{4.9}$$

$$\mu^u = 1 \left/ \left(1 - (1 - \frac{\beta^u}{\delta}) \frac{1}{\varepsilon^u_{xp}} \right) \right., \tag{4.10}$$

$\beta^i = \lambda^i(\partial W/\partial V^i)$ is the social marginal utility of income to a worker in sector i, and λ^i is the (positive) private marginal utility of income to a worker in sector i.

Expression (4.7) implies that social welfare is increased by increasing or decreasing the rural food price depending on whether the current price is lower or higher than $P\mu^r$. A similar rule for changing the urban food price is given by (4.8). These rules are more detailed than those we obtained earlier. This should not be surprising as rules (4.2) and (4.3) were limited to Pareto-efficiency considerations only. The present rules, being concerned with the question of social welfare, require more information. Specifically, they need two social valuation parameters (the social weights associated with rural and urban incomes relative to the social weight on investment) in addition to the two behavioural parameters (ε^r_{Qp} and ε^u_{xp}) which were needed for our earlier rules of reform.

Interpretation. The critical parameters in the price reform rules (4.7) and (4.8) are μ^r and μ^u. From (4.9) it is clear that if the social marginal value of consumption in the rural sector is less than the social marginal value of investment, then μ^r is less than unity. Similarly (4.10) shows that if the social marginal value of consumption in the urban sector is less than the social marginal value of investment, then μ^u is greater than unity. In these cases: Social welfare can be increased by: (*a*) increasing urban prices if they are below international prices, or (*b*) lowering rural prices if they are above international prices.

Egalitarian Price Reforms

If the social marginal utility of income to rural workers is greater than that for urban workers (i.e. $\beta^r > \beta^u$), then we can derive a condition for the prices (or taxes) in the urban and rural sectors such that if this condition is not satisfied, then there exist potential price reforms. These price reforms involve an increase in the rural as well as the urban price which leaves investment unchanged, but raises social welfare.

To derive this rule, recall that $t^r = (P - p^r)/p^r$ denotes the tax on food in the rural sector, and $t^u = (p^u - P)/p^u$ denotes the corresponding tax in the urban sector. The effects of price changes on the investible surplus are given (see fn. 14 and 15) by

$$\frac{\partial I}{\partial p^r} = N^r Q(t^r \varepsilon^r_{Qp} - 1) \quad \text{and} \quad \frac{\partial I}{\partial p^u} = N^u x^u (1 - t^u \varepsilon^u_{xp}). \tag{4.11}$$

We assume that the possibilities of Pareto-improving price reforms (see the previous section, especially expressions (4.2a) and (4.3a)) have already been exhausted. That is, current prices are such that the first expression in (4.11) is negative and the second expression is positive. Equivalently,

$$t^r < \frac{1}{\varepsilon^r_{Qp}} \quad \text{and} \quad t^u < \frac{1}{\varepsilon^u_{xp}}. \tag{4.12}$$

Next, we determine the increase in the rural price, with a corresponding increase in the urban price, which will leave the investible surplus unchanged. From (4.11),

$$\left(\frac{dp^u}{dp^r}\right)_I = -\frac{\partial I}{\partial p^r} \bigg/ \frac{\partial I}{\partial p^u} = -\frac{(t^r \varepsilon^r_{Qp} - 1)N^r Q}{(1 - t^u \varepsilon^u_{xp})N^u x^u} > 0. \tag{4.13}$$

The positive sign of the above expression follows from (4.12).

The effect of such a price change on social welfare is given by

$$\left(\frac{dH}{dp^r}\right)_I = \frac{\partial H}{\partial p^r} + \frac{\partial H}{\partial p^u}\left(\frac{dp^u}{dp^r}\right)_I = N^r Q \beta^r - N^u x^u \beta^u \left(\frac{dp^u}{dp^r}\right)_I. \tag{4.14}$$

Substitution of (4.13) into (4.14) yields

$$\left(\frac{dH}{dp^r}\right)_I = N^r Q \left(\beta^r + \beta^u \frac{t^r \varepsilon^r_{Qp} - 1}{1 - t^u \varepsilon^u_{xp}} \right). \tag{4.15}$$

Now recall (4.12) and that $\beta^r > \beta^u$. It follows from (4.15) that

$$\left(\frac{dH}{dp^r}\right)_I > 0 \quad \text{if } t^r \varepsilon^r_{Qp} - t^u \varepsilon^u_{xp} > 0. \tag{4.16}$$

This result has some useful implications. We assume that the government revenue collected is positive. Then there are two possible reforms:

(a) Suppose $t^r > 0$ and $t^u < 0$. In this case (4.16) shows that an increase in the rural as well as the urban food price will improve welfare. That is, if the rural sector is being taxed and the urban sector is being subsidized, then a reduction in the rural tax and a reduction in the urban subsidy is desirable.

(b) Suppose $t^r > 0$ and $t^u > 0$. In this case (4.16) shows that an increase in the rural as well as the urban food price will improve welfare, as long as the ratio of current taxes, t^r/t^u, exceeds the ratio of the elasticities in the two sectors, $\varepsilon^u_{xp}/\varepsilon^r_{Qp}$.

These rules, like the previous rules for price reform, are remarkably parsimonious in their informational requirements. They require, at most, knowledge of the two price elasticities, in addition to the qualitative value-judgement that the social marginal utility of income to a rural worker exceeds that to an urban worker. We suspect that in practice many instances can be found where current prices can be reformed using condition (4.16).

Optimal Prices

The optimal prices are those at which the possibilities of reform have been fully exhausted. Diagrammatically, the optimum represents that point on the utility possibilities surface (see Fig. 4.2) which is tangent to the social indifference curve. An immediate consequence of rules (4.7) and (4.8) is that the optimum is represented by

$$p^r = P\mu^r, \text{ and} \tag{4.17}$$

$$p^u = P\mu^u. \tag{4.18}$$

We have thus obtained optimal pricing formulae of a remarkably simple form in terms of the welfare weights and the price elasticities. The optimal price in the agricultural sector depends only on the social weight on the income of peasants (relative to investment) and the price elasticity of agricultural surplus. Similarly, the optimal price in the industrial sector depends only on the social weight on the income of industrial workers and the price elasticity of their demand for agricultural goods.

The above results have some natural implications. In the early stages of development, the social weight on investment might be thought to exceed those on private incomes, that is, $\delta > \beta^r$ and $\delta > \beta^u$. In this case:

(a) Peasants should receive less than the international price of food, and city-dwellers should pay more than the international price of food. That is, both sectors should be taxed.

(b) A higher elasticity of agricultural surplus should imply a higher price paid to peasants. This is because the marginal decrease in the public revenue from a price increase is smaller. Also, a higher demand elasticity of food in the industrial sector should imply a lower price charged to city-dwellers. This is because the marginal increase in the public revenue from a price increase is lower.

(c) The smaller the social weight on peasants' income, the lower the price in the agricultural sector should be; the smaller the social weight on city-dwellers' income, the higher the price paid by them should be. More generally, a sector should be subsidized if and only if its social weight exceeds that of investment.

(*d*) Even if the government is unconcerned about the welfare of peasants and city-dwellers, there is a limit to the amount of surplus it can extract. Investment-maximizing prices are obtained by using (4.17) and (4.18), and by setting $\beta^i/\delta = 0$ in (4.9) and (4.10). It is easily verified that the investment-maximizing rural and urban prices are $\bar{p}^r$ and $\bar{p}^u$, respectively.

A special case of the relationship between the investible surplus and the rural price is depicted in Fig. 4.1. In general, this relationship need not be strictly concave. However, if the elasticity ε^r_{Qp} is not greatly sensitive to the rural price p^r (within the range of prices under consideration), then it can easily be shown that I has a single peak with respect to p^r. The more general point, that there is an upper limit to the investible surplus that can be extracted by changing p^r, holds even if I has multiple peaks with respect to p^r.

Implicit Tax-Rate

The optimal pricing formulae derived above can also be stated in terms of tax-rates. Recall that

$$t^r = (P - p^r)/p^r$$

is the tax-rate on the output of peasants. If we denote the food output and the consumption of a peasant by X and x^r, respectively, then the marketed surplus per peasant is $Q = X - x^r$. Further, if we define

$$\varepsilon^r_{Xp} = \partial \ln X / \partial \ln p^r \quad \text{and} \quad \varepsilon^r_{xp} = - \partial \ln x^r / \partial \ln p^r$$

as the price elasticities of food output and consumption of a peasant,[20] then the surplus elasticity can be expressed as

$$\varepsilon^r_{Qp} = (1 + a) \, \varepsilon^r_{Xp} + a\varepsilon^r_{xp} \,, \tag{4.19}$$

where $a = x^r/Q$ is the ratio of peasants' consumption to their marketed surplus. Using these definitions, the optimal rural tax-rate is obtained from (4.9) and (4.17) as

$$t^r = \frac{P - p^r}{p^r} = \left(1 - \frac{\beta^r}{\delta} \right) \frac{1}{(1 + a) \, \varepsilon^r_{Xp} + a\varepsilon^r_{xp}} = \left(1 - \frac{\beta^r}{\delta} \right) \frac{1}{\varepsilon^r_{Qp}} \,. \tag{4.20}$$

The corresponding expression for the optimal urban tax-rate is obtained from (4.10) and (4.18) as

---

[20] Since the choice of peasants' labour hours is endogenous, the elasticities ε^r_{Xp} and ε^r_{xp} are not the standard partial elasticities in which income is held constant.

$$t^u = \frac{P - p^u}{p^u} = -\left(1 - \frac{\beta^u}{\delta}\right)\frac{1}{\varepsilon^u_{xp}} . \qquad (4.20')$$

The above expression for the tax-rate has some similarities with those in the traditional tax literature, but there are also some important differences. According to (4.20) the magnitude of the tax-rate is inversely proportional to the price elasticities of output and consumption. This dependence is similar to the one which was suggested in some of the earliest writings on taxation, for example, those by Ramsey (1927) and Pigou.[21] However, there is a basic difference between the present policy problem and the standard taxation problem in which production and consumption decisions are made separately by firms and consumers. In the latter case, the relative roles played by output and consumption elasticities depend heavily on the government's taxation of profits. The output elasticity does not appear in the tax formula, for example, if profits are entirely taxed away (see Stiglitz and Dasgupta 1971, and Atkinson and Stiglitz 1980, p. 467).

In the problem currently under consideration, it is nearly impossible for the government to distinguish between producers and consumers within the agricultural sector, since peasants are simultaneously producers as well as consumers. The key elasticity is therefore that of marketed surplus. Even though this elasticity can be restated in terms of output and consumption elasticities, as in (4.20), it is the combined effect that matters. This should not be surprising. In the formulations of standard general-equilibrium models what matters is the net trade: for farmers, this is just their marketed surplus.

Reform Analysis versus Optimal Pricing

An important qualification in implementing the optimal pricing formulae of the type obtained above is that we require knowledge of the values of the relevant parameters at the optimum. If we believe that we may be at some distance from the optimum, then the values of the elasticities as well as the welfare weights at the optimum may be quite different from their values at the current equilibrium. Thus, given the paucity of data, and the possibly quite non-linear nature of the relevant functions, it may not be possible to estimate the values at the optimum on the basis of currently available information.

This observation has led some economists to conclude that the appropriate policy is a sequence of gradual reforms, or to argue even more strongly, that only 'reform' analysis is relevant. However, such a view ignores an equally important aspect of policy: that changes in policy are costly. Firms and

[21] In Pigou's formula, the magnitude of the tax-rate is proportional to the inverse of the demand and supply elasticities (see Atkinson and Stiglitz 1980, p. 467).

consumers need to know which policies are likely to prevail in the future if they are to make reasonable economic decisions. There are significant costs associated with uncertainties concerning future government policies. There are, furthermore, significant costs associated with frequent policy changes. These include not only the direct governmental costs of implementing them, but also the indirect costs imposed on consumers, firms, and peasants in adapting to them, as well as the transitional distortions induced by individuals attempting to take advantage of differential tax-rates at different moments. Thus, 'optimal policy' does not always entail a process of continual revision, but rather a careful balancing among the factors we have identified.

4.4 PRICE–PRODUCTIVITY EFFECTS

Several hypotheses have been advanced in the recent literature which contend that the wages received by workers affect their net productivity. Among the sources of this relationship which have been discussed are the effects of wages on the nutrition (and hence health), quality, effort, and turnover of workers. A fuller description of these effects is postponed until Chapter 11. However, it is useful at this stage to see, in a preliminary manner, the impact of these effects on pricing and taxation.

Past analyses of the effect of wages on productivity have been conducted in an environment of fixed prices, and it has been argued that productivity increases with wages, at least up to a point. One of the contributions of this book is to describe a crucial generalization of this hypothesis which implies that prices may affect the productivity of workers, for economic reasons analogous to those underlying the effect of wages on productivity. This generalization is especially important in the context of the analysis of taxation and pricing policies, because it emphasizes the price–productivity effects of these policies, in addition to their other consequences. We provide here a simple framework within which to assess such effects and to examine their consequences for the analysis of taxation and pricing.

The output of an industrial worker is represented as

$$Y = Y\,(k,\, L^u,\, p^u,\, w^u) \tag{4.21}$$

where the first two arguments on the right-hand side of the above expression represent the conventional inputs, namely capital, k, and labour hours, L^u, per worker. The last two arguments represent, in a reduced form, the effects of urban prices and wages on the net output per worker. We define

$$\sigma_p = -\frac{\partial \ln Y}{\partial \ln p^u} \tag{4.22}$$

as the elasticity of output with respect to the urban price. For expositional brevity, we assume that σ_p is positive, that is, that a higher food price lowers productivity. This assumption is a natural counterpart of the standard assumption that productivity increases with the wage in an environment of fixed prices.

The consequences of incorporating the above price–productivity effect on the rules for price reform and optimal prices are quite intuitive. The effect of an increase in the urban food price on the investible surplus is now given by the following expression (which generalizes the expression derived in n. 15):

$$\frac{\partial I}{\partial p^u} = N^u \left[\frac{\partial Y}{\partial p^u} + (p^u - P) \frac{\partial x^u}{\partial p^u} + x^u \right]$$

$$= \frac{N^u Y}{p^u} \left[-\sigma_p + \alpha^u \gamma^u \left(\frac{P - p^u}{p^u} \varepsilon_{xp}^u + 1 \right) \right], \qquad (4.23)$$

where

$\alpha^u = p^u x^u / w^u L^u$ = share of urban workers' income spent on food, and
$\gamma^u = w^u L^u / Y$ = share of urban workers' income in urban output.

The corresponding modification required in our earlier results can be seen from the following illustrations.

(*a*) Pareto-inefficient pricing:

$$\frac{\partial I}{\partial p^u} < 0 \ \text{ if }$$

$$p^u > P \left/ \left[1 - \left(1 - \frac{\sigma_p}{\alpha^u \gamma^u} \right) \frac{1}{\varepsilon_{xp}^u} \right] \equiv \bar{p}^u \ \text{ and} \right. \qquad (4.24)$$

$$\varepsilon_{xp}^u > 1 - \frac{\sigma_p}{\alpha^u \gamma^u}. \qquad (4.25)$$

As in (4.3), any price above $\bar{p}^u$ is Pareto-inefficient. A comparison between (4.24) and (4.3) immediately reveals that this critical level is lower when price–productivity effects are taken into account. This is what we would expect because there are productivity gains associated with a lower urban food price. Also (4.24) shows that in order for the above Pareto reform to hold, the urban demand elasticity no longer needs to exceed unity. The modified condition, (4.25), would be satisfied at sufficiently high urban prices (where we would expect σ_p to be large) even if ε_{xp}^u is small in magnitude.

(*b*) Other reform rules and optimal prices:
Recall the reform rule (4.8) that an increase or a decrease in the urban price improves social welfare depending on whether the current price p^u is less than or greater than $P\mu^u$. Also recall the expression (4.18) for the optimal price: $p^u = P\mu^u$. These results now hold with[22]

---

[22] As before (see n. 19), we assume that $\mu^u > 0$. This implies, from (4.26):

$$\mu^u = 1 \bigg/ \left[1 - \left(1 - \frac{\sigma_p}{\alpha^u \gamma^u} - \frac{\beta^u}{\delta} \right) \frac{1}{\varepsilon^u_{xp}} \right]. \tag{4.26}$$

Once again, a comparison of (4.26) with the earlier expression (4.10) points to the desirability of keeping the urban price lower than what would have been desirable in the absence of price–productivity effects.

APPENDIX

In this appendix, we present the essential details of the model analysed in this chapter. Some of these details are also helpful in the next two chapters.

Agricultural Sector

A is the agricultural land per peasant. The output of the agricultural good per peasant is $X \equiv X(A, L^r)$, where L^r is the variable number of hours a peasant works. (x^r, y^r) denotes a peasant's consumption of agricultural and industrial goods. $Q \equiv X - x^r$ is the surplus of the agricultural good per peasant. Q is positive. p^r represents the rural price of the agricultural good in terms of the industrial good. A peasant's budget constraint is

$$p^r Q = y^r. \tag{4.A1}$$

A peasant's utility function is $U^r(x^r, y^r, L^r)$. His indirect utility level, denoted by $V^r(p^r)$, is obtained from

$$V^r(p^r) = \max_{x^r, y^r, L^r} : \quad U^r + \lambda^r \left\{ p^r [X(A, L^r) - x^r] - y^r \right\}. \tag{4.A2}$$

The envelope theorem yields

$$\partial V^r / \partial p^r = \lambda^r Q \tag{4.A3}$$

where λ^i is the positive marginal utility of income of a person in sector i.

To understand why the sign of the surplus elasticity, $\varepsilon^r_{Qp} = \partial \ln Q / \partial \ln p^r$, is not predictable from the standard restrictions on the utility and production functions, we must first consider the simpler case in which a farmer faces a fixed market wage and buys or sells labour services. There are then three effects on the surplus of an increase in p^r: output increases because its price is higher; consumption increases because the net profit or rent from land is higher (we assume here that the agricultural good is normal); and consumption decreases because the price of the consumption good is higher. The overall effect is, therefore, ambiguous. In our present model of a peasant working on his own farm, there is an additional source of ambiguity: the 'implicit wage', $p^r \, \partial X/\partial L^r$, is also altered by an increase in p^r, and the sign of the resulting effect on the surplus cannot be predicted on the basis of the standard restrictions on the utility function and the production function. Thus, for instance, labour supply curves may be backward bending. An extensive empirical literature suggests, however, that farmers' surplus is positively related to the price of the surplus. An early study of economy-wide surplus is by Behrman (1968); a collection of recent micro-econometric studies of farm household behaviour is by Singh, Squire, and Strauss (1986).

Industrial Sector

An industrial worker's consumption is denoted by (x^u, y^u), and his wage-rate and labour hours are w^u and L^u, respectively. His budget constraint is thus

$$p^u x^u + y^u = w^u L^u. \tag{4.A4}$$

The indirect utility of an urban worker, $V^u(p^u, w^u)$, is defined by

$$V^u(p^u, w^u) = \max_{x^u,\, y^u} \quad U^u + \lambda^u \, (w^u L^u - p^u x^u - y^u) \,, \tag{4.A5}$$

where $U^u \equiv U^u(x^u, y^u, L^u)$ denotes the worker's utility level. The envelope theorem yields

$$\partial V^u / \partial p^u = - \lambda^u x^u \,. \tag{4.A6}$$

Investible Surplus

We finally derive expression (4.1) for the investible surplus. If T_x and T_y denote the net imports of agricultural and industrial goods respectively, then trade balance implies

$$T_y = -PT_x \,, \tag{4.A7}$$

where P is the fixed international terms of trade. The investible surplus, defined in terms of the industrial good, is

$$I = N^u Y - N^r y^r - N^u y^u + T_y \,, \tag{4.A8}$$

where Y is the output of an industrial worker. Substitution of (4.A1), (4.A4), and (4.A7) into the preceding expression yields (4.1).

5

THE PRICE SCISSORS IN OPEN ECONOMIES

5.1 INTRODUCTION

The analysis of the preceding chapter assumed that the government has the ability to maintain separate sets of prices in the urban and rural sectors. Obviously, if transportation costs between the sectors are low, then the presence of large price differences between the two sectors would provide strong incentives for tax arbitrage. For instance, if the urban price is higher than the rural price, an underground market might develop through which farmers would try to sell directly to the urban sector, capturing the difference in prices. Similarly, if the urban price is lower than that in the rural sector, farmers may have an incentive to tranship, that is, buy food in the urban sector and resell it back to the government at a higher price. Rationing of food in the urban sector may serve to alleviate the latter problem, but not without incurring significant administrative costs.

Some tax evasion of the kind described above is inevitable. If it is very extensive, government revenues will be significantly less than what was intended, and the legitimacy of the government (or at least of its tax-pricing policies) may be called into question. In any event, it is clear that the problems associated with maintaining different sets of prices in rural and urban sectors imply that some LDC governments may be constrained to having the same set of prices in both sectors.

The problem of the government in these circumstances is similar to some of those faced by the British Government after the Napoleonic wars and by the American government prior to the Civil War. In the former case, the question was whether the Corn Laws, which raised the price of agricultural goods above the international price, should be repealed. In the latter case, the question concerned how high tariffs on industrial goods should be. Similar problems were also faced by the Soviet government during the pre-collectivization period, when an important question was to what extent prices should be twisted to squeeze the peasant sector. In fact, the term 'price scissors' originated in the Soviet debate where it was extensively employed to represent the ratio of the price of industrial goods to the price of agricultural goods. The ratio under consideration was an economy-wide one. Setting different ratios in the rural and urban sectors (as was done in Chapter 4) was considered infeasible or costly, given the limited administrative capacity of the Soviet state at that time.

It should be apparent that in a general-equilibrium model, it makes no difference whether the price of the agricultural good is raised or the price of the industrial good is lowered. Likewise, the effects of a tariff on the import of industrial goods are analogous to those of a tax on the export of agricultural goods.[1] Thus the consequences of these equivalent policies can be analysed in a simple modification of the basic model of Chapter 4.[2] The key difference is that now there is a single set of prices in both the urban and the rural sectors. We continue to model the economy as an open economy. The case of a closed economy is more appropriate for understanding the Soviet industrialization debate as well as the pricing and taxation policies in some but not all of today's non-socialist LDCs. The latter case will be analysed in the next two chapters.

5.2 EFFECTS ON THE INVESTIBLE SURPLUS OF CHANGES IN THE PRICE SCISSORS

Let the economy-wide price of the agricultural good (in terms of the industrial good) be denoted by p. Recalling the notation of the previous chapter, this implies: $p \equiv p^r = p^u$. Then the investible surplus can be expressed as

$$I = N^u (Y - w^u L^u) + (P - p) (N^r Q - N^u x^u) . \tag{5.1}$$

That is, the investible surplus equals profits in the urban sector plus revenues from export taxes or import duties.

For later use, we define $\theta = (N^u x^u - N^r Q)/N^u x^u$ to be the net import of the agricultural good expressed as a fraction of urban food consumption. A negative (positive) θ implies that the country exports (imports) the agricultural good. Also, $1 > \theta$, because it is assumed that the rural sector's surplus of the agricultural good is always positive. Another symbol which we shall use extensively is the tax- or subsidy-rate $t = (P - p)/p$. Note an interesting feature of the present problem: if one sector is being taxed then the other sector is being subsidized. If t is positive (negative) then the rural sector is being taxed (subsidized) and the urban sector is being subsidized (taxed).

The effects of a price change on the investible surplus can be ascertained by differentiating (5.1) with respect to p:

$$\frac{\partial I}{\partial p} = -(N^r Q - N^u x^u) + (P - p)\left(N^r \frac{\partial Q}{\partial p} - N^u \frac{\partial x^u}{\partial p} \right) + N^u \frac{\partial Y}{\partial p} .$$

We rearrange this derivative as

---

[1] Such equivalences are not always recognized. For instance, as we noted earlier the framers of the US constitution were not cognizant of some of these equivalences.

[2] We are abstracting here from the differences in the administrative costs associated with policies which are otherwise equivalent.

$$\frac{\partial I}{\partial p} = N^u x^u \left\{ \theta + t\,[\,(1 - \theta)\,\varepsilon^r_{Qp} + \varepsilon^u_{Xp}] - \frac{\sigma_p}{\alpha^u \gamma^u} \right\}, \tag{5.2}$$

where $\sigma_p = -\partial\ln Y/\partial\ln p$ is the productivity effect of a change in price, $\alpha^u = px^u/w^u L^u$ is the share of urban workers' income spent on food, $\gamma^u = w^u L^u/Y$ is the share of wages in urban output, $\varepsilon^r_{Qp} = \partial\ln Q/\partial\ln p > 0$ is the price elasticity of agricultural surplus, and $\varepsilon^u_{Xp} = -\partial\ln x^u/\partial\ln p > 0$ is the price elasticity of urban food consumption.

There are three distinct effects of raising the terms of trade, p. These effects can be seen in the three terms within the brace brackets on the right-hand side of (5.2). First, a higher domestic price of the agricultural good decreases or increases the tariff revenue depending on whether the country is currently an exporter or an importer of this good. Second, a higher price implies a larger rural surplus and a smaller urban demand and, hence, a larger net export (or a smaller net import) of the agricultural good. As a result, the net tariff revenue increases if the current domestic price is lower than the international price of the agricultural good, and the net tariff revenue decreases if the converse is the case. Third, a higher price reduces the investible surplus because of its deleterious effects on productivity.[3]

The overall impact of the terms of trade on the investible surplus depends, of course, on the combination of the above effects. However, we would expect that lowering the terms of trade below some level lowers the investible surplus. At a low p, the rural surplus will be small and the urban demand large, and the country would be importing food (that is $\theta > 0$ at a sufficiently low p). Also, by definition, the domestic price would be below the international price (so, $t > 0$). For specific results of this kind, we derive the following expression from (5.2):

$$\frac{\partial I}{\partial p} \gtrless 0, \quad \text{if} \quad t \equiv \frac{P - p}{p} \gtrless \frac{-\theta + \dfrac{\sigma_p}{\alpha^u \gamma^u}}{(1 - \theta)\,\varepsilon^r_{Qp} + \varepsilon^u_{Xp}}. \tag{5.3}$$

To see some of the implications of the above expression, assume that the price–productivity effect is negligible (that is, $\sigma_p/\alpha^u\gamma^u$ is close to zero). Then it follows from (5.3) that:

If the country is currently an importer of the agricultural good and if the current domestic price is lower than the international price, then a price increase would increase the investible surplus.

Conversely:

If the country is currently an exporter of the agricultural good and if the current domestic price is higher than the international price, then a price decrease would increase the investible surplus.

---

[3] The nature of this effect may be different if urban wages increase as a result of higher prices. Here we ignore such induced changes, and assume that the urban wage remains unaltered in terms of the (numeraire) industrial good. See ch. 10 for a detailed discussion.

5.3 WELFARE EFFECTS OF CHANGING
THE PRICE SCISSORS

It is clear that in the present set-up, a change in the terms of trade has opposite effects on the welfare of those in the rural and urban sectors. Those in the rural sector gain from an increase in the price of the agricultural good, that is,

$$\frac{\partial V^r}{\partial p} = \lambda^r Q > 0,$$

whereas those in the urban sector lose, that is,

$$\frac{\partial V^u}{\partial p} = -\lambda^u x^u < 0.$$

As before, therefore, we evaluate social welfare using the Hamiltonian

$$H = N^r W(V^r) + N^u W(V^u) + \delta I, \tag{5.4}$$

where $N^r W(V^r) + N^u W(V^u)$ is an additive Bergson–Samuelson social welfare function representing society's valuation of current consumption, and δ is the marginal social evaluation of investible surplus. Differentiating (5.4) and using (5.2), we obtain

$$\frac{1}{N^u x^u \delta} \frac{\partial H}{\partial p} = \frac{\beta^r (1-\theta)}{\delta} - \frac{\beta^u}{\delta} + \theta + t \left[(1-\theta) \, \varepsilon^r_{Qp} + \varepsilon^u_{xp} \right] - \frac{\sigma_p}{\alpha^u \gamma^u}, \tag{5.5}$$

where, as before, β^i is the marginal social utility of income to an individual in the i-th sector.

We analyse the above expression in the neighbourhood of non-intervention (that is, at $t \approx 0$) and under the assumption that the social weight on investment exceeds the weights on current incomes (that is, δ is larger than β^r and β^u). Expression (5.5) can then be rearranged as

$$\frac{\partial H}{\partial p} \gtreqless 0 \text{ if } \beta^r \gtreqless \beta^u - \frac{\theta (\delta - \beta^u)}{1-\theta} + \frac{\sigma_p \delta}{\alpha^u \gamma^u (1-\theta)} . \tag{5.6}$$

We call attention to four cases.[4]

(a) First consider an economy whose natural comparative advantage is in agriculture; that is, $\theta < 0$ at $t = 0$. Then (5.6) shows that a small increase in the price of the agricultural good would increase social welfare only if rural incomes are so low relative to urban incomes that the marginal social utility of rural income exceeds, by a significant amount, that of urban income.

[4] In evaluating (5.6) or (5.7), presented later, it should be emphasized that the variables on the right-hand side, including θ, are themselves functions of p. They are not, in general, constants. As p changes, θ might even change sign, the country being an importer of food at low p and an exporter at high p.

(b) Conversely, it can be shown that if the natural advantage of the economy is in industrial production, and if productivity effects are not significant, then a small decrease in the price of the agricultural good would increase social welfare only if rural incomes are sufficiently large compared to urban incomes. This conclusion would only be reversed if there were large price–productivity effects.

(c) In the absence of productivity effects, if the country's external trade is negligible, then whether agriculture or industry should be taxed depends on whether incomes in the rural sector are higher or lower than those in the urban sector.

(d) If the urban wage level is such that $\beta^u = \beta^r$, and if external trade is negligible, then, because of price–productivity effects, the agricultural sector should always be taxed.

Thus, in light of the present simple model, whether the imposition of tariffs on industrial imports in pre-Civil War America was or was not an unreasonable policy, given an egalitarian social welfare function, depends primarily on the magnitudes of the differences in incomes between the two sectors and the relative importance of international trade.[5]

5.4 OPTIMAL PRICE SCISSORS

It is now an easy matter to solve for the optimal price, or the optimal tax:

$$t \equiv \frac{P-p}{p} = \frac{\dfrac{\beta^u}{\delta} - \dfrac{\beta^r(1-\theta)}{\delta} - \theta + \dfrac{\sigma_p}{\alpha^u \gamma^u}}{(1-\theta)\,\varepsilon^r_{Qp} + \varepsilon^u_{xp}}. \tag{5.7}$$

Of course, the variables on the right-hand side of the above expression are all evaluated at the optimal tax-rate. We thus obtain the following result for the case in which, at the optimum, agricultural exports or imports are a small fraction of urban food consumption, and in which productivity effects are not significant:

$$t \approx \frac{(\beta^u - \beta^r)/\delta}{\varepsilon^r_{Qp} + \varepsilon^u_{xp}}. \tag{5.8}$$

In these cases, food is subsidized (taxed) if and only if the individual income in the rural sector is less (more) than that in the urban sector. The magnitude of taxation or subsidy is determined by the social valuation of investment.

---

[5] Note that a major justification for industrial tariffs is the infant-industry argument, which has not yet been incorporated into our analysis. We agree with the general consensus that the infant-industry argument is invoked far more often than is justified.

5.5 CONCLUDING REMARKS

Pricing policies in economies in which relative prices in the rural and urban sectors must be the same involve a more complicated set of trade-offs than in the case, discussed in the previous chapter, in which prices may be set independently in the two sectors. In the present case, there is almost always a direct conflict between the interests of the rural and urban sectors. In addition, the calculation of the effects of the terms of trade on the investible surplus must now take into account the simultaneous effects that price changes have in each of the two sectors.

This chapter has contributed to an understanding of these issues in three ways. First, we have identified intuitive conditions under which an increase or a decrease in the price of agricultural goods leads to an unambiguous increase in the investible surplus. The results show, for instance, that taxation (subsidization) of the agricultural sector is inconsistent with the maximization of the investible surplus if the economy is currently importing (exporting) the agricultural good.

Second, we have provided qualitative conditions under which agriculture should or should not be taxed. In particular, in many LDCs in which rural incomes are much lower than urban incomes, and the natural comparative advantage of the economy is in agriculture, there is some presumption against a tax on the agricultural sector. On the other hand, if a plausible case exists that the marginal social utility of income in the rural sector is less than that in the urban sector (which would be the case if most of the agricultural land was owned by plantations or large landlords, and if most of the benefits of higher food prices did not accrue to farm-workers), and the natural comparative advantage of the country is in industry, then there is some presumption that in these cases the rural sector should be taxed.

Third, we derived a simple formula characterizing the optimal price scissors, expressed in terms of the price elasticity of urban demand, the price elasticity of rural surplus, the price–productivity effect, and the magnitude of international trade.

6

THE PRICE SCISSORS IN CLOSED AND PARTIALLY CLOSED SOCIALIST ECONOMIES

6.1 INTRODUCTION

This chapter addresses the same issues that were examined in the previous chapter but in the context of a closed economy. Before beginning the analysis, we need to address two questions:

1. Why should it make any difference whether an economy is open or closed?
2. Which assumption is more appropriate for modern-day LDCs?

Closed economies differ from open economies in one critical way: in closed economies, domestic demand for each good must equal the domestic supply if markets are to clear. (In the literature on socialist economies, these conditions were sometimes referred to as material balance equations.) In the previous chapter, we did not have to worry about the demand for food equalling its supply or the demand for manufactured goods equalling the supply of them; there was a single, overall balance of payments constraint. This in turn meant that the government could vary the price of food without varying urban wages or some other variable in the economy. By contrast, in a closed economy, if the government lowers the price of food, supply will decrease and demand increase; to restore equilibrium, demand must somehow be decreased. In the model explored in this chapter, the primary way demand is decreased is through lowering the urban wage. That is, a change in the price of food is accompanied by a change in the urban wage. Underlying this equilibrating mechanism is an assumption that the government has the ability to change the urban wage. This assumption is appropriate for socialist countries rather than for non-socialist LDCs. We also investigate other equilibrating mechanisms.

The question of whether it is more appropriate to model an economy as open or closed does not, in general, have a definitive answer. No economy is completely open—there are always some non-traded goods. The analysis of the previous chapter assumed, of course, more than an open economy. It also assumed that import and export prices were identical and fixed. This assumption is also not quite accurate. There are goods for which the difference between the import and export prices is large. Most countries exporting goods other than primary products believe that they cannot sell an arbitrarily large amount of their exports at a fixed price. Even for agricultural commodities, markets must be cultivated,[1] and governments often commit many resources to doing just that.

At the same time, neither is any economy completely closed. Most countries can make up for some part of a food shortage by importing food. What is critical, however, is not the level of trade (say, relative to the national income), but the ability of the government to change the level of trade at the margin. If the government cannot do so (for instance, because the short-run demand for the country's exports is very inelastic, or because the country faces constraints in the international credit market which limit its ability to trade), then the analysis of the price scissors in these economies is quite similar to that in a closed economy.[2]

Another general question is whether pricing policies for some goods—e.g. the price of food—affect wages or prices of other goods in ways which the government cannot or does not perfectly offset. Except under certain idealized conditions, perfect offsetting will not be possible. Thus, in our view, the models of the previous chapters should be viewed as limiting cases, useful in helping to fix our ideas. But in some cases of interest, an analysis of the inter-sectoral links of the kind undertaken here will be required. The model on which we focus in this chapter is an extreme one in which, at the margin, there is no external trade. Its central results however extend to the case in which the economy can, to some limited degree, increase or decrease its external trade of some tradable commodities.

A final reason for our interest in closed (or partially closed) economies is that such models provide insights into important historical episodes; for example, the debate in the Soviet Union concerning the size of the scissors. In the next chapter, we show how the model developed here can be used to interpret that debate.

6.2 THE MODEL

The model is identical to that presented in the previous chapter, except that now there is an explicit equation representing the balance between the demand and supply of the agricultural good.

Rural food surplus + Net imports = Urban food consumption

$$N^r Q + T_x = N^u x^u, \tag{6.1}$$

where T_x is the net quantity of food imports (which can be positive or

[1] Indeed, even a supposedly homogeneous grain such as rice has enough variation in quality that markets have to be cultivated. Thai rice is not a perfect substitute for American rice.
[2] For a discussion of why market equilibrium, particularly with sovereign debt, will be characterized by credit rationing, see Eaton, Gersovitz, and Stiglitz (1986). For empirical evidence that many LDCs do face credit rationing, see Eaton and Gersovitz (1981).

negative). Throughout the analysis T_x is kept fixed. We assume, in other words, that the economy is 'marginally closed'. A completely closed economy can be represented as the special case in which $T_x = 0$. As in the previous chapter, we assume that prices in the rural and urban sectors are identical; that is, $p = p^r = p^u$ denotes the economy-wide price of food relative to industrial goods.

Using the notation defined above, it follows that the investible surplus can be represented as

$$I = N^u(Y - w^u L^u) \quad + \quad (p - P) T_x .$$

$$\begin{array}{cc} \text{Profit of the} & \text{Tax} \\ \text{industrial sector} & \text{revenue} \end{array} \qquad (6.2)$$

The Adjustment of Wages in Response to Price Changes

We first calculate the change in the urban wage, w^u, which must accompany a change in the terms of trade, in order that the quantity balance in the market for the agricultural good (6.1) is maintained. Let

$$\varepsilon^u_{wp} = \frac{\text{dln } w^u}{\text{dln } p}$$

represent this change in wage in the form of an elasticity. Then a perturbation of (6.1)[3] shows that

$$\varepsilon^u_{wp} = [(1 - \theta) \varepsilon^r_{Qp} + \varepsilon^u_{xp}] / \varepsilon^u_{xm} , \qquad (6.3)$$

where, as before, $\theta = (N^u x^u - N^r Q)/N^u x^u$ is the net import of the agricultural good as a fraction of its consumption in the industrial sector, $1 > \theta$, and $\varepsilon^u_{xm} = \partial \ln x^u / \partial \ln (w^u L^u)$ is the income elasticity of urban food demand. The special case of a closed economy corresponds to $\theta = 0$.

It is clear from (6.3), that $\varepsilon^u_{wp} > 0$. That is, in an economy with constraints on traded quantities, a decrease in the price of the agricultural good must be accompanied by a decrease in the urban wage. The reason is simple. Lowering the price of the agricultural good lowers rural surplus and raises the urban food demand. To balance demand and supply, the urban wage

---

[3] The total derivative of (6.1) is

$$N^r \frac{\partial Q}{\partial p} dp = N^u \left(\frac{\partial x^u}{\partial p} dp + \frac{\partial x^u}{\partial w^u} dw^u \right) .$$

Thus,

$$N^r Q \frac{\partial Q}{\partial p} \frac{p}{Q} \frac{dp}{p} = N^u x^u \left(\frac{\partial x^u}{\partial p} \frac{p}{x^u} \frac{dp}{p} + \frac{\partial x^u}{\partial w^u} \frac{w^u}{x^u} \frac{dw^u}{w^u} \right) .$$

Now, noting that $N^r Q = (1 - \theta) N^u x^u$, and using the definitions of elasticities in the text, we obtain (6.3).

must be reduced. Moreover, as we would expect (6.3) shows that the reduction in the urban wage, corresponding to a decrease in the price of the agricultural good is larger if the peasants' surplus elasticity is larger, or if the net import of the agricultural good is smaller in relation to its urban consumption (see Fig. 6.1).

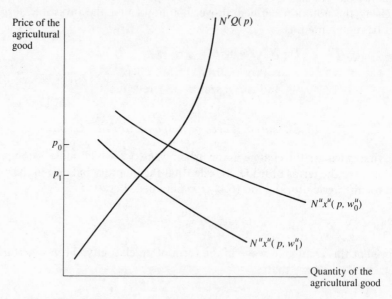

Fig. 6.1 Equilibrium in the market for the agricultural good

The upward-sloping curve represents the rural surplus of the agricultural good. The downward-sloping curves represent the urban demand at two different levels of urban wage, w_0^u and w_1^u, where $w_0^u > w_1^u$. If the price of the agricultural good is lowered from the original equilibrium, p_0 to p_1, then the demand exceeds the supply. To restore the equilibrium at the new price, it is necessary to lower the wage from w_0^u to w_1^u. For any decrease in price, the required decrease in the urban wage is smaller if the curve representing the surplus supply is steeper.

The Effect on Individuals' Welfare

It is clear that peasants become worse off if the price of the agricultural good is lowered. The effect on the industrial workers, on the other hand, would appear at first to be ambiguous: they face a lower price but also a lower wage. We now show that the wage effect always dominates the direct price effect. Thus, in an economy with constraints on traded quantities, a decrease in the price of the agricultural good hurts industrial workers as well as peasants.

The overall effect on the welfare of an industrial worker is

$$\frac{dV^u}{dp} = \frac{\partial V^u}{\partial p} + \frac{dw^u}{dp} \frac{\partial V^u}{\partial w^u} . \tag{6.4}$$

This can be re-expressed[4] as

$$\frac{dV^u}{dp} = \lambda^u x^u \rho , \tag{6.5}$$

where

$$\rho = -1 + \frac{\varepsilon_{wp}^u}{\alpha^u} , \tag{6.6}$$

and $\alpha^u = px^u/w^u L^u$ is the share of food in an industrial worker's expenditure. Substituting (6.3) into (6.6), we obtain

$$\rho = [(1 - \theta) \varepsilon_{Qp}^r + e_{xp}^u]/\alpha^u \varepsilon_{xm}^u > 0 , \tag{6.7}$$

where e_{xp}^u is the compensated price elasticity of food in the urban sector.[5] From (6.5) it thus follows that $\dfrac{dV^u}{dp} > 0$.

The Effect on Productivity

In an earlier chapter, we noted that a change in prices can alter productivity. But as we have just observed, a change in prices entails a change in wages, and this may also have an effect on productivity. Our objective in this subsection is to attempt to ascertain the nature of these productivity effects.

The reduced-form representation of the net output per worker is

$$Y = Y (k, L^u, p, w^u)$$

where the last two arguments on the right-hand side of the above expression represent the productivity effects. We define as before

$$\sigma_p = -\partial \ln Y/\partial \ln p \text{ and } \sigma_w = \partial \ln Y/\partial \ln w^u.$$

Whether an increase in either p or w increases or decreases productivity cannot be predicted without additional restrictions. To see the reason, suppose productivity increases with the consumption quantities of various goods. Then an increase in the price of one good increases the consumption of some goods (gross substitutes) and reduces the consumption of other goods (gross complements). Consequently, the nature of the overall effect on productivity cannot be predicted in general.

---

[4] In deriving (6.5) we have used the identities: $\partial V^u/\partial p = -\lambda^u x^u$ and $\partial V^u/\partial w^u = \lambda^u L^u$.

[5] Here we have used the Slutsky relationship between compensated and uncompensated elasticities: $e_{xp}^u = \varepsilon_{xp}^u - \alpha^u \varepsilon_{xm}^u$. Also, to avoid inessential details, we assume that e_{xp}^u is positive (rather than non-negative, as it always is). Here, as elsewhere, the price elasticity of demand is defined as the absolute value of the logarithmic derivative of demand with respect to price.

We therefore consider two particular specifications here. Under the first specification, a worker's productivity depends on, and increases with, his utility level. That is

$$Y = Y[k, L^u, V^u(p, w^u)], \quad \text{where} \quad \frac{\partial Y}{\partial V^u} > 0.$$

In this case, a higher price of the agricultural good lowers productivity, whereas a higher urban wage raises productivity. It is easily verified[6] that

$$\sigma_p > 0, \ \sigma_w > 0, \quad \text{and} \quad \sigma_p - \alpha^u \sigma_w = 0. \tag{6.8}$$

Under the second specification, a worker's productivity depends on, and increases with, the quantity of his food consumption. That is,

$$Y = Y[k, L^u, x^u(p, w^u)], \quad \text{where} \quad \frac{\partial Y}{\partial x^u} > 0.$$

In this case also, a higher price of the agricultural good lowers productivity, whereas a higher urban wage raises productivity. Further, it is straightforward to establish[7] that

$$\sigma_p > 0, \ \sigma_w > 0, \quad \text{and} \quad \sigma_p - \alpha^u \sigma_w > 0. \tag{6.9}$$

Finally, for later use, we determine the total effect of a price change on productivity, taking into account the induced wage effect (6.3). This is given by

$$\frac{dY}{dp} = \frac{\partial Y}{\partial p} + \frac{\partial Y}{\partial w^u} \frac{dw^u}{dp}$$

$$= \frac{Y}{p} (\sigma_w \varepsilon_{wp}^u - \sigma_p). \tag{6.10}$$

Now, consider the special case in which a worker's productivity depends on his utility level. Substituting (6.6) and (6.8) into (6.10), and re-arranging the resulting expression, we obtain

[6]

$$\sigma_p = -\frac{p}{Y} \frac{\partial Y}{\partial p} = -\frac{p}{Y} \frac{\partial Y}{\partial V^u} \frac{\partial V^u}{\partial p} = \lambda^u \frac{\partial Y}{\partial V^u} \frac{p x^u}{Y}.$$

$$\sigma_w = \frac{w^u}{Y} \frac{\partial Y}{\partial w^u} = \frac{w^u}{Y} \frac{\partial Y}{\partial V^u} \frac{\partial V^u}{\partial w^u} = \lambda^u \frac{\partial Y}{\partial V^u} \frac{w^u L^u}{Y}.$$

[7]

$$\sigma_p = (\partial \ln Y / \partial \ln x^u) \ \varepsilon_{xp}^u \quad \text{and}$$
$$\sigma_w = (\partial \ln Y / \partial \ln x^u) \ \varepsilon_{xm}^u.$$

Thus,

$$\sigma_p - \alpha^u \sigma_w = (\partial \ln Y / \partial \ln x^u) \ e_{xp}^u,$$

where e_{xp}^u is the compensated price elasticity of food demand in the urban sector. As explained earlier, e_{xp}^u is assumed to be positive.

$$\frac{dY}{dp} = \sigma_p \rho > 0.$$

That is, the overall effect of an increase in the price of the agricultural good is to increase an industrial worker's productivity. This is what we would expect because the price increase raises the worker's utility level, which, in turn, raises his productivity.

The Effect on the Investible Surplus

The total effect of a change in the price of the agricultural good on the investible surplus is

$$\frac{dI}{dp} = \frac{\partial I}{\partial p} + \frac{dw^u}{dp} \frac{\partial I}{\partial w^u}.$$ (6.11)

Using the expression (6.2) for I, the above is evaluated as

$$\frac{dI}{dp} = N^u \left(\frac{dY}{dp} - L^u \frac{dw^u}{dp} \right) + T_x.$$ (6.12)

An increase in the price of food has three effects on the investible surplus:

(a) It leads to higher wages, which decrease the investible surplus.
(b) It leads to higher government tariff revenue from imported food (or, lower expenditure on food subsidies), which increases the investible surplus.
(c) It affects productivity. If productivity depends on the utility of an urban worker or on his food consumption, then productivity increases. In this case, the investible surplus increases.

The net effect would appear to be ambiguous. We now show that, provided the productivity effect is not too large, the net effect is negative. That is, an increase in the price of the agricultural good raises the welfare of both peasants and urban workers, but at the expense of future generations (the investible surplus). The decrease in profits induced by the increase in wages dominates the gain in tariff revenues (or the reduction in urban food subsidies).

Substitution of (6.10) and the definition $\theta = T_x/N^u x^u$ allow us to rearrange (6.12) as

$$\frac{dI}{dp} = \frac{N^u Y}{p} (\sigma_w \varepsilon^u_{wp} - \sigma_p) - N^u \frac{w^u L^u}{p} \varepsilon^u_{wp} + N^u x^u \theta$$

$$= -N^u x^u \left[\frac{1}{\alpha^u \gamma^u} (\sigma_p - \alpha^u \sigma_w) + \rho \left(1 - \frac{\sigma_w}{\gamma^u} \right) + (1 - \theta) \right] \quad (6.13)$$

where, it will be recalled $\gamma^u = w^u L^u / Y$ is the share of wages in the industrial output, and $\alpha^u = px^u/w^uL^u$ is the share of an industrial worker's expenditure spent on food.

The above equation has several interpretations. First, note that since $1 - \theta > 0$, and $\rho > 0$ it follows from (6.13) that in the absence of wage–productivity effects, an increase in the price of the agricultural good leads to a decrease in the investible surplus.

The above result continues to hold even in the presence of productivity effects provided these effects are not very large. Recall from (6.8) and (6.9) that $\sigma_p - \alpha^u\sigma_w \geq 0$ if productivity depends on the utility level or on food consumption. In these cases, it follows from (6.13) that: A sufficient condition for the investible surplus to decrease with an increase in the price of the agricultural good is: $\gamma^u \geq \sigma_w$.

The sufficient condition $\gamma^u \geq \sigma_w$ has a natural interpretation. Consider the impact of an increase in the urban wage on industrial profits. The net increase in industrial profits can be expressed as

$$\frac{\partial}{\partial w^u} N^u(Y - w^uL^u) = N^u\frac{Y}{w^u}(\sigma_w - \gamma^u) \cdot$$

The condition $\gamma^u \geq \sigma_w$ thus means that, given the current prices and urban wages, the productivity effects are such that a dollar increase in an industrial worker's income would raise his net output by no more than a dollar.[8]

The Consequences of a Higher Price Elasticity of the Agricultural Surplus

Recalling from (6.7) the definition of ρ, it is clear that so long as the productivity effect is not too large, (that is, so long as $\gamma^u \geq \sigma_w$), the absolute value of the right-hand side of (6.13) is larger if ε'_{Qp} is larger. That is, the response of the investible surplus to a change in the terms of trade is larger if peasants' surplus elasticity is larger. This should not be surprising since a reduction in the terms of trade necessitates a larger decrease in the urban wage if ε'_{Qp} is larger. But these results contrast markedly with those of Chapter 4, where prices in the rural and urban sectors could be set independently. There, a smaller surplus elasticity made government revenue more sensitive to price changes. For instance, in the presence of a smaller rural surplus elasticity, the government could raise a larger amount of revenue for a given decrease in the price of the agricultural good (and, the resulting dead-weight costs on peasants were smaller in relation to the revenue raised). Now, in a

---

[8] It might be tempting to assert that this condition will always be satisfied because if it were not, then firms (or the government) could increase industrial profits by increasing the urban wage. However, the urban wage is not set in such a manner within the present model. Instead, corresponding to any given price, the urban wage is adjusted to balance the demand and supply of the agricultural good. As we shall see below, the condition $\gamma^u \geq \sigma_w$ is not satisfied, if the government sets the prices optimally to maximize the investible surplus.

closed economy with only one price instrument, p, a larger rural surplus elasticity is more favourable to raising government revenue because it requires a larger decrease in wages in the urban sector.

6.3 REFORM IN THE PRICE SCISSORS

The above analysis shows that a change in the terms of trade affects individuals' welfare and the investible surplus in opposite directions. A lowering of the terms of trade increases the investible surplus (provided productivity effects are not very large) but lowers the welfare of peasants as well as that of industrial workers. As a consequence, Pareto-improving reforms in the terms of trade are typically not possible. In the analysis below, therefore, we study the combined effects of a change in the terms of trade on individuals' welfare and on the investible surplus. Since the aim of a policy reform analysis is to identify rules for an improvement in society's overall welfare, any such rule is more useful if less information is required to apply it. The rules for price reform that we obtain here require only limited information.

The first step in the analysis of reform is to define the aggregate social welfare. For this, we again use an additive Bergson–Samuelson social welfare function, ψ, to aggregate over individual utilities:

$$\psi = N^r W(V^r) + N^u W(V^u), \tag{6.14}$$

where W is concave and increasing in V. If δ is the social value of the marginal investment, then the current value of the aggregate social welfare is given by the Hamiltonian

$$H = \psi + \delta I. \tag{6.15}$$

The above expression is now perturbed with respect to p, while ensuring a corresponding perturbation in the urban wage to preserve the balance in the supply and demand of the agricultural good (6.1). Using (6.5) and (6.13), we obtain

$$\frac{dH}{dp} = \beta^r N^r Q \qquad \text{gain to the rural sector}$$

$$+ \beta^u N^u x^u \rho \qquad \text{gain to the urban sector}$$

$$- N^u x^u \left[\frac{1}{\alpha^u \gamma^u} (\sigma_p - \alpha^u \sigma_w) + \rho(1 - \frac{\sigma_w}{\gamma^u}) + (1 - \theta) \right]$$

$$\text{loss of investible surplus.} \tag{6.16}$$

As before, $\beta^i = \lambda^i \partial W / \partial V^i$ denotes the social value of a marginal increase in the income of a worker in sector i. The three terms on the right-hand side of (6.16) respectively represent the welfare gain to the rural sector, the welfare gain to the urban sector, and the loss of investment due to an increase in the price of the agricultural good. Naturally, these gains and losses are weighted by their respective social weights.

An alternative expression for $\dfrac{dH}{dp}$ is obtained by recalling from (6.6) that $\rho = -1 + \varepsilon^u_{wp}/\alpha^u$, and rearranging (6.16) to yield

$$\frac{dH}{dp} = N^u x^u \left[\beta^r(1-\theta) - \beta^u + \delta\left(\theta - \frac{\sigma_p}{\alpha^u \gamma^u}\right)\right] \qquad \text{direct effect}[9]$$

$$+ N^u x^u \left[\beta^u - \delta\left(1 - \frac{\sigma_w}{\gamma^u}\right)\right] \frac{\varepsilon^u_{wp}}{\alpha^u} \qquad \text{induced wage effect.} \qquad (6.17)$$

The above expression clearly separates the two distinct effects of a change in the terms of trade. The first term is the direct effect of an increase in p, which benefits peasants, hurts urban workers, increases (respectively, decreases) tax revenue if the country is a net importer (respectively, exporter) of the agricultural good, and lowers industrial productivity. The second term represents the effects of the induced increase in the urban wage, which benefits urban workers, increases the wage bill, and increases industrial productivity.

Expressions (6.16) or (6.17) can now be used to obtain sufficient conditions which will guarantee that a specific change in the relative price will increase social welfare. For brevity, the discussion below abstracts from productivity effects, but it can be easily expanded to include them. With this abstraction, we rewrite (6.17) as

$$\frac{dH}{dp} = N^u x^u [(\beta^r - \delta)(1-\theta) + (\beta^u - \delta)\rho]. \qquad (6.18)$$

Recalling that $\rho > 0$ and $1 > \theta$, it follows that

$$\frac{dH}{dp} < 0, \text{ if } \beta^r \le \delta \text{ and } \beta^u \le \delta \qquad (6.19)$$

(with at least one strict inequality), and

$$\frac{dH}{dp} > 0, \text{ if } \beta^r \ge \delta \text{ and } \beta^u \ge \delta \qquad (6.20)$$

(with at least one strict inequality).

From (6.19) and (6.20) we find that moving the terms of trade against or in favour of peasants is desirable depending on whether the social weight on the investible surplus is larger or smaller than the social weights on rural

---

[9] In calculating the direct effect we use equation (6.1) and the definition of θ to obtain $N^r Q / N^u x^u = 1 - T_x / N^u x^u = 1 - \theta$.

and urban incomes. Note that this rule holds regardless of whether the social weight on rural income is larger or smaller than that on urban income. That is, if the marginal social valuation of a dollar of government investment exceeds the marginal social valuation of a dollar of consumption in both sectors then the gains from moving the prices against peasants exceed the losses, regardless of which one of the two sets of workers is worse off.

What is important about these rules is that they do not require knowledge of the behavioural parameters, such as the response of rural surplus and urban consumption to price changes. The rules can be used solely on the basis of the marginal social weights in the existing regime, that is, on the basis of the current social weights associated with a dollar of rural and urban income versus a dollar of government investment. It is also noteworthy that, abstracting from productivity effects on urban workers, the issues of incentive and efficiency play no role in these reforms.

6.4 OPTIMAL PRICE SCISSORS

We are now in a position to identify some of the features of the optimal price structure. For simplicity, we continue to ignore productivity effects. Assuming that there is a unique interior maximum for social welfare as defined in (6.15), we should have $dH/dp = 0$ at the optimum. From (6.19) and (6.20), this implies that the optimal price structure must satisfy

$$\beta^r > \delta > \beta^u \text{ or } \beta^u > \delta > \beta^r .$$

That is, if the marginal social weight on the investible surplus does not lie between the marginal social weights on the rural and the urban individuals' income, then the current price regime is not optimal, and it can be improved through a change in price policy.[10] This result needs to be contrasted with a view often held in the literature on project evaluation that the social weight on investment should be larger than the social weight on consumption.[11] This view is incorrect if the terms of trade can be used as an instrument of policy and if the government has chosen the terms of trade optimally.

An Interpretation in Terms of the Tax- or Subsidy-Rate

One way to analyse the optimal terms of trade is to look at the issue of implicit taxation. Additional insights can sometimes be obtained by comparing market prices with shadow prices, rather than by comparing producer and consumer prices. This is especially relevant here since producer and consumer prices are identical. In fact, a rural worker is simultaneously a

[10] To keep our exposition uncluttered, we are ruling out the exceptional possibility in which $\beta^r = \beta^u = \delta$.

[11] See Yotopoulos and Nugent (1976, p. 385) for a summary of such a view.

producer and a consumer. Therefore, in the analysis below, we define the 'tax' as the difference between the social opportunity cost of producing a good and the market price of the same good. If η is the shadow price of the agricultural good, then the shadow price of this good in terms of investment is η/δ. The tax-rate is therefore defined as

$$t = \left(\frac{\eta}{\delta} - p\right) \Big/ p \ .$$

Thus, if $t < 0$, then the urban sector is paying a tax while the rural sector is receiving a subsidy.

To analyse the optimal tax, we define the following Lagrangian by explicitly incorporating the condition for equilibrium in the market for the agricultural good, (6.1), into the maximand (6.15):

$$\mathcal{L} = \psi + \delta I + \eta \left(N^r Q + T_x - N^u x^u\right) , \tag{6.21}$$

where ψ is given by (6.14), and p and w^u are the control variables. Recalling (6.2) and the definition of net import of the agricultural good, $T_x = N^u x^u - N^r Q$, we use the following expression for the investible surplus

$$I = N^u (Y - w^u L^u) + p (N^u x^u - N^r Q) - P T_x \ . \tag{6.22}$$

From (6.21) and (6.22), the first-order conditions for an interior optimum with respect to p and w^u, after some manipulation, yield the following expressions respectively (the derivations are given in the Appendix to this chapter):

$$-t = \frac{(\beta^r - \beta^u) + \theta \, (\delta - \beta^r) - \delta \sigma_p / \alpha^u \gamma^u}{\delta \, [(1 - \theta) \, \varepsilon^r_{Qp} + \varepsilon^u_{xp}]} \quad \text{and} \tag{6.23}$$

$$\frac{\beta^u}{\delta} = 1 - \frac{\sigma_w}{\gamma^u} + t \alpha^u \varepsilon^u_{xm} \ . \tag{6.24}$$

Next, the substitution of (6.24) into (6.23) allows the latter to be rewritten as

$$t = \frac{(1 - \theta) \, (1 - \beta^r/\delta) + (\sigma_p - \alpha^u \sigma_w)/\alpha^u \gamma^u}{(1 - \theta) \, \varepsilon^r_{Qp} + e^u_{xp}} \ . \tag{6.25}$$

Now recall that $1 > \theta$, and, from (6.8) and (6.9), $\sigma_p \geq \alpha^u \sigma_w$ for the productivity hypotheses under consideration. From (6.25), therefore, t is positive if $\delta > \beta^r$. On the other hand, t is negative if $\beta^r > \delta$, and σ_p and σ_w are negligible. Next, consider the special case in which society maximizes the investible surplus, that is $\beta^i/\delta \rightarrow 0$. In this case, t is positive from (6.25). In turn, from (6.24), $\sigma_w > \gamma^u$ at the optimum. The following results are therefore immediate. Note that these results are entirely independent of the volume or the direction of external trade.

(a) Peasants are taxed if the marginal social weight on their income is smaller than that on the investible surplus.

(b) Peasants are subsidized if the marginal social weight on their income is larger than that on the investible surplus and if urban productivity effects are not significant.

(c) If the urban productivity depends on utility, the optimal tax-rate is independent of the magnitude of the productivity effects. The tax is negative or positive as the marginal social weight on the rural income is larger than or smaller than that on the investible surplus.

(d) In an economy concerned solely with maximizing the investible surplus, peasants are taxed. The wages and prices faced by industrial workers are such that an increase in their wage would more than proportionately increase their output.

At first sight the last result appears counter-intuitive because one would expect a society to be willing to increase the industrial wage at least to the point where it can recover, through increased productivity, more than what it paid. The reason why this is not true is that increasing the industrial wage also increases the food consumption of industrial workers. This, in turn, leads to a loss in the public revenue because the optimal food price is lower than the shadow price (that is, $t > 0$). This indirect revenue effect makes it undesirable for the society to take full advantage of the productivity gains from increasing the industrial wage.

Next, consider the special case of a closed economy without productivity effects (that is, θ, σ_p and σ_w are close to zero). Since a higher β corresponds to a lower level of utility, it is clear that expression (6.23) demarcates, in this case, the location of the optimal tax or subsidy between the two sectors. The workers who are better off should be taxed, and the workers who are worse off should be subsidized. This result is independent of the behavioural responses in the economy or the social valuation of investment. Moreover, the result holds regardless of whether it is the peasants or the industrial workers who are better off.

The importance of the last result can be seen as follows. Suppose there is a country in which peasants are worse off than industrial workers (as is usually the case) but where peasants are being taxed and industrial workers are being subsidized. Then, under the set of assumptions on which the last result is based, such a pattern of taxation cannot be consistent with an egalitarian social welfare function giving the same weight to an individual's welfare irrespective of his location.

The above conclusions regarding the terms of trade remain essentially unaltered in those more realistic cases in which the modern capital good produced in the urban sector can be productively employed in the rural sector, and where the government exercises a choice over the inter-sectoral allocation of investment. As a simple example, consider the case in which there is positive investment in both sectors and the return on rural capital accrues to the rural sector. Then it can be verified that the taxation rules we have derived continue to characterize the optimum. Of course, the magnitude of the tax will be affected in fairly complicated ways by how capital is allocated. A shift in capital from the urban to the rural sector not only affects marginal social weights but also potentially affects the surplus elasticity, the urban demand elasticity, and the sensitivity of productivity to wages.

Expression (6.25) provides additional insights which are important, but, for reasons indicated below, they are somewhat partial. For instance, recall that $\sigma_p - \alpha^u \sigma_w$ is zero when productivity depends on workers' utility, and it is positive when productivity depends on food consumption. Expression (6.25) thus suggests that the optimal food price is lower if productivity is more sensitive to workers' food consumption than to their consumption of other goods. This is what one would expect, since the marginal social gain from lowering the food price is higher if workers' productivity is more sensitive to food consumption.[12]

Expression (6.25) also suggests that the magnitude of the optimal tax- or subsidy-rate is smaller if the peasants' surplus elasticity is larger. This is intuitive since a higher ε'_{Qp} implies that there is a larger change in the supply of the agricultural good (and hence both in the induced change in the urban wage and in industrial profits) due to a given change in the terms of trade.

Alternative Characterizations

In the above analysis we employed the terms of trade as the instrument of control. The analysis was thus within the context of the problem of price scissors. However, there are several alternative ways in which the same problem can be characterized. First, consider the control of the nominal urban wage. It can be verified that an increase in the nominal urban wage corresponds to a movement in the terms of trade in favour of the rural sector. Second, the economic content of the analysis remains unchanged if either the investible surplus, I, or the rural surplus, Q, is viewed as the focus of policy analysis, so long as additional instruments (other than relative prices and the urban wage) are not available. In these cases the analysis will correspond to the problems sometimes called the 'investment problem', and the 'marketed surplus' problem. Finally, we can reinterpret our analysis for a decentralized economic setting. To see this, first imagine that the government instructs its public-sector managers to maximize profits based on the

[12] The reason why this insight is partial is as follows. Note that the variables on the right-hand side of (6.25) are endogenous functions of the tax-rate. This endogeneity complicates a precise assessment of how the optimal tax-rate will differ under the two productivity hypotheses under consideration here. The result just noted in the text is based on the simplification that variables such as β^r, δ, and θ are not significantly different under the alternatives being compared. An analogous caveat applies to the results noted below.

nominal prices they face, but introduces either a commodity tax on the industrial good or an urban wage tax. Naturally then, the government can control the terms of trade. In particular, the optimum analysed earlier can be implemented in this manner. Next, assume that industrial production is privately owned, but that the government imposes a 100 per cent profits tax, and that it also imposes one of the two taxes mentioned above. It follows that the desired public policy can be implemented through a private market equilibrium.[13]

6.5 ECONOMIES WITH TRADED AND NON-TRADED GOODS

The preceding analysis was based on the simplifying assumption that a single aggregate good is produced in each of the two sectors. This assumption focuses our attention on the central trade-offs associated with changes in the terms of trade between the two sectors. Indeed, as we shall see in the next chapter, these trade-offs underlie some of the longstanding controversies concerning the conflict between agriculture and industry.

An assumption in the analysis of this chapter was that if international trade opportunities faced by a country are restricted, then a change in the terms of trade needs to be accompanied by a change in the urban wage so that the balance between demand and supply of the agricultural good can be maintained. We now consider the more general case in which many commodities are produced and consumed in each of the two sectors and where some of the commodities are traded while others are not traded.

In the general case, we can represent the equilibrium of the economy by (*a*) an investment equation, such as (6.2), and (*b*) a set of equations representing the balance between the demand and supply of each of the marginally non-traded goods. (In the preceding analysis, expression (6.1) represented the balance between the demand and supply of the single non-traded good, the agricultural good.) If the price of a marginally non-traded good is altered, then the restoration of the equilibrium would require a change in the price of at least some other goods (traded or non-traded) or a change in the urban wage.

Formally, we can represent the equilibrium of the economy by the balance of trade condition and a set of market-clearing equations for the non-traded

---

[13] The relationship between optimal pricing in public enterprises and optimal taxation of private enterprises has been discussed in the literature. See, for instance, Stiglitz and Dasgupta (1971). If 100 per cent profits taxes are not imposed (and they seldom are) then the optimal tax rules need to be modified to take this into account.

Both the scenarios just depicted—public-sector managers maximizing public enterprise profits and private firms maximizing profits but with 100 per cent profits taxation—ignore essential issues of incentives. Though these idealizations have played a central role in discussions of taxation and pricing, they need to be treated with considerable caution.

goods. Let the vectors P and p respectively denote the international and domestic prices of traded goods. Let the vectors q and t denote producer prices of and taxes on non-traded goods. Let the vector Q^r denote the surplus of non-traded goods per rural individual, and let the vector x^u denote the consumption of these goods per urban individual (we assume for simplicity that all non-traded goods are produced in the rural sector, and that all industrial goods are tradable). Let the vector T denote the net imports of traded goods. Then the market-clearing equations for the non-traded goods are:

$$N^r Q^r(p, q + t) - N^u x^u(p, q + t, w^u) = 0. \qquad (6.26)$$

The investible surplus is

$$I = (Y - w^u N^u) + (p - P) T, \qquad (6.27)$$

where Y is the total value of the industrial sector's output calculated (in terms of the numeraire good) using international prices. It is clear that if the government changes the domestic price of a traded good, or the tax on a non-traded good, then it can balance the market-clearing equations, (6.26), by altering the domestic prices of some other traded goods or the taxes on some other goods.

To see an implication of the above model, suppose that one category of food, say millet, is not traded, but another category of food, say rice, is traded. When the government lowers the price of millet, the rural surplus of this good will decrease while the urban demand will increase. The government can restore equilibrium in the market for millet either by reducing the urban wage or by lowering the price of rice (which will induce individuals to shift their demand towards rice and away from millet). The welfare consequences of these two policies are markedly different. In the former case urban workers are likely to be worse off, rural workers are unambiguously worse off, and investment may increase or decrease depending on whether or not the lowered urban wage payments exceed the likely loss of tax revenue. In the latter case, urban workers are unambiguously better off, rural workers are worse off if their surplus of rice is positive, and the investible surplus decreases.

Note that the preceding argument assumes that non-traded goods can be taxed. This is not always the case for many non-traded goods (including low-quality cereals) which are produced and consumed almost entirely within the rural sector. For a variety of economic reasons (elaborated upon in the introductory chapters), it is not possible (or it is too expensive) for the government to tax or subsidize such goods. This does not mean that these goods do not matter for the analysis of pricing and taxation. A change in the government's tax and price policy has induced effects on the prices of such non-traded goods. These induced effects, in turn, affect the welfare of producers and consumers of these goods in the rural sector. In Chapter 8 we show how these induced effects can easily be taken into account in analysing taxation and pricing policy.

In the model presented earlier in this chapter, the government's instruments were severely limited. It can only achieve equilibrium in the market for agricultural goods by adjusting the urban wage. In practice, governments often resort to other instruments, in particular to rationing. Rationing can be thought of as a way of introducing a non-linear pricing scheme: that is, there is a low price for the rationed quantity (sometimes zero) and a higher price for the remainder. When the rations can be exchanged in secondary markets (and it is often difficult for the government to prohibit such exchange, even if it is thought to be desirable to do so) and when there is no effective tax border between the two sectors, then such a rationing scheme is equivalent to providing a lump-sum subsidy to urban residents. Apart from the treatment of the unemployed, this subsidy is equivalent to an increase in the urban wage.

6.6 CONCLUDING REMARKS

A central message of this chapter is that when there are non-traded goods— or when there are binding constraints on the magnitude of trade—the government cannot change one price (the size of the scissors) alone. For the balance between the demand and supply of non-traded goods to be maintained, the price of some other commodity or the level of the urban wage must change. This chapter focused on a simple model in which the urban wage adjusts to ensure that the demand for food equals its supply. This has some dramatic effects on conclusions concerning the effects of increasing the size of the scissors, that is, increasing taxes on the rural sector. The induced wage adjustments reinforce the positive effects that such taxes have on government revenue, and they more than offset the direct welfare effects of the price changes on the urban sector. In the next chapter, we show how the analysis may be further used to shed light on certain aspects of the Soviet industrialization debate.

APPENDIX

Derivation of (6.23) and (6.24)

From (6.14), (6.21), and (6.22),

$$\mathcal{L} = N^r W\left[V^r(p)\right] + N^u W\left[V^u(p, w^u)\right] + \delta\left[N^u(Y - w^u L^u)\right.$$
$$\left. + p\left(N^u x^u - N^r Q\right) - PT_x\right] + \eta\left(N^r Q + T_x - N^u x^u\right). \tag{6.41}$$

The partial derivative of $\mathcal{L}$ with respect to p can be re-arranged as

$$\frac{1}{\delta}\frac{\partial \mathcal{L}}{\partial p} = \frac{\beta^r}{\delta} N^r Q - \frac{\beta^u}{\delta} N^u x^u + N^u\frac{\partial Y}{\partial p} + (N^u x^u - N^r Q)$$
$$+ \left(p - \frac{\eta}{\delta}\right)\left(N^u\frac{\partial x^u}{\partial p} - N^r\frac{\partial Q}{\partial p}\right) \tag{6.42}$$

$$= N^u x^u\left\{\frac{\beta^r}{\delta}(1 - \theta) - \frac{\beta^u}{\delta} - \frac{\sigma_p}{\alpha^u \gamma^u} + \theta + t\left[(1 - \theta)\,\varepsilon^r_{Qp} + \varepsilon^u_{xp}\right]\right\}. \tag{6.43}$$

Equating the last expression to zero, we obtain (6.23). Next, the partial derivative of $\mathcal{L}$ with respect to w^u can be rearranged as

$$\frac{1}{\delta}\frac{\partial \mathcal{L}}{\partial w^u} = \frac{\beta^u}{\delta} N^u L^u + N^u\left(\frac{\partial Y}{\partial w^u} - L^u\right) + \left(p - \frac{\eta}{\delta}\right) N^u\frac{\partial x^u}{\partial w^u}$$

$$= N^u L^u\left(\frac{\beta^u}{\delta} + \frac{\sigma_w}{\gamma^u} - 1 - t\alpha^u \varepsilon^u_{xm}\right). \tag{6.44}$$

Equating the last expression to zero, we obtain (6.24).

7

THE SOVIET INDUSTRIALIZATION
DEBATE AND COLLECTIVIZATION

7.1 INTRODUCTION

An economic question which became pivotal in the Soviet Union in the after-
math of the October Revolution concerned how to raise the resources required to finance industrialization. The need for industrialization was not a
matter of debate: it was commonly agreed that this was the next stage in the
inevitable process of social transformation. The issue of the appropriate
source of revenue (in particular, the role of the price scissors in squeezing
resources out of the rural sector), on the other hand, became a raging controversy in the ensuing debate on Soviet industrialization. Every important
Soviet leader had to grapple with it.[1] This debate is important, despite its
polemics, because it anticipated some of the difficult but central trade-offs
which confront many LDCs today.

The Soviet debate over-emphasized the price squeeze of peasants as a
source of investible surplus, and under-emphasized the possible increase in
surplus through a wage squeeze of the industrial proletariat. This bias, however, need not be surprising given the general bias of the early Soviet state
in favour of the proletariat.[2] What was surprising was the lack of attention
given to the behavioural responses of peasants. This lack of concern for incentives is especially glaring since the economic events faced by the early
Soviet state (especially the sharp swings in the rural supply of food surplus),[3]
as well as Lenin's warning,[4] had already pointed out the importance of
incentives. Be that as it may, our analysis in the preceding chapters has
clearly demonstrated that the behavioural responses of peasants are central
to any analysis of the price scissors.

Before we begin our discussion, it might be useful to note that the term
'price scissors' was not only used extensively in the Soviet debate, but it
perhaps originated there. As we have noted earlier, price scissors refer to the
price of industrial goods relative to that of agricultural goods. A graph of

---

[1] For example, Bukharin (1920); Lenin (1919, 1921); Preobrazhensky (1926); Stalin (1926);
and Trotsky (1909). For a review of this debate see Erlich (1960).
[2] A bias which Marx himself shared. 'The bourgeoisie has . . . created enormous cities, has
greatly increased the urban population as compared with the rural, and has thus rescued a
considerable part of the population from *the idiocy of rural life*' (Marx and Engels 1848: p. 488,
our emphasis).
[3] See Dobb (1966, ch. 7) for a description of some of these events.
[4] 'It is impossible to increase the production and collection of grain . . . except by improving
the condition of the peasantry' (1921, p. 593).

industrial prices and agricultural prices in the Soviet Union during 1922–4 (see Fig. 7.1) shows why these price movements might have been referred to as first a closing and then an opening of price scissors. An unambiguous use of this term, employed sometimes in this book, is that a movement of price scissors against (respectively, in favour of) agriculture is simply another way of stating that the prices of agricultural goods have decreased (respectively, increased) relative to the prices of industrial goods.

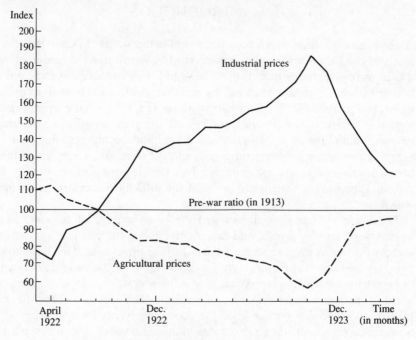

FIG. 7.1 THE 'PRICE SCISSORS'.
The ratio of retail prices of industrial and agricultural goods.

Source: Dobb (1966, chapter 7).

7.2 PREOBRAZHENSKY'S PROPOSITIONS

A seminal contributor to the Soviet industrialization debate was Evgeny Preobrazhensky. Unlike most other participants in this debate, he based his arguments on an explicit model of a peasant sector existing side-by-side with a state-controlled industrial sector.[5] He discussed the role of a number of policy instruments besides the terms of trade, such as railway tariffs, printing

---

[5] See Preobrazhensky (1926) and the collection of his papers edited by Filtzer (1979). As Dixit (1973, p. 325) has correctly pointed out, Preobrazhensky's verbal model can be considered a precursor of modern models of dual developing economies.

money, and credit policy. The centre-piece of his analysis, as well as the focus of the most significant controversies he faced, was a set of propositions which he advanced concerning the effects and the role of the terms of trade. The objective in this section is to use the analysis of the preceding chapters to clarify some of these propositions. The discussion below is based on the model in Chapter 6 in which rural and urban prices are the same and there are binding constraints on trade. In our view, a model with, rather than without, constraints on external trade is the more appropriate one with which to understand the Soviet situation during the period under consideration. This and other issues concerning the appropriate model are taken up later. For brevity, our discussion in this chapter abstracts from the effects of wage and price changes on a worker's productivity.

First Proposition

Preobrazhensky's most important claim was that the state can increase its capital accumulation by moving the terms of trade against peasants. For ease of reference, we will call this Preobrazhensky's first proposition. Naturally, this proposition is quite basic because it asserts the feasibility of using the terms of trade as an instrument for society's accumulation of capital.

Recall that moving the terms of trade against peasants means a decrease in p. The above proposition thus says that $dI/dp < 0$. Expression (6.13) showed that this proposition is valid because a lowering of the terms of trade necessitates a lowering of the urban wage which, in turn, increases the investible surplus.

Furthermore, recall from our earlier discussion of expression (6.13) that turning the terms of trade against peasants leads to a larger increase in the investible surplus if the price response of the rural surplus is larger. This result needs to be contrasted with the suggestion made by several authors that increasing the squeeze on farmers through the price scissors may not lead to accumulation if the rural surplus is highly price-responsive. (See, for example, Lipton 1977, pp. 129–30, and Mitra 1977, p. 54.) What is relevant here, however, is the distinction between the rural surplus of the agricultural good and the state's investible surplus, as well as the distinction between the state's surplus and consumption by industrial workers. A decrease in the relative price of the agricultural good will lead to a greater decrease in the rural surplus if the price response of the rural surplus is higher. This in turn will require a larger curtailment of urban demand of the agricultural good. This larger decrease in the urban wage necessarily increases the investible surplus by a larger amount.[6]

[6] A parallel conclusion does not always hold, however, when external trade is unconstrained. In fact, as our analysis in ch. 5 (see especially equation (5.2)) has pointed out, the investible surplus in an open economy may not increase if the terms of trade are turned against the peasants. This is true even if one abstracts, as we are doing here, from productivity effects. It

Second Proposition

The economic content of another important claim by Preobrazhensky can be expressed as follows: By turning the terms of trade against peasants, it is possible to accumulate in a manner that does not cause the economic position of the industrial proletariat to deteriorate. This proposition, which we shall refer to as Preobrazhensky's second proposition, can be expressed in our notation as: $dV^u/dp \leq 0$, while $dI/dp < 0$. From (6.5) and (6.7), this proposition is obviously not correct. That is, a price squeeze hurts the proletariat just as it hurts the peasants. Furthermore, expressions (6.5) and (6.7) show that turning the terms of trade against peasants leads to a larger decline in the welfare of industrial workers if the price response of the rural surplus is larger. The crucial point, once again, is the constraint generated by the demand and supply balance of the rural good.[7] This constraint dictates the feasible combinations of the terms of trade and the urban wage and, hence, it determines the full consequences of a change in the terms of trade.

It is of some interest to note here that much of the criticism faced by Preobrazhensky in the Soviet debate was that he was anti-peasant. 'They accused him of favouring the "exploitation" of the peasant, of advocating a kind of internal colonialism' (Nove 1965, p. xi). In fact, Preobrazhensky himself devoted much of his energy to trying to prove that he was not as anti-peasant as his book might at first have suggested.[8] Some of this criticism might have been avoided, we suspect, had he not claimed (incorrectly, as suggested by our analysis) that the industrial proletariat would not have to pay any price for the state's accumulation.[9]

---

also follows from equation (5.2) that whether the sensitivity of the investible surplus to price (that is, the magnitude of dI/dp) increases or decreases when the surplus elasticity, ε'_{Qp}, is larger depends on the tax regime (that is, on whether peasants are being taxed or subsidized). Thus, those who have emphasized the negative effect of the rural surplus elasticity on the price sensitivity of the investible surplus may have had in mind particular sub-cases of an open economy. Alternatively, they may have had in mind alternative means of equilibrating the economy.

[7] It is possible, however, that some governments are unaware of such a constraint. If this is the case, the government may decide to increase the nominal price of the industrial good without changing the real urban wage (that is, keeping the urban wage unchanged in terms of the industrial good). This would simply increase the nominal price of the agricultural good, without changing the terms of trade. Of course, the government could employ additional policy instruments, such as urban rationing or different sets of prices in the two sectors (see ch. 4), but then the economic problem is different from that of price scissors.

[8] See his reply to Bukharin and other opponents in Preobrazhensky (1926, Appendix).

[9] Michael Ellman's empirical studies (1975; 1987) are suggestive in this context. He assesses the contributions of the agricultural versus the industrial sector to the Soviet accumulation during the First Plan period and concludes that most of the accumulation came from industry. Ellman's analysis, however, refers to the post-collectivization period when the central policy instrument was coercion rather than the terms of trade. See Mody (1981) for an analysis of the First Plan period in the Soviet Union as well as of some other historical experiences. Another study that should be noted here is by Gregory and Stuart (1991). Using data for the 1920s, they show, as one analysis assumes, that the price elasticity of the Soviet agricultural surplus was positive.

The Fundamental Law of Primitive Socialist Accumulation

... the smaller the inheritance received by the socialist accumulation fund of the proletariat ... when the social revolution takes place, by so much the more, in proportion, will socialist accumulation be obliged to rely on alienating part of the surplus product of presocialist forms of economy and the smaller will be the relative weight of accumulation on its own production basis; that is, the less will it be nourished by the surplus product of the workers in socialist industry (Preobrazhensky 1926, p. 124).

This 'law' suggests that a smaller current stock of industrial capital:

(*a*) necessitates the state to put a greater price squeeze on peasants, and
(*b*) implies that the profit from the industrial sector would be a smaller fraction of the total investible surplus.

For brevity, we shall refer to the above as Preobrazhensky's third and fourth propositions, respectively. Within our model, a smaller current capital stock would imply a larger value of the social weight on investment, δ. With this interpretation, the third proposition is correct in the sense that the optimal terms of trade would tend to be lower if δ is larger (see expression (6.25) for example). The fourth proposition may also be correct in the sense that, at given wages and prices, a lower capital stock means that the profit from the industrial sector is lower, and so is the proportion of the total investible surplus coming from that sector. But a lower capital stock also affects δ, as well as the relevant behavioural parameters, and hence, the optimal industrial wage and the terms of trade. As we have argued earlier, the optimal p and w^u and, therefore, the optimal proportions of the sources of the investible surplus, are determined by society's value-judgements concerning the welfare of peasants versus the welfare of the proletariat, as well as by the behavioural parameters.[10]

7.3 THE CORRECT SIZE OF THE PRICE SCISSORS

We have shown that the optimal size of the scissors (or, equivalently, the correct level of the implicit 'tax' imposed upon peasants) depends on the social valuation of the welfare of the peasants and the industrial proletariat, as compared to the social valuation of investment. On this score, it has often been believed that the peasants' welfare was irrelevant to the early Soviet state. A better interpretation of the pre-collectivization debates might perhaps

[10] An increase in δ/β' will increase the tax on the rural sector. This increases the contribution from the rural sector. But it also leads to lower wages, which increase the revenues received from the urban sector.

Note that in Preobrazhensky's third and fourth propositions, it is implicitly assumed that as the economy grows through capital accumulation, most of the capital is allocated to the industrial sector. This assumption was pervasive in the Soviet debate, but its justification should at least be questioned in the context of present-day less developed countries. See our discussion of the sources and uses of investment in the introductory chapters.

be that Preobrazhensky represented the lower end of the concern for the peasants, in contrast to Lenin who represented the middle position (see Lenin 1919), and to Bukharin who represented the higher end.[11] On the other hand, the early Soviet leadership appears to have been fairly unanimous in placing a higher social weight on investment than on consumption, and in placing a higher social weight on the consumption of the industrial proletariat than on the consumption of the peasants.[12]

From this interpretation of the initial Soviet situation, our analysis shows that a movement in the terms of trade against peasants emerges as desirable, at least to the point where the investible surplus, and the consumption of the industrial proletariat have the same social weight (see Chapter 6 above, expression (6.19)). The direction of change in the terms of trade (from what it would have been in the absence of government intervention), therefore, remains the same even though the magnitude of relative concern for peasants versus the industrial proletariat might differ. The level of tax to be imposed on peasants, on the other hand, will be affected by the precise magnitude of relative concern: a higher concern for peasants will correspond to a lower tax.

7.4 COLLECTIVIZATION

It is clear from this analysis that there is a limit to how low the prices to peasants should be pushed, regardless of whether the state values them or not. Correspondingly, there is a limit to how large a surplus can be extracted from the peasants. If a state wants to extract more surplus than this limit, it must discover an alternative way of organizing the rural sector. One can interpret Soviet collectivization as a response to these problems.[13] According to this interpretation, collectivization was seen as a form of organization which would allow for the extraction of a significantly larger surplus from the rural sector, enabling not only a faster accumulation of capital (deemed by early Soviet leaders to be urgently needed), but also a betterment of the proletariat. As is now well recognized, collectivization did not solve the conflicts of incentive which are at the heart of the issue, and, in fact, created problems whose enormity is now widely recognized (see Swarup 1954 for an early analysis of some of these problems).

Using economic terminology, collectivization can be viewed as a substitution of a supervisory-command system in the place of a price-incentive

---

[11] Bukharin, in fact, exhorted the peasants to enrich themselves.

[12] Stated differently, it appears that there was unanimity on $\delta > \beta^u$ and on $\delta > \beta^r$. But there were differences on the relative size of β^r compared to β^u. It is obvious that, in the present context, the welfare evaluations are not necessarily based on an anonymous social welfare function.

[13] This, of course, is a purely economic interpretation. At the other extreme, one can argue that the reasons for collectivization were entirely non-economic, for example the commitment of the Soviet state to destroy the power of a potentially reactionary peasantry or simply to abolish private property.

system. Some aspects of the comparison between the two systems (such as the workers' incentives to shirk under the former) have been extensively studied. Here, we would like to point to an aspect which has received insufficient attention. Most of the literature has focused on a comparison of the ability of alternative organizations to induce workers to achieve certain work norms. However, in agriculture in particular (where there are wide variations in the quality of land from plot to plot and in the climatic conditions from season to season), a critical problem is the setting of norms.[14] What should be the output from a plot of land? How much work is reasonable to expect from someone? When individuals work on their own plots, they make these decisions for themselves. And, in a competitive environment, supervisory systems may work better, because workers can choose among a variety of farms, where differences in pay may correspond to differences in work norms. But: there is virtually no endogenous basis for norm-determination in a collective economy.

This analysis also suggests that productivity in collectives may decline over time relative to the contemporaneous performance of price-incentive systems. In the early days of a collective, historical productivity may provide a reasonable basis for norm determination; but as technology changes it provides a less and less adequate basis. Moreover, in the early days there may be a cadre of individuals committed to making the collective work; these individuals may not need much economic incentive. As time progresses, the necessity of economic incentives may increase.

One method of obtaining some of the information needed to determine norms for different locations would have been to allow private plots in the neighbourhood of collectives. Another possible method would have been to establish contests among collectives such that high performers receive large rewards whereas low performers receive significant punishments.[15] Both of these methods, however, were inconsistent with certain interpretations of socialist ideals.

7.5 A POSTSCRIPT ON THE SOVIET DEBATE

Since the publication of our initial interpretation of the Soviet debate (Sah and Stiglitz 1984), several economists have considered the same issue. We discuss here two of the alternative approaches that have been proposed, and our evaluation of these alternatives (see Sah and Stiglitz 1986 for details).

First, it has been proposed that a better vehicle to examine the Soviet debate is an open economy model of the form analysed in Chapter 5.[16] As we

---

[14] The problem of norm-setting also arises in industrial production, especially in connection with setting appropriate piece-rates against a background of changing technology.

[15] See Nalebuff and Stiglitz (1983), and Lazear and Rosen (1981) for analyses of contests.

[16] See Carter (1986) for arguments in favour of such a model.

emphasized in Chapter 6, the question is not so much whether a country engages in external trade, because almost all countries do, but whether there are binding constraints on the magnitude of that trade, at least in the short run. The trade figures for the Soviet Union during the relevant period (that is, between the October Revolution and the beginning of the industrialization debate in 1924) exhibit an extreme decline in trade compared to the period before World War I. Trade was negligible until 1920; even in 1923, the import volume was less than 11 per cent, and the export volume less than 15 per cent, of the respective 1913 levels (see Gregory and Stuart 1981, p. 267). Though these or any other trade figures could, in principle, be consistent with a model with or without constraints on external trade, historical facts suggest the former model. Not only was the Soviet Union facing blockades by the allies during much of this period (augmenting the Soviets' fear of 'capitalist encirclement'), but even after the Treaty of Rapallo (April 1922), it faced significant isolation in trade and current business credit.[17]

The importance of these constraints is explicit in Preobrazhensky's views. Though he emphasized the potential usefulness of external trade to the Soviet state, he clearly noted that there were 'all kinds of external complications that might not only sever our economic ties with the capitalist countries but will also most effectively retard even that part of socialist construction that is based on the domestic resources of the Republic' (1921, p. 14).[18] Obviously, the specific trade and credit constraints faced by an economy can be formalized in many ways, particularly when the full disaggregation of goods is modelled. However, in aggregate models such as those being discussed at present, the facts concerning the Soviet Union during 1917–24 (and the understanding that the participants in the Soviet debate had of these facts) suggest that a model with constraints on trade is more plausible than one without any constraints.

Second, it has also been suggested that a model of the kind analysed in Chapter 4 (in which the government can impose different sets of taxes in the rural and urban sectors) is more appropriate for examining the Soviet debate.[19] There can be little doubt that the key policy instrument in Preobrazhensky's scheme of primitive socialist accumulation was the terms of trade between agricultural and industrial goods, although he did mention a multitude of other instruments.[20] The reason for the primacy of the terms

---

[17] See Dobb (1966, ch. 7) for some of the details of these constraints and their consequences. Long-term international credit to the Soviet Union was obviously not available at the time, in part as a reaction to the Soviet repudiation of the Tsarist debts. Preobrazhensky, for instance, did not anticipate foreign capital 'to flow on a large scale into an economic system of a type alien to itself' (1928, p. 298).

[18] For a similar interpretation of Preobrazhensky's belief that though external trade was beneficial to some extent to the Soviet state, its ability to trade was constrained, see Gregory and Stuart (1981, pp. 73–4).

[19] See Blomqvist (1986) for views supporting this model.

[20] Such as railway freights, credit and banking policy, printing money, etc.

of trade was simple. The state's monopoly of industry made it possible to alter the terms of trade without additional administrative costs, and without the administrative abilities of the sort the Soviet Union was clearly lacking during 1917–24. Basing his conclusions on quotations from Preobrazhensky's writings, Erlich (1960, pp. 49–50) makes this point succinctly:

The concentration of the whole of big industries . . . in the hands of the workers' state increases to an extraordinary extent . . . the possibility of carrying out . . . a price policy on the basis of monopoly. . . . Preobrazhensky did not, to be sure, renounce direct taxation as an instrument of the redistribution of income in favor of socialist industry . . . . Taxation through price, however, was in his view the most effective single device—both because of the 'extreme convenience of collection which did not require a penny for a special fiscal apparatus' and for reasons of political expediency. 'The way of direct taxation is the most dangerous way, leading to a break with the peasants.'

Implicit in Preobrazhensky's view is the equivalence of taxation of rural output and an increase in the prices of manufactured goods. In contrast, a model with distinct sets of rural and urban prices entails not only large administrative costs but, as discussed earlier, also requires the administrative ability to monitor the tax border. Therefore, it should not be surprising that the participants in the Soviet debate, as well as those who have subsequently analysed this debate, have viewed the terms of trade, and not rural–urban pricing differentials, as the central instrument in Preobrazhensky's scheme.[21]

[21] Our view on this issue is corroborated by Michael Lipton: 'The "scissors" discussion always was, and is, mostly about changing the price of the rural good relative to the urban good—not about changing the relative price paid by the two sectors for the same good' (personal communication, 1982, Lipton's emphasis).

PART III

The Rural Sector

Part III extends the basic analysis of Part II in several ways. In Chapter 8, we study the effects of taxation policies on the distribution of welfare and real incomes of diverse individuals within the rural sector. We then show how the analysis can be expanded to incorporate specific institutions (such as share-cropping, the extended family, and plantations), and rigidities (leading, for instance, to unemployment in the rural sector) which might be important in particular LDCs. Chapter 9 addresses the question of the structure of taxes and prices on different goods in the rural sector. Should all goods be taxed at the same rate? If at different rates, what principles should guide the rates at which the taxes or subsidies are levied? We derive rules for reform in taxes on certain categories of goods in the rural sector. These rules are not only parsimonious in the information required to implement them, but also lead to Pareto-improving reforms; that is, no member of society is hurt in the implementation of these rules.

8

INCOME DISTRIBUTION AND ALTERNATIVE ORGANIZATIONAL FORMS WITHIN THE RURAL SECTOR

8.1 INTRODUCTION

In many LDCs, there are wide disparities in the incomes of those in the rural sector. At one extreme there are landlords with very large landholdings, while at the other there are impoverished landless workers. While changing the prices of agricultural and industrial goods alters the distribution of income between urban and rural sectors, it also influences the income distribution within each of these sectors. In this chapter, we examine how changes in the price of the agricultural good affect the welfare and real incomes of different groups of individuals in the rural sector. It is then shown that the earlier analysis can be modified to incorporate these distributive effects.

The importance of distributive effects hardly needs to be emphasized. For those who believe that the individual is the basic unit of analysis for evaluating policy changes, the distribution of welfare across individuals is of concern. It is inequality among individuals, not across sectors, which should ultimately be the centre of analysis. On the other hand, at a practical level, policies do focus on larger units such as the urban and rural sectors. Indeed, one seldom has the data to conduct an analysis at the individual level. Even with good data on the intra-sectoral inter-household distribution of consumption, rarely is there sufficient data on how the household consumption is divided among family members. Policies can have important effects on intra-family distribution of income, which is no less important than effects on the distribution of income among households. This observation is particularly important in societies where certain tasks are traditionally performed by individuals of one sex or another. For instance, in Western industrial societies subsidizing dishwashers undoubtedly has an intra-family distribution effect, as do those provisions of the corporate income tax which encourage expensive business meals.

In addition, political reasons (including the role of pressure groups) may make governments more sensitive to extremes of poverty, or to inequalities within the urban rather than the rural sector. Politicians may find specific types of real income comparisons to be central, and they may find an anonymous individualistic social welfare function—giving equal weight to inequality irrespective of the sector—unpersuasive.

The distributional consequences of price changes in the rural sector have often been a source of controversy. An extensive debate has taken place in India, for instance, on whether past agricultural pricing policies of the Indian government have worsened or improved the distribution of income within the rural sector. See Mitra (1977) and Kalhon and Tyagi (1980) for differing views on this debate.

In general, the distributional consequences of price changes in the rural sector depend not only on income and land distribution within agriculture, but also on the induced effects which prices have on variables such as the rural wage, migration, reallocation of land entailed by migration, the terms of share-cropping and credit, and intra-family arrangements for sharing work and output. For brevity, we first focus on the induced effect on the rural wage (or, on the corresponding payments to individuals in the case of an extended family or share-cropping). However, as we show later, other induced effects (say, on the demand and supply of a multitude of goods which cannot be taxed or subsidized) can be similarly analysed.

The importance of the induced effects can be seen as follows. If there were no induced effects, then an increase in food prices would hurt the net buyers of food (the landless workers and farmers with small landholdings) and help the net sellers of food (large landlords). Quite the reverse may be the case if the wage is highly responsive to the food price. If an increase in food price increases the rural wage, then the net sellers of labour (who are typically poor) will gain at the expense of the net buyers of labour (for instance, large landlords). In fact, if the supply of labour is sufficiently inelastic and the demand sufficiently elastic, then it is possible (as we shall see later) that the beneficial distributional effect of the induced increase in the rural wage will offset the deleterious direct distributional effects of a food price increase.

Taking account of the induced changes in wages, which are simply transfers within the rural sector (with the workers' income gains just equalling the landlords' income losses), we are able to obtain formulae for price reforms and for the optimal set of prices and taxes. These resemble the formulae obtained in Part II, but the marginal social utility of income in the rural sector, β^r, is now a weighted average of the marginal social utilities of incomes to different groups of rural individuals.

The form of the results derived below are remarkably robust to alternative organizational forms within the rural sector. To demonstrate this, we extend the analysis (in Sections 8.3 and 8.4) to several forms of rural organization, such as plantations, share-cropping, and extended family systems. Certain aspects of rural unemployment are briefly discussed in Section 8.4.

8.2 DISTRIBUTIONAL EFFECTS

A person belonging to rural group h is denoted by a superscript h. Correspondingly, A^h is his fixed farm size, and Q^h is his surplus of the agricultural good which can be positive, negative, or zero. y^{rh} is his consumption of the industrial good L^{rh}. is his net labour supply hours (that is, labour hours he supplies minus the labour hours employed on his farm). Thus L^{rh} is positive or negative depending on whether a person is a net supplier or net demander of labour. For the landless, it is obvious that $A^h = 0$, $L^{rh} > 0$, and $Q^h < 0$. An individual's budget constraint is

$$p^r Q^h + w^r L^{rh} = y^{rh} > 0 , \tag{8.1}$$

where p^r is the price of the agricultural good in terms of the industrial good, and $w^r(p^r)$ represents the rural wage per hour which, in general, depends on the rural price. The sign of (8.1) is positive because we assume that the consumption of industrial goods is positive for every individual. Let $\varepsilon^r_{wp} =$ dln w^r/dln p^r denote the elasticity of the rural wage-rate with respect to p^r.[1] Then, using (8.1), the envelope theorem yields

$$\frac{dV^{rh}}{dp^r} = \lambda^{rh} \left(Q^h + \frac{w^r L^{rh}}{p^r} \varepsilon^r_{wp} \right) , \tag{8.2}$$

where V^{rh} and λ^{rh} respectively are the utility level and the positive marginal utility of income for a rural individual belonging to group h. It is apparent that the term inside the parentheses on the right-hand side of (8.2) is the marginal income change (which will be positive or negative depending on whether the income increases or decreases) for a person in group h from an increase in the rural price.[2] We can rewrite the above expression as:

$$\frac{dV^{rh}}{dp^r} = \frac{\lambda^{rh}}{p^r} [(p^r Q^h + w^r L^{rh}) + w^r L^{rh}(\varepsilon^r_{wp} - 1)] .$$

This, in turn, can be expressed, using (8.1), as

$$\frac{dV^{rh}}{dp^r} = \frac{\lambda^{rh}}{p^r} [y^{rh} + w^r L^{rh}(\varepsilon^r_{wp} - 1)] . \tag{8.3}$$

Now note from (8.1) that y^{rh} is positive. Expression (8.3), therefore, yields the following results. A movement of prices in favour of agriculture improves the welfare of:

(a) every rural individual, rich or poor, if the elasticity of the rural wage-rate with respect to the price of the agricultural good is close to one;

(b) the net sellers or demanders of labour depending on whether the elasticity is significantly greater or smaller than one.

Further, suppose we define a 'labour self-sufficient' farmer to be one who

[1] This is the elasticity arising out of rural labour-market equilibrium. It describes the change in equilibrium wage in the rural sector when the rural price of the agricultural good is increased. We show below how this elasticity may be calculated.

[2] The direct change is captured by Q^h, and the indirect change (through the induced change in wage) by $w^r L^{rh} \varepsilon^r_{wp}/p^r$.

neither buys nor sells labour services, that is, for whom $L^{rh} = 0$. Then it is apparent from (8.3) that a labour self-sufficient farmer is better off if the price of the agricultural good is higher. Categories such as labour self-sufficient farmers and marginal farmers (those who are not landless but are sufficiently poor) have often been used in policy discussions, particularly in South Asia. It should be clear that the boundary lines of such categories, whether defined on the basis of net trade of labour or goods, or on the basis of a given level of welfare or real income, are themselves dependent on the rural wage and prices.

Elasticity of the Rural Wage

The elasticity of the rural wage depends on the nature of the labour market and on the labour demand and supply responses of individuals. Here we consider the case in which there are constant returns to scale in agricultural production, and the rural wage-rate is determined in a competitive rural labour-market. The labour-market equilibrium is described by

$$\Sigma_h N^{rh} L^{rh} = \Sigma_h N^{rh}(L^{sh} - A^h L^d) = 0, \tag{8.4}$$

where N^{rh} is the number of individuals in the rural group h, $L^{sh}(p^r, w^r)$ is the labour supply of an individual in group h, and $L^d(p^r, w^r)$ is the labour employed per unit of land. Thus, $L^{rh} = L^{sh} - A^h L^d$ is the net labour supply of individual h.

We define $\varepsilon^d_{Lw} = -\partial \ln L^d/\partial \ln w^r$ and $\varepsilon^d_{Lp} = \partial \ln L^d/\partial \ln p^r$ as elasticities of labour demand on one unit of land with respect to wage and price. Now, if the wage-rate equals the value of the marginal product; that is, if $w^r = p^r \partial X(L^d)/\partial L^d$, then $\varepsilon^d_{Lw} = \varepsilon^d_{Lp}$. The preceding relationship between the elasticities is what one would expect, since in the present case, labour demand depends only on the ratio of the wage to the output price.[3] Next, we define $\varepsilon^{sh}_{Lw} = \partial \ln L^{sh}/\partial \ln w^r$ and $\varepsilon^{sh}_{Lp} = -\partial \ln L^{sh}/\partial \ln p^r$ as elasticities of labour supply with respect to wage and price, for an individual belonging to group h. A perturbation of (8.4) yields

$$\varepsilon^r_{wp} - 1 = \Sigma_h N^{rh} L^{sh}(\varepsilon^{sh}_{Lp} - \varepsilon^{sh}_{Lw})/(\Sigma_h N^{rh} L^{sh} \varepsilon^{sh}_{Lw} + N^r A L^d \varepsilon^d_{Lw}) , \tag{8.5}$$

where $A = \Sigma_h N^{rh} A^h/N^r$ is the average land area per rural individual. Substitution of the above into (8.3) makes it possible to express an individual's gain or loss from a change in the price of the agricultural good solely in terms of the behavioural parameters which, in principle, can be estimated.

Note that the right-hand side of (8.5) is zero if $\varepsilon^{sh}_{Lw} = \varepsilon^{sh}_{Lp}$, which occurs if the individual's labour supply depends on the rural price and on the wage, but not on the price of the industrial good. The right-hand side of (8.5) is

---

[3] For the results derived below, therefore, what is important is not that the wage-rate equals the value of the marginal product, but that farm labour demand depends only on w^r/p^r. That is, farm labour demand is homogeneous of degree zero in the wage-rate and output price.

also zero if an individual's labour supply is fixed, in which case the labour supply elasticities are zero. In both cases, the net labour supply of an individual (and hence of the entire sector) depends only on the ratio of the rural wage to the output price. From (8.3) and (8.5), therefore: A movement of prices in favour of (respectively, against) agriculture helps (respectively, hurts) every rural individual if the rural wage-rate equals the value of the marginal product, and if one of the following two conditions are met: (*a*) individuals' labour supplies are fixed, or (*b*) the elasticities of an individual's labour supply with respect to the rural wage and price are close to one another.

Normative Analysis

Normative analysis in the context of heterogeneous agricultural individuals requires only a slight restatement of the corresponding analysis in earlier chapters. The aggregate social welfare can now be defined as

$$\psi = \Sigma_h N^{rh} W(V^{rh}(p^r, w^r; A^h)) + N^u W(V^u), \tag{8.6}$$

where for simplicity we continue to model the urban sector as consisting of homogeneous individuals. Using (8.6) we can do an analysis analogous to that found in those those sections of Chapters 4 to 7 that deal with normative analysis. It turns out that this entire analysis remains unchanged, provided we express β^r as

$$\beta^r = \Sigma_h \beta^{rh} \Gamma^{rh}, \text{ where} \tag{8.7}$$

$$\Gamma^{rh} = \frac{N^{rh}}{N^r Q} \left(Q^h + \frac{w^r L^{rh}}{p^r} \varepsilon_{wp}^r \right), \tag{8.8}$$

$\beta^{rh} = \lambda^h \partial W(V^{rh})/\partial V^{rh}$ is the social weight on the marginal income of individual h in the rural sector, and $Q = \Sigma_h N^{rh} Q^h / N^r$ is the average surplus per rural individual.[4]

---

[4] To see the reason for (8.7) and (8.8), note that the only change introduced in the Hamiltonian $H = \psi + \partial I$ by the heterogeneity in the rural sector is due to the first term on the right-hand side of (8.6). In the absence of heterogeneity, the derivative of this term with respect to p^r is:

$$\partial N^r W(V^r(p^r))/\partial p^r = N^r(\partial W/\partial V^r)(\partial V^r/\partial p^r).$$

This, in turn, equals $N^r Q \beta^r$, because $\partial V^r/\partial p^r = \lambda^r Q$ and $\beta^r = \lambda^r \partial W/\partial V^r$. In the presence of heterogeneity, the corresponding derivative is

$$d\Sigma_h N^{rh} W(V^{rh}(p^r, w^r; A^r))/dp^r = \Sigma_h N^{rh}(\partial W/\partial V^{rh})(dV^{rh}/dp).$$

Using (8.2), and $\beta^{rh} = \lambda^h \partial W/\partial V^{rh}$, the preceding expression becomes

$$\Sigma_h N^{rh} \beta^{rh}(Q^h + w^r L^{rh} \varepsilon_{wp}^r/p^r).$$

This, once again, equals $N^r Q \beta^r$, provided definitions (8.7) and (8.8) are employed.

As (8.7) makes clear, the social weight to be associated with the gain to the rural sector as a whole, β^r, is a weighted average of the social weights, the β^{rh}, to be associated with the marginal incomes of different individuals in the rural sector. The weighting factor Γ^{rh} corresponding to the individuals in rural group h is the income gain to this group (accruing directly or indirectly from an increase in the price of the agricultural good) as a fraction of the aggregate income gain to the rural sector. This can be seen from (8.8), in which the numerator is the income gain to group h and the denominator is the income gain to the rural population as a whole. Using (8.4), it is easily verified that the weighting factors sum to one. That is

$$\Sigma_h \Gamma^{rh} = 1. \tag{8.9}$$

The reinterpretation of the analysis presented in earlier chapters is not only straightforward but is also unaffected by certain aspects of the economy's model, such as whether the economy is open or closed, or whether the prices in the two sectors can or cannot be set at different levels. As an example, in a closed economy in which prices in the two sectors cannot be set at different levels, the optimal price scissors are given by

$$t = \left(\frac{\eta}{\delta} - p\right) \Big/ p = \frac{(1 - \theta)(1 - \beta^r/\delta) + (\sigma_p - \alpha^u \sigma_w)/\alpha^u \gamma^u}{(1 - \theta)\varepsilon^r_{Qp} + e^u_{xp}}, \tag{8.10}$$

where $p \equiv p^r = p^u$ denotes the common price of the agricultural good in the two sectors, and $\varepsilon^r_{Qp} = \partial\ln Q/\partial\ln p$ represents the elasticity of per capita rural surplus with respect to price. Expression (8.10) is thus the same as the expression for the optimal tax in the model with homogeneous rural individuals (see expression (6.25) in Chapter 6), but now, to account for the intra-sectoral heterogeneity of individuals in the rural sector, β^r is given by (8.7). Similarly, in an open economy in which the prices in the two sectors can be set at different levels, the earlier rules for price reform or for optimal prices (see expressions (4.7) to (4.10) in Chapter 4) remain unchanged, provided that the parameter β^r is calculated according to (8.7).

The parameter β^r can obviously be viewed as the 'average' distributional consequence of raising the rural good's price. An important feature of this distributional parameter is that it explicitly takes into account the general-equilibrium effects faced by individuals, due to the induced change in the rural wage. Parallel induced effects are typically absent in the standard tax models, which assume that wages or incomes are fixed, or that the government can control wages.[5] Either assumption is not fully satisfactory in the context of the agricultural sector of an LDC.

Expression (8.7) also enables us to understand, to some degree, the role

---

[5] See Atkinson and Stiglitz (1980, lecture 14), for example, where parameters similar to (8.7) are called the 'distributional characteristic of a good', and where the general-equilibrium effects are missing because it is assumed that wages and incomes are fixed.

that the social weights of different groups (poor versus rich) play in the determination of the distributional parameter β^r. First, note that under extreme circumstances, it is possible for β^r to be negative. For instance, if the government has a Rawlsian welfare function then only the welfare of the poorest (say, the landless) is relevant; that is, only the β^{rh} corresponding to landless workers is positive, while all other values of β^{rh} are zero. Further, if the elasticity of the wage with respect to price is close to zero, then (8.7) is negative because the food surplus, Q^h, is negative for the landless. In this case, some of the qualitative observations made in earlier chapters (where β^r was assumed to be positive) would have to be altered. For instance, in the absence of productivity effects, expression (8.10) would then imply that rural output should be taxed (equivalently, the consumption of food by the landless and by those in the urban sector should be subsidized)[6] regardless of how large or small the social weight on investment might be. Clearly, the conditions underlying this result are extreme, yet the result does illustrate the sensitivity of taxation and pricing policies to value-judgements and to the nature of induced effects of prices on wages.

Another special case is the one in which all rural individuals gain from an increase in the rural price. As pointed out earlier, a sufficient condition for this to happen is that the elasticity of the rural wage with respect to price is close to one. Focusing on that case, from (8.3), the corresponding marginal income gain to a person in group h from an increase in the rural price, is y^{rh}/p^r. This income gain increases with the income (or land area) of the individual.[7]

Finally, it is perhaps useful to explain the difference between applying the rules for optimal prices based on the assumption of a representative farmer (that is, where β^r is the social weight corresponding to that person whose income is the average of the rural sector's income), and applying the rules in which the intra-sectoral heterogeneity of individuals is explicit (that is, rules which use distributional parameters such as (8.7)). In both cases the required information on sectoral price elasticities is the same, since the government's budget is the same. The application of rules based on heterogeneous individuals requires additional information about the quantities of goods, net labour supply, and the social weights corresponding to different groups of individuals. How a distributional parameter like (8.7) differs from the social weight for the representative rural person would clearly depend on how skewed land ownership and income distribution are within the rural sector, as well as on how β^{rh} varies with income. If income disparities are

[6] Recall that, in the model under consideration here, taxing the agricultural goods means that p is lower than the shadow price, η/δ.

[7] Recall that y^{rh} is an individual's consumption of urban goods, and it is assumed here that these goods are normal. Moreover, it can be verified from (8.3) that the income gain to a person (from an increase in p^r) may be increasing with land area even when the elasticity ε^r_{wp} is smaller than one, provided the net labour supply of an individual is a decreasing function of his land area. We would normally expect the latter condition to hold.

large (as they typically are) and if the society cares about the intra-sectoral distribution of welfare, then, clearly, the government should use distributional parameters such as (8.7).

Non-Taxable Goods

It is difficult, if not impossible, for most LDC governments to tax or subsidize those goods which are produced, traded, and consumed primarily within the rural sector (millet, for example). Yet, government pricing and tax policies towards taxed and internationally traded goods (rice, for example) will, in general, affect the prices of the non-taxable goods. Incorporating these induced price effects into our analysis is not only straightforward but also very similar to the treatment of the induced effect on the rural wage. In fact, we simply need to modify the weighting term (8.8) as:

$$\Gamma^{rh} = \frac{N^{rh}}{\sum_h N^{rh}Q^r}\left(Q^h + \frac{1}{p^r}\, w^r L^{rh}\varepsilon^r_{wp} - \frac{1}{p^r}\sum_i c^h_i\, \varepsilon^r_{ip} \right), \qquad (8.8')$$

where Q^h is the net surplus of individual h of the taxable agricultural good, c^h_i is his net expenditure on the non-taxable good i (this expenditure can be positive or negative), and ε^r_{ip} is the elasticity of the price of the non-taxable good i with respect to p^r (these elasticities are obtained by perturbing, with respect to p^r, the market-clearing conditions for the non-taxable goods).[8] Since good i is not traded outside the rural sector, it follows that

$$\sum_h N^{rh}c^h_i = 0 \quad \text{for all } i .$$

Using the above property, it is easily verified that the new weighting terms (8.8') continue to satisfy the adding-up property (8.9).[9]

To see an implication of (8.8'), suppose that a higher price of rice (which is taxable) raises the price of non-taxable millet. Then (8.8') shows that Γ^{rh} for the poor (who are net consumers of millet) will be lower (compared to the base case in which the rice price does not affect the millet price), whereas the Γ^{rh} will be higher for the rich (who are net suppliers of millet). Since the social weight on an individual's income, β^{rh}, is higher for a poor person than for a rich person, it follows that the aggregate welfare gains from raising the rice price will be lower than that in the base case.

---

[8] The derivation of (8.8') is straightforward. First, note that the prices of the non-taxable goods under consideration here do not affect the investible surplus or the urban individuals, but they do affect rural individuals. Let q_i denote the price of the i-th non-taxable good, and let $\varepsilon^r_{ip} = \mathrm{d}\ln q_i/\mathrm{d}\ln p^r$ denote the elasticity of this price with respect to p_r. Then,

$$\frac{\mathrm{d}V^r}{\mathrm{d}p^r} = \lambda^{rh}\left(Q^h + L^{rh}\frac{\mathrm{d}w^r}{\mathrm{d}p^r} - \sum_i \frac{c^h_i}{q_i}\frac{\mathrm{d}q_i}{\mathrm{d}p^r} \right) = \lambda^{rh}\left(Q^h + \frac{w^r L^{rh}}{p^r}\varepsilon^r_{wp} - \frac{1}{p^r}\sum_i c^h_i\, \varepsilon^r_{ip} \right) .$$

The preceding expression along with the steps described in n. 4 yields (8.8').

[9] For non-taxable goods which are tradable across sectors but are not imported, $\sum_h N^{rh}c^h_i < 0 .$

8.3 ALTERNATIVE FORMS OF RURAL ORGANIZATION

There is a wide variety of organizational forms which have been observed within the rural sector of LDCs. In fact, numerous variations in the details of arrangements are found even within common organizational forms, such as household farming with family and hired labour, extended family systems, share-cropping, and plantations. An understanding of the consequences of pricing and taxation policies in the presence of such organizational forms requires a two-step analysis: first, a positive economic explanation of why a particular set of organizational forms is observed in an economy and, second, an analysis of how individuals' responses (for instance, their surplus response) and their welfare levels are altered when prices are altered. It is also possible that the tax regime will affect the observed mix of organizational forms; for example, the prevalence of farming based on an extended family. In this section, we briefly demonstrate how the earlier analysis can be modified in the context of two specific types of organizations: joint or extended families, and share-cropping. A discussion of another important organizational form, namely plantations, is postponed until the next section, where we also address the issue of involuntary unemployment in the rural sector.

Extended-Family Farming

One mode of rural organization which has received extensive attention in development economics is the extended-family organization. In this model, family members co-operate in sharing income, but they do not fully co-operate in providing labour. As a result, there is an undersupply of family labour on the farm, because each individual receives not his marginal but his average product. Accordingly, in a Nash equilibrium, the increment to his income from extra effort which an individual imputes is much less than what it would have been if he were paid his marginal product (the ratio between these two increments is approximately equal to the inverse of the number of individuals in the family).

Such a model is a peculiar hybrid. The family is neither fully co-operative (in which case the labour supply would be determined in a way which maximized family welfare) nor is it fully non-cooperative (in which case each individual would receive his marginal contribution plus the share in the rents determined by whatever property-right conventions are adopted by the society). The fact that this model appears to be a hybrid does not, of course, imply that it might not represent an element of reality in some economies.

Consider a family with farm size A^F consisting of N^F homogeneous adult workers. Let (x^r, y^r, L^r) denote the consumption of the agricultural and industrial goods and the labour supply of an individual. Then in a symmetric Nash equilibrium, an individual chooses (x^r, y^r, L^r) to maximize

$$U(x^r, y^r, L^r) + \lambda^r \left[p^r \frac{X(A^F, L^r + (N^F - 1)L^{r*})}{N^F} - p^r x^r - y^r \right], \quad (8.11)$$

where U denotes an individual's utility function, and X is the total family output which is divided into N^F equal parts with each part going to an individual. Denote the resulting level of utility to an individual as V^r. An individual determines his own optimal choices based on the assumption that the labour supplied by others, denoted by L^{r*} per person, will not change as a result of his choice. In a symmetric equilibrium, $L^r = L^{r*}$. Then, it is straightforward to verify that

$$\frac{\partial V^r}{\partial p^r} = \lambda^r Q + \lambda^r p^r \left[\frac{N^F - 1}{N^F} \right] \frac{\partial X}{\partial L^r} \frac{\partial L^r}{\partial p^r}, \quad (8.12)$$

where $Q = \frac{X}{N^F} - x^r$. Here the second term can obviously be considerably larger than zero. Thus, there may be an additional benefit from increasing the price because, at the margin, the increased utility from the increased output more than offsets the corresponding marginal disutility from the increased labour input. This reflects the fact that there is an undersupply of labour.

Share-Cropping

In some LDCs a part of agricultural production takes place under share-cropping arrangements with various kinds of landlord–tenant contracts concerning inputs, outputs, and credit. An economic analysis of such arrangements has recently been the subject of research. This research has questioned one of the earlier views that share-cropping is an inefficient social arrangement because it provides workers with incomplete incentives since they receive only a fraction of the value of their marginal product. It is now recognized that share-cropping might play a role in sharing risks between landowner and workers.

Stiglitz (1974c), for instance, has argued that a central reason behind a share-cropping contract is that it provides work incentives in situations where measuring the labour input is difficult. Wage contracts are better than share-cropping contracts in risk-sharing, but they provide insufficient incentives and necessitate costly supervision. At the other extreme, rental contracts provide better incentives to workers, since workers keep all the value of their marginal product, but they force workers to absorb all the risk. Thus, share-cropping contracts can be viewed as a compromise between incentives and risk-sharing.

What is important from our point of view is how the share-cropping equilibrium is altered by a change in prices and, more importantly, how this change in equilibrium affects the welfare of various groups of landowners and share-croppers. Such an analysis has not yet been undertaken in the literature on share-cropping, which has focused on an environment of fixed prices. The analysis below establishes the central point that there is an asymmetry in how a price change affects the welfare of tenants versus landlords. This asymmetry arises because, while the marginal utility of a change in the labour supply of a tenant (induced by the change in prices) is offset by the change in income he receives, there is no corresponding offset for the landowner. To see this in the simplest setting, let the superscript $h = 0$ and 1 respectively denote the tenant and the landlord (who does not supply labour). S denotes the share of output X received by the landlord. We assume for simplicity that this share is unchanged within the range of prices under consideration. Using the envelope theorem, it is straightforward to show that

$$\frac{dV^{r0}}{dp^r} = \lambda^{r0}Q^0 \text{ and} \tag{8.13a}$$

$$\frac{dV^{r1}}{dp^r} = \lambda^{r1}Q^1 + \lambda^{r1}p^rS\frac{dX}{dp^r}, \tag{8.13b}$$

where $Q^0 = (1 - S)X - x^{r0}$ is a tenant's surplus of the rural good, and $Q^1 = SX - x^{r1}$ is a landowner's surplus. In the second term in (8.13b) dX/dp^r is the change in the output due to the effect of a price change on the supply of effort by the tenant. This last term is the source of asymmetry referred to earlier. As can easily be verified, an analogous asymmetry arises even when the possible price responses of sharing rules are explicitly taken into account.

The average social weight for the rural sector can be expressed, using (8.13a) and (8.13b) as

$$\beta^r = \left[\beta^{r0}Q^0 + \beta^{r1}\left(Q^1 + p^rS\frac{dX}{dp^r} \right) \right] / (Q^0 + Q^1). \tag{8.14}$$

For simplicity, we have assumed in (8.14) that there is an equal number of landowners and tenants, but the expression can easily be modified for alternative assumptions. If we make a plausible assumption that dX/dp^r is positive (that is, a higher price increases a tenant's effort which, in turn, increases the total output), then it is clear from (8.14) that the presence of share-cropping adds an extra positive term in the expression for β^r (provided, of course, that the social weight associated with the marginal income of landowners is not zero). From the expressions for optimal prices and taxes, such as (8.10), a possible consequence of this extra term is to make the tax on the agricultural good lower than it would have been in the absence of share-cropping.[10] The reason for this is that in making labour-supply decisions, workers fail to take into account the benefits of increased output which accrue to landlords. In other words, share-cropping acts just like a pre-existing tax. Thus, share-cropping with a 50 per cent share already has some of the efficiency consequences of a 50 per cent output tax. Now, since the distortion associated with a tax increases rapidly with the magnitude of the tax, it is apparent that there is an efficiency-based argument against high taxes on agriculture in the presence of share-cropping.

8.4 EFFECTS OF WAGES AND PRICES ON RURAL PRODUCTIVITY

The analysis in Chapters 4, 5, and 6 emphasized potential consequences which arise when the net productivity of urban workers is affected by urban wages and prices. A discussion of various sources of such productivity effects is presented in Chapter 11. Below, we briefly examine some aspects of productivity effects in the rural sector. It is worth noting here that the earliest version of the relationship between productivity and wages (the efficiency–wage hypothesis) was first discussed in the context of agricultural workers in LDCs, where it was hypothesized that there may be a decline in the productivity of workers below some level of nutrition (see Leibenstein 1957; Mirrlees 1975; and Stiglitz 1976*a*).

In economies where wage productivity effects play a significant role, it is obvious that the rural wage may be set above the market-clearing level, creating involuntary unemployment. It does not pay farmers to lower wages to hire the unemployed, because the lowered productivity at lower wages reduces profit. The central issues from our point of view are the effects which changes in prices have on the employment level (or more specifically on who gets employed and who does not), on the welfare of different groups of workers (say, employed versus unemployed), and on the aggregate marketed surplus. To illustrate this, we focus our attention on a plantation economy in which labour is supplied only by landless workers.

Plantations

Assume for simplicity that the number of hours, L^r, which a plantation worker works is fixed but his productivity level, denoted by $b(p^r, w^r)$, depends on the wage-rate he receives and on the prices he faces. The effective labour hours per worker (that is, labour hours in productivity units) are $L^r b$.

---

[10] In the presence of alternative organizations such as share-cropping and joint family farms, it should also be apparent that the values of some of the crucial behavioural elasticities (for instance, the price elasticity of rural surplus, ε_{Qp}^r, in (8.10)) will depend on the nature of the organization under consideration.

We assume that output exhibits constant returns to scale in land and effective labour.[11] If E denotes the number of workers employed on land area $\bar{A}$, then E and w^r are determined from

$$\underset{E,w^r}{\text{Max: }} p^r X \left[\bar{A}, EL^r b(p^r, w^r) \right] - w^r EL^r. \tag{8.15}$$

The conditions of optimality are

$$p^r X_L b = w^r \quad \text{and} \quad p^r X_L b_w = 1, \tag{8.16}$$

where X_L is the partial derivative of X with respect to its second argument and $b_w = \partial b / \partial w^r$. The above expressions yield the following characterization of the rural wage-rate

$$b_w = b/w^r. \tag{8.17}$$

The solution to (8.17) is called the efficiency wage.

The economic rationale underlying the above relationship is simple. The employer can choose a higher effective labour input by paying a higher wage or by hiring an extra hour of work at the current wage. At the optimum, therefore, the marginal increase in labour effectiveness from a wage increase is equated to the average labour effectiveness. At the resulting efficiency wage, the labour demand may be lower than the supply. Consequently, there may be rural unemployment. In fact, if A is the plantation land per landless worker, then $EA / \bar{A}$ will be the rural employment rate, and $(1 - EA / \bar{A})$ will be the rural unemployment rate.

A change in the rural price will affect the rural wage, so as to maintain the wage determination equation (8.17). Let b_{ww} and b_{wp} denote the partial derivatives of b_w with respect to w^r and p^r. Then, a perturbation of (8.17) yields: $dw^r/dp^r = (b_p/w^r - b_{wp})/b_{ww}$. It is reasonable to assume that $b_p < 0$ and $b_{ww} < 0$. That is, productivity declines at higher prices and that it is concave in wages. It follows that:

$$\frac{dw^r}{dp^r} \gtrless 0 \quad \text{as} \quad b_{wp} \gtrless \frac{b_p}{w^r}. \tag{8.18}$$

Moreover, the level of employment will change to restore, at changed prices and wages, the plantations' optimality conditions (8.16). These changes, along with the changes in the profits of plantation-owners, will determine the consumption responses of the three groups in the present stylized economy: employed rural workers, unemployed rural workers, and plantation-owners. The resulting effects on government revenue and on the welfare of

[11] We also assume here that there are many competing plantations and, therefore, the food prices faced by all plantation workers are the same. Note, however, that a plantation might find it desirable to provide food to workers at a subsidized price, if it could prevent workers from arbitraging across price differences. In fact, it is not unusual to find plantations providing benefits (that is, goods and services in kind) to workers, particularly in those isolated areas where a plantation can exercise significant monopolistic influence and where arbitrage is not easily possible.

each of the three groups can be studied by using the approach developed in the earlier sections.

Selectivity in Employment

Next consider a model of the rural sector with a continuum of farm sizes. Suppose the primary mechanism through which wage productivity effects arise in the economy is through nutrition (and, hence, consumption). Then, since land ownership is systematically related to an individual's income and consumption, it is apparent that the productivity of different individuals may also be related to land ownership. In such an economy, the benefits from hiring a landless worker to work full-time would be lower than, say, hiring two farmers (who have small farms of their own) to work half-time each, if the wage-rate per hour were the same for all workers. Obviously, one would not expect productivity to increase with land endowment beyond some level, nor would one expect individuals with large land endowments to hire themselves out to work on others' farms.

There are two consequences of the dependence of productivity on wages in such a framework. First, wage-rates may tend to differ for workers with different land endowments, to the extent that productivity differences are captured in wage-rate differences. Second, to the extent that productivity differences are not fully captured in wage differences, there might be a higher demand (and, hence, a higher rate of employment) for workers with some land endowment and a lower rate of employment for landless workers.[12] In the presence of such productivity effects, the consequences of an increase in food price can be additionally deleterious at the lower end of the income distribution. The reason is simple. The poorest and the landless workers are net buyers of food to a greater degree than those who are less poor. An increase in food price worsens the welfare of the poor directly. It also reduces their productivity (and, hence, their earning power) to a greater degree than the corresponding reduction in the productivity of a less poor person.

8.5 CONCLUDING REMARKS

A primary contribution of this chapter has been to analyse who gains and who loses in the rural sector when the terms of trade are altered. These distributional questions (in particular, whether a higher price for the agricultural good improves or worsens real income distribution within the rural sector) have been of critical political importance in many LDCs.

---

[12] When there are different groups of rural workers, the groups which have higher productivity at the same wage will have lower unemployment (see Stiglitz 1987c). The more general consequences for rural income distribution have been examined by Dasgupta and Ray (1986; 1987).

The basic analysis incorporates direct effects of price changes, as well as induced effects including those on the rural wage. We have developed simple rules to delineate who gains and who loses, and then shown how these rules can be related to individuals' elasticities of labour demand and supply. We have derived a coefficient, 'the generalized social weight on rural income', which plays the same role in the relevant formulae for pricing and taxation as was earlier played by the marginal social valuation of income of the representative peasant. The generalized social weight on rural income turns out to be simply a weighted average of the marginal social valuation of different rural individuals' incomes. We have also shown how the analysis can be extended to the case in which there are many goods produced and consumed solely within the rural sector (such as low-quality millet) which are administratively difficult to tax or subsidize.

Another objective of this chapter was to show how the positive and normative analysis of pricing and taxation can be adapted to include the presence of alternative rural organizational forms, such as the extended family, share-cropping, and plantations. In contrast to the earlier analysis, where we decomposed the effects of a pricing policy into distributional effects and tax-induced dead-weight losses, there is now a third set of effects, showing that there may be a corrective role for taxes because of the pre-existing distortions induced by specific organizational forms. As a result, the generalized social weight on rural income is no longer a weighted average of the social valuation of the incomes of different rural individuals. This can have important consequences for pricing and taxation policy. For instance, in an economy where there is share-cropping or income-sharing within extended families, it might be desirable to set prices in the rural sector higher than they would otherwise be. To put it another way, since the existing organizational form already leads to an undersupply of labour (and a corresponding dead-weight loss), any further tax imposed on the margin has an additional effect of exacerbating the total dead-weight loss.

Finally, we briefly analysed the effects of changes in the rural wage and prices on the productivity of workers, and, in turn, the effect of tax policy on the wages that are paid to hired workers. In the presence of productivity effects, there is not only a possibility of unemployment but also a selectivity in employment which works against the poor. In these cases, it is important for government policy to take into account the level of unemployment as well as its incidence.

9

TAXES AND SUBSIDIES ON DIFFERENT GOODS IN THE RURAL SECTOR

9.1 INTRODUCTION

A major issue facing many LDCs is whether cash-crops and agricultural inputs such as fertilizers and tractors should be subsidized to increase agricultural production, or taxed to raise the investible surplus. It is argued by some that cash-crops are more commonly grown by the wealthier farmers, and that such crops thus provide a desirable basis for taxation by a government concerned with equality. Similarly, it has been argued that fertilizer, tractors, and other modern inputs are used predominantly by the wealthier farmers, and that modern inputs should therefore be subjected to taxation.

On the face of it, in many LDCs, government policies in this area often seem contradictory. While the government provides a subsidy on fertilizer, allegedly to encourage production, it taxes the output, which discourages production. Would it not be better to eliminate the subsidy, and reduce the tax? In short, would it not be better to reduce the extent of government intervention? The model developed in earlier chapters can easily be extended to obtain insights into these issues. The main extension required is that, instead of dealing with an aggregate agricultural good and an aggregate industrial good, as in much of the preceding analysis, we now deal with a multitude of goods being produced, used, and consumed in each of the two sectors.

We obtain two basic sets of results. The first shows that the earlier formulae for pricing and taxation in the rural sector may be extended to determine the optimal taxes on a variety of inputs and outputs. Associated with each commodity i (input or output) in the rural sector is a distributional coefficient, β_i^r, representing an appropriately weighted average of the social marginal valuation of the income of different rural individuals. β_i^r is larger if the net surplus of this good for the poor is larger (equivalently, for a consumption good, the demand of the poor is smaller). We show that if β_i^r is larger, then the optimal rural price of the commodity is typically higher. As a summary of the distributional consequences of a change in the price of a good, our commodity-specific distributional coefficients differ from those previously noted in the literature in that they take into account the general-equilibrium effects of the price change on the rural wage.[1]

---

[1] Although we do not pursue these extensions here, the distributional coefficient β_i^r can be

Another difference between the multi-commodity analysis conducted in this chapter and the earlier single commodity analysis is that we now take into account the interactions among commodities. A tax on the output of a commodity may induce a shift in production towards another commodity, and thus may increase government revenue (if the latter commodity is being taxed) or decrease government revenue (if the latter commodity is being subsidized).

The second set of results deals with the tax policy concerning cash-crops (such as sugar-cane, tobacco, and cotton) and manufactured agricultural inputs (such as fertilizer, tractors, and pesticides). We refer to these goods as 'production goods', to emphasize that they do not enter an individual's consumption basket. We show how Pareto-improving price reforms can be implemented for production goods, based on very limited information. This reform analysis requires knowledge only of how inputs and outputs per unit land respond to certain kinds of price changes. Economy-wide information on the distribution of land ownership and on the consumption responses of individuals is not required for these reforms. The reason for this, fully described later, is that the prices of production goods affect individuals' welfare and consumption only through their effects on the full income (that is, on farm profit plus the value of their labour endowment). Further, these effects bear a systematic relationship to the individual's farm size, if the production technology is homothetic (the assumption of homotheticity seems to describe well many agricultural environments). These Pareto-improving reforms are relevant even when certain types of induced wage effects are taken into account.[2]

In a related result, we show that, at the optimum, the proportional reduction in the quantities of different production goods per unit land, due to taxation or subsidization, should be equal. These results concerning the taxation of production goods are quite general. Our model allows for:

(a) a variety of goods other than the production goods, which peasants produce, use as inputs, or consume, and

(b) a non-taxable transaction, namely, the buying and selling of labour services.

Finally, a version of our Pareto-improving reform analysis indicates that there is an a priori case against the simultaneous taxation of some production goods and subsidization of other such goods. Such policies are often justified on grounds of equality. We show that this justification is weak.

---

easily modified to take into account the interaction of taxation with previously existing inefficiencies, such as those associated with share-cropping or with the extended family (see ch. 8 for a discussion of alternative forms of rural organization).

[2] This analysis can be extended to more general Pareto-improving tax reform rules that are applicable at the economy-wide level; that is, in the agricultural as well as industrial sector.

9.2 A GENERAL FORMULATION

The range of goods produced and employed in the agricultural sector can be divided into several distinct categories. Among them are those goods which are consumed by peasants and also sold to outsiders (like some food grains), those which are produced solely for sale (cash-crops like rubber and fibres), and those which are inputs to agricultural production itself (like manure). Similarly, the agricultural sector buys some manufactured goods from the outside for consumption (like textiles and radios) and others for use as inputs in production (like fertilizers and tractors).[3]

All these goods can be incorporated within the earlier model by defining Q^h as a vector, of which an element Q_i^h represents the net supply of the i-th good from the rural household h to the rest of the economy. Q_i^h is positive if the peasant is a net seller of good i, and negative if he is a net buyer. For the rural sector as a whole, the per capita surplus of good i is denoted by $Q_i = \Sigma_h N^{rh} Q_i^h / N^r$, where N^{rh} is the number of individuals in rural group h. For those goods which are produced and used solely within the agricultural sector, Q_i is zero. We assume in this section that the economy is open, that the government can maintain different sets of prices in the two sectors, and that there are no taxes on trade within the agricultural sector.[4] As we shall see, however, the reform analysis presented in the next two sections holds even if the government cannot set different sets of prices in the two sectors. The investible surplus is represented by

$$I = N^u(Y - w^u L^u) + (P - p^r) N^r Q + (p^u - P) N^u x^u \qquad (9.1)$$

which is the same as (4.1) except that Y now denotes the value of the entire vector of industrial outputs, measured at the international price vector P. The numeraire good is any one of the pure consumption goods produced in the industrial sector. The quantity of this good consumed by a rural individual in group h is y^{rh}. The vector x^u denotes the per capita consumption

---

[3] The same good sometimes belongs to more than one category. For example, tractors are primarily employed as inputs in agricultural production but are also occasionally used for transportation.

[4] The underlying model of the economy here is thus the same as that in ch. 4. Note, however, that there are some ambiguities in practice in the precise geographical definition of a tax border between the two sectors. This is because agricultural activities are sometimes undertaken on the fringe areas of cities which fall under cities' tax jurisdiction. Moreover, our assumption that trade within the agricultural sector cannot be taxed somewhat overstates the constraints on the government. What is crucial for our purpose is whether a transaction can be monitored so that a tax can be imposed. If a farmer can sell directly to another farmer, then it is unlikely that a tax can be collected. LDC governments can and frequently do attempt to impose taxes and marketing controls on transactions within the agricultural sector. One of the consequences of such interventions is to encourage individuals to avoid using formal markets, and thereby avoid taxes.

of non-numeraire goods in the urban sector, and p^u denotes the corresponding vector of urban prices.[5]

The effects of a change in the price of good i on a rural individual's utility and on the investible surplus are respectively given by

$$\frac{dV^{rh}}{dp_i^r} = \lambda^{rh}\left(Q_i^h + \frac{dw^r}{dp_i}L^{rh}\right) \quad \text{and} \tag{9.2}$$

$$\frac{dI}{dp_i^r} = N^r(P - p^r)\frac{dQ}{dp_i^r} - N^rQ_i, \tag{9.3}$$

where L^{rh} denotes the net labour hours supplied by person h. Also note that dQ/dp_i^r includes the induced effect due to a change in the rural wage, that is,

$$\frac{dQ}{dp_i^r} = \frac{\partial Q}{\partial p_i^r} + \frac{\partial Q}{\partial w^r}\frac{dw^r}{dp_i^r}. \tag{9.4}$$

We can immediately calculate the effect of a change in prices on social welfare. Recall that the Hamiltonian $H = \psi + \delta I$ represents the current value of the time-discounted social welfare, where ψ is given by (8.6). Using (9.1), (9.2), and (9.3), we obtain

$$\frac{\partial H}{\partial p_i^r} \gtreqless 0,$$

if

$$(P - p^r)\frac{dQ}{dp_i^r} \gtreqless \left(1 - \frac{\beta_i^r}{\delta}\right)Q_i, \tag{9.5}$$

where

$$\beta_i^r = \Sigma_h \beta^{rh} N^{rh}\left(Q_i^h + \frac{w^r L^{rh}}{p_i^r}\varepsilon_{wp_i}^r\right) \Big/ N^r Q_i, \tag{9.6}$$

$\beta^{rh} = (\partial W/\partial V^{rh})\lambda^{rh}$ is the social marginal utility of income of the rural household h, and $\varepsilon_{wp_i}^r = \partial \ln w^r/\partial \ln p_i^r$ is the elasticity of the rural wage with respect to the price of good i.

We thus obtain a straightforward modification of the earlier analysis. Note that the above expressions take into account the fact that different commodities have different distributional effects depending on the marketed surplus of the commodity for the rich versus the poor. These expressions also emphasize the need to take into account not only the direct effects (for example, large surplus suppliers are hurt more by a reduction in the prices they receive) but also the indirect effects due to price-induced changes in rural wages. These indirect effects, represented by $\varepsilon_{wp_i}^r$, would be different for changes in the prices of different goods. A tax on a crop which is largely

---

[5] The precise specification of the urban sector (for instance, the nature of heterogeneity among urban individuals, and the nature of price–productivity effects) is not central to the present analysis of rural taxes and prices.

a cash-crop may have deleterious distributional effects if it depresses labour demand and agricultural wages significantly. The small landholders and the landless, who are net suppliers of labour, may be hurt more than the large landholders. The above expressions differ from the earlier analysis in another way: when there are other taxes in place, a change in the tax on one commodity may change the net demands for other commodities, increasing or decreasing tax revenues. These effects have been incorporated on the left-hand side of (9.5).

Following the earlier analysis, it is obvious that the optimal prices are characterized by (9.5) in which the inequality is replaced by an equality. This equality yields a multi-person Ramsey-like rule, with the difference that induced general-equilibrium effects on wages and earnings are now taken into account. This rule can be re-expressed to provide the standard interpretation of how the proportional reduction in the net purchase of a good should be related to its distributional characteristics.[6] A more direct interpretation is that, at the optimum,

$$\frac{\mathrm{d}I}{\mathrm{d}p_i^r} = -\frac{\beta_i^r}{\delta} N^r Q_i .$$

That is, the change in revenue from a marginal increase in the price of the i-th good equals $-\beta_i^r/\delta$ times the net rural surplus of this good. In the special case in which β_i^r is the same for all goods, the change in revenue from a price increase is proportional, at the optimum, to the net surplus of the good under consideration.

9.3 INFORMATIONALLY PARSIMONIOUS PARETO-IMPROVING PRICE REFORMS FOR CASH-CROPS AND MANUFACTURED INPUTS

Implementation of the optimum described in the previous section requires a knowledge of, among other things, the intra-sectoral distribution of income, the social weights corresponding to different groups of individuals, the own- and cross-elasticities of the consumption quantities with respect to prices, and the elasticities of the rural wage with respect to various prices. The use of (9.5) for reform analysis may also be inhibited because the same set of information is required, although only the knowledge of local derivatives is necessary. Therefore, instead of focusing on the characterization of the optimum, we present here a novel and more useful result which shows how Pareto-improving price reforms can be achieved for certain goods on the basis of very limited information.

---

[6] The conventional case is analysed in Atkinson and Stiglitz (1980, pp. 386–90).

We focus on price reforms for those goods which are produced or used within the rural sector but which do not enter into the consumption basket of individuals. We refer to this class of goods as 'production goods'. This class consists of cash-crops produced in the agricultural sector as well as manufactured inputs (fertilizers, pesticides, machine inputs) which the agricultural sector buys from the industrial sector or from abroad. The objective of this section is to show that Pareto-improving price reforms can be made for production goods solely on the basis of the elasticities of inputs and outputs per unit land with respect to the prices of production goods. We do not need any information concerning consumption responses, distribution of land, or social weights.

Before presenting the analysis, it is worth noting that a change in the prices of what we have defined as production goods has no effect on the consumption or welfare of urban individuals (because production goods do not enter into individuals' consumption baskets). It should be apparent, therefore, that the analysis of a reform in the prices of production goods remains the same whether the government can or cannot set different sets of prices in the two sectors (that is, whether the vectors p^r and p^u are different, or the vector $p = p^r = p^u$ denotes the economy-wide price vector). To simplify the notation, thus, we use p to denote the price vector faced by those in the rural sector.

We assume that the agricultural production technology is characterized by constant returns to scale. Actually, a weaker assumption that the technology is homothetic is sufficient for the results derived below. We assume constant returns to scale, however, because this simplifies the exposition. Thus, if the j-th good is a production good, and z is the vector of inputs and outputs per unit land, then $Q_j^h = A^h z_j$, where A^h is the farm size for a rural household in group h. Note that inputs and outputs are represented as respectively negative and positive elements of vector z.[7]

We consider here the case in which the rural wage is determined in a competitive labour-market and assume that all production goods have the same (but not constant) elasticity with respect to the wage,[8] that is

$$\frac{\partial z_j}{\partial w^r} = g_1 z_j , \qquad (9.7)$$

where the symbol g_1, as well as the symbols g and B to be used below, are defined in the Appendix to this chapter; their precise definitions are irrelevant here. As we shall see, the above assumption is entirely unnecessary

---

[7] In general, the vector of net supply from a household in group h is $Q^h = -x^{rh} + A^h z$, where the consumption vector x^{rh} contains zeros for those goods which are not consumed by the household and the unit-land net output vector z contains zeros for those goods which are neither agricultural inputs nor outputs.

[8] This happens if the unit-land profit function is separable between the prices of production goods and other prices (see the Appendix to this chapter). For details on the underlying production technologies see Lau (1978).

if the induced effects of changes in the prices of production goods on the rural wage are not significant. Using (9.7) we show in the Appendix that

$$\frac{dw^r}{dp_j} = gz_j \cdot \tag{9.8}$$

That is: The change in the rural wage due to a change in the price of a production good is proportional to the quantity of this production good per unit land. This result holds regardless of the nature of individuals' labour supply responses.

Next, we define

$$c_j = \Sigma_i \, t_i \, \varepsilon_{ji}^r , \tag{9.9}$$

where $t_i = (P_i - p_i)/p_i$ represents the rates of taxes or subsidies, and $\varepsilon_{ji}^r = \partial \ln z_j / \partial \ln p_i$ represents the price elasticities of inputs and outputs per unit of land. Thus (9.9) represents the proportional change, due to taxation or subsidization, in the unit-land quantity of the production good j. Using (9.3), (9.8), and (9.9), we show in the Appendix that the effect of a price change on the investible surplus depends on c_j in a simple way:

$$\frac{dI}{dp_j} = (c_j + B)N^r A z_j , \tag{9.10}$$

where $A = \Sigma_h N^{rh} A^h / N^r$ is the average land area per rural individual. A special case of (9.10) occurs, of course, when the induced effects of price changes on the rural wage are insignificant: that is, when $g \approx 0$ in (9.8). In this case (9.10) holds even if assumption (9.7) is not satisfied.

Expression (9.10) provides a basis for the following price reforms. Consider two production goods, j and i. If their prices are changed by Δp_j and $-(z_j/z_i)\Delta p_j$ respectively, then, using (9.2) and (9.8), it follows that the net change in the utility of an individual in the rural group h is:

$$\Delta V^{rh} = \left(\frac{dV^{rh}}{dp_j} - \frac{dV^{rh}}{dp_i} \frac{z_j}{z_i} \right) \Delta p_j$$

$$= \lambda^{rh} \left[\left(A^h z_j + \frac{dw^r}{dp_j} L^{rh} \right) - \left(A^h z_i + \frac{dw^r}{dp_i} L^{rh} \right) \frac{z_j}{z_i} \right] \Delta p_j = 0 .$$

That is, these price changes have no effect on the welfare of any rural individual.

Next, we calculate the impact of these price changes on the investible surplus. Using (9.10),

$$\Delta I = \left(\frac{dI}{dp_j} - \frac{dI}{dp_i} \frac{z_j}{z_i} \right) \Delta p_j = (c_j - c_i) N^r A z_j \Delta p_j . \tag{9.11}$$

The rules for price reforms follow immediately. Calculate the c_i for all the production goods. If $c_j > c_i$, and j and i are both outputs (respectively, inputs), then increase (respectively, decrease) the price of the j-th good by a small amount, say Δp_j, and decrease (respectively, increase) the price of the i-th good by $(z_j/z_i)\Delta p_j$. Parallel rules apply if the j-th good is an output (respectively, input) and the i-th good is an input (respectively, output).

The above reforms lead to an unambiguous increase in the investible surplus, without affecting the welfare of any individual. Therefore, the rules of reform are Pareto-improving. A remarkable property of these rules is the extreme parsimony of information required to implement them. The information required to use the above rule of reform consists solely of the current taxes on inputs and outputs, current quantities of inputs and outputs per unit land, and the response of these quantities to the changes in the price of production goods.

Our rules of reform take into account the induced effects of price changes on rural wages, albeit under assumption (9.7) which restricts the nature of these effects. If this assumption appears too restrictive, then the relevant empirical question is: How different are the observed induced wage effects from those with the above restriction? If the differences are not significant, then our rules of reform can be employed with extreme parsimony of information.

Finally, note from (9.11) that a necessary condition for the optimality of taxation is that

$$c_i \text{ is the same for all production goods.} \tag{9.12}$$

That is: The proportional reductions in the quantities of different production goods per unit land, due to taxation or subsidization, should be equal.

It is useful to keep in mind the generality of our model. It allows for: (*a*) a variety of goods, other than production goods, which peasants produce, use as inputs, or consume, and (*b*) a non-taxable transaction, namely, the buying and selling of labour services.

Further, we can relax the assumption of constant returns to scale in agricultural production. The Pareto-improving rules of reform and condition (9.12) for efficiency hold under a weaker assumption, namely, that the production function is homothetic. To see this intuitively, let us assume that the induced wage effects are negligible so that changes in the prices of production goods have effects on individual welfare only through changes in the profit from land. (If the induced wage effects are significant, the relaxation of the constant-returns-to-scale assumption requires only a slight modification of the specification of a separable profit function.) Consider two production goods, j and i. With homotheticity, isoquant contours indicating different production scales (i.e. different farm sizes) have the same slope along a ray through the origin. Thus, the ratio of quantities of good i and j, Q_i^h/Q_j^h, is the same for all individuals and can be written as, say, θ_{ij}. If the prices of these goods are changed respectively by Δp_i and $\Delta p_j = -\theta_{ij}\Delta p_i$, the income and the welfare of each individual remain unchanged. Moreover, since own- and cross-price elasticities of inputs and outputs are also independent of farm sizes, the response of the investible surplus to these price changes can be written in a manner similar to (9.11). (The only difference is that $N^r A z_j$ on the right-hand side of (9.11) is now $\Sigma_h Q_j^h$.) In turn, the result (9.12) follows.

9.4 SHOULD SOME CASH-CROPS OR MANUFACTURED INPUTS BE TAXED AND OTHERS SUBSIDIZED?

To obtain insights into this question, assume for a moment, that changes in the prices of production goods have negligible cross-price effects on the quantities of inputs and outputs (that is, $\varepsilon_{ji}^r = 0$ if $i \neq j$). Then, using (9.9) and (9.12), a necessary condition for Pareto optimality is that $t_j \varepsilon_{jj}^r$ should be the same for all j. Next, we know from the standard properties of profit functions that $\varepsilon_{jj}^r > 0$ for an output and $\varepsilon_{jj}^r < 0$ for an input. Also, from our definition of t_j, a negative (respectively, positive) t_j implies a tax (respectively, subsidy) on an input and a subsidy (respectively, tax) on an output. It follows then that either all of the production goods (inputs as well as outputs) should be taxed, or that they all should be subsidized, but not both.

These results are important not because we believe that the cross-price effects are negligible, or that the induced wage effects are always of the type considered above. They are important because we have isolated the reasons why the sign of taxes might differ among different production goods. Specifically, we often find that a fertilizer is being subsidized, while a pesticide is being taxed, or vice versa. Similarly, cotton may be subsidized while another cash-crop is being taxed. It is obvious from our analysis that the justification for such taxation must lie in the presence of large cross-price effects or in the presence of specific types of induced wage effects. If it is found from empirical analysis that such is not the case, then the existing tax structure is not optimal and can be improved regardless of the social weights.

This analysis thus casts some doubt on the frequently given advice that, on grounds of equity, some agricultural inputs (such as tractors) should be taxed since they are primarily used by rich farmers, while other inputs (such as fertilizer) should be subsidized since they are used by poor as well as rich farmers.

9.5 SOME CAVEATS

As indicated at the beginning of the chapter, the assumption of constant returns to scale or of homotheticity in agricultural production (and the resulting invariance of the ratios of input and output quantities to farm size) underlies some of the results obtained in this section. The assumption of constant returns to scale has been empirically validated in the past based on household level data (see Strauss 1986 and references given there). At the same time, there might be particular instances where it would appear that the ratios of inputs and outputs are not even approximately invariant to farm size. In these instances, parts of our analysis may need to be modified, and it might appear that there may be scope for differential taxation. However, even under these circumstances one must be cautious about the use of differential taxation. In particular, one must enquire into the reasons why the ratios of inputs and outputs are not invariant to farm size; one needs to ask whether it reflects, for instance, differences in land quality, deviations from homotheticity, deviations from uniform prices across individuals, or differences in individuals' knowledge about best practices. Policies should accordingly attempt to correct price distortions, if these are the underlying reasons, or to provide better information, if lack of knowledge is the underlying reason.

Market Imperfection

One aim of this book has been to explore the implications of market imperfections commonly associated with LDCs for the design of pricing and taxation policies. We have focused on various types of imperfection including those in the labour market and those arising endogenously due to alternative organizational arrangements. An important set of imperfections that are not explicitly studied in this book are those which might arise in credit markets.[9] However, if the poor do not use as much fertilizer per unit land as the rich because they do not have access to credit markets, it does not necessarily follow that a policy of taxing fertilizer is an appropriate one for attaining distributional objectives. For if the availability of credit to the poor is constrained, the value of the marginal product of fertilizer for them may be significantly higher than that for the rich farmers, and the adverse consequences of an induced reduction in fertilizer usage by the poor, as a result of the tax, may be larger. Accordingly, a fertilizer tax, although collecting more revenue from rich farmers, may have a more deleterious effect on the welfare of the poor farmers.

---

[9] Some of the reasons for market imperfections may lie in costly monitoring and information-gathering. Moral hazard considerations—the inability to monitor the usage and care of credit or rental property—may be important in explaining the absence of rental markets, and in explaining why prices in these markets seem so high when these markets do exist.

Technological Change

The qualitative results we have derived not only hold at each point in time, but are also consistent with a number of extensions including the presence of an exogenous process of technological change affecting agricultural production. There is one important set of dynamic effects, however, which will require some modifications of the model: when current output or input decisions of individuals have direct effects on outputs in other periods. For then, changes in the current prices of goods will have effects on individuals' utility levels and on the investible surplus in subsequent periods. These effects need to be taken into account for they have both equity and efficiency implications.

The most obvious examples of inter-temporal effects are those associated with endogenous aspects of technological change. If, for instance, there are important learning-by-doing effects in the use of modern technology, then the level of output in future periods, for given levels of future inputs, will depend on current production choices. Individuals, in deciding on their current production, will take into account the future benefits which accrue from current production. Thus, it is still true that the change in the discounted present value of utility of farmers as a result of an increase in the price of agricultural goods can be represented by an expression such as (9.2). However, the framework of analysis presented earlier would have to be modified to take into account future changes in tax revenues resulting from a price-induced change in current production.

In such cases, it may turn out that those new production processes which have significant externality effects due to learning-by-doing should be subjected to a smaller tax (or should receive a larger subsidy). By the same token, since direct monitoring of (and, hence, a direct subsidy to) a particular production process may not be administratively feasible or economical, the government can affect the rate of learning-by-doing by subsidizing inputs which are more intensively used in the new processes. Thus, if the new process is fertilizer-intensive, a fertilizer subsidy may be desirable.

Moreover, if learning is farm-specific (that is, future learning benefits accrue only to farmers currently using the new process) then there may be considerable diversity across different groups of farmers concerning when and to what extent they adopt new processes. It has often been argued that new technologies and processes are relatively less attractive to smaller farmers because (*a*) their credit constraints increase the cost of future learning (*b*) poorer individuals may be more averse to risk-taking and hence less willing to try out new processes, and (*c*) learning about new technology may involve some fixed costs and it may accordingly not be worthwhile for small farmers.

One of the central characteristics of most LDCs is that many peasants do not use the best available practices because the diffusion of new technologies is slow. It is often argued that pricing policies can be used to help overcome peasants' resistance to the adoption of new techniques, or to protect them while they learn the new technology. (The analogy to the infant-industry argument should be obvious.) If this argument is correct, then it suggests that there is another dimension to the equity–efficiency trade-off in input subsidies. Subsidizing tractors may indeed yield more benefits, in the short run, to faster learners (those who adopt the new technology more quickly); but subsidizing bullocks may simply serve to perpetuate inefficient technologies. Similarly, while efficiency considerations may argue for the subsidization of fertilizer, the main beneficiaries of these subsidies may be large farmers. As a consequence, such subsidies might appear to be regressive.

The argument that subsidies encourage the adoption of new technologies is even stronger if learning is not farm-specific. That is, if some of the benefits of learning on one farm spill over to those on neighbouring farms. Large farmers, in making decisions on whether to switch from the old to the new technology, will not take into account these socially productive externalities.

Though we have couched the analysis in terms of learning-by-doing effects, a similar kind of analysis applies if there is uncertainty about the appropriateness of a particular technology for a particular region. The demonstration of the success of a particular technology by one farmer conveys information to other farmers, and thus stimulates the diffusion of the new technology.[10] There is thus a potentially important externality. Input subsidies (such as seed and fertilizer subsidies) may comprise parts of the appropriate second-best corrective tax policy.

At the same time, it is important to examine whether taxation and pricing are the appropriate instruments, from the point of view of costs and benefits to society, to promote certain technologies or discourage others. A direct subsidization of information (through extension and demonstration services and through media campaigns) may be more socially profitable.

APPENDIX

Derivation of (9.7)

Denote the profit function on unit land as $G = G(G^1(p^1, w^r), G^2(p^2)) = pz - w^r L^d$, where p^2 is the sub-vector of the prices of production goods in the rural sector, p^1 is the sub-vector of all other prices relevant to production decisions, and L^d is the labour

---

[10] Arguments given earlier suggest why small farmers may not undertake even limited usage of a new technology in such situations. Also, given the variability of soil and other conditions which exist even within a local area, and given the variability in the manner in which the new technology may be employed (for example, the timing of planting and harvesting, the extent of utilization of fertilizer and weeding), it is apparent that the more extensive and varied the experimentation with a new technology, the more information potential adopters will have.

input per unit land. Recall that p_j denotes the price of production good j. Then, it is easily shown that:

$$z_j = \frac{\partial G}{\partial G^2}\frac{\partial G^2}{\partial p_j},$$

$$L^d = -\frac{\partial G}{\partial G^1}\frac{\partial G^1}{\partial w^r} \quad \text{and}$$

$$\frac{\partial z_j}{\partial w^r} = -\frac{\partial L^d}{\partial p_j} = g_1 z_j, \tag{9.A1}$$

where

$$g_1 = \frac{\partial^2 G}{\partial G^1 \partial G^2}\frac{\partial G^1}{\partial w^r} \bigg/ \frac{\partial G}{\partial G^2}.$$

It follows from (9.A1) that the elasticity

$$\frac{\partial \ln z_j}{\partial \ln w^r} = g_1 w^r \tag{9.A2}$$

is the same for all j.

Derivation of (9.8)

The market-clearing condition for labour is $\Sigma_h N^{rh} L^{rh}(p, w^r) = 0$, which upon differentiation yields

$$\frac{dw^r}{dp_j} = -\left[\Sigma_h N^{rh}\frac{\partial L^{rh}}{\partial p_j}\right] \bigg/ \Sigma_h N^{rh}\frac{\partial L^{rh}}{\partial w^r}. \tag{9.A3}$$

Denote the full income of the rural individual h as $m^{rh} = w^r \overline{L}^h + A^h G$, where $\overline{L}^h$ is his endowment of labour. Thus, from the definition of the unit profit function:

$$\frac{\partial m^{rh}}{\partial p_j} = A^h z_j. \tag{9.A4}$$

Next, recall that an individual's net labour supply is expressed as $L^{rh} = L^{sh} - A^h L^d$, where L^{sh} is his labour supply. Now, the prices of production goods only affect an individual's labour supply through his full income. Using (9.A4) it therefore follows that

$$\frac{\partial L^{rh}}{\partial p_j} = A^h z_j \frac{\partial L^{sh}}{\partial m^{rh}} - A^h \frac{\partial L^d}{\partial p_j}.$$

Substituting (9.A1) and the preceding expression into (9.A3), we obtain

$$\frac{dw^r}{dp_j} = g z_j, \tag{9.A5}$$

where

$$g = -\Sigma_h N^{rh} A^h \left[g_1 + \frac{\partial L^{sh}}{\partial m^{rh}}\right] \bigg/ \Sigma_h N^{rh}\frac{\partial L^{rh}}{\partial w^r}.$$

Also, for later use, note the symmetry property

$$\frac{\partial z_i}{\partial p_j} = \frac{\partial z_j}{\partial p_i} \, . \tag{9.A6}$$

Derivation of (9.10)

We evaluate the derivative (9.3), where the i-th good is a production good. Using (9.4), $Q_i = Az_i$, and $Q_i = \sum_h N^{rh} Q_i^h / N^r$, (9.3) becomes

$$\frac{dI}{dp_i} = -N^r A z_i + (P - p) \left(\sum_h N^{rh} \frac{\partial Q^h}{\partial p_i} + \sum_h N^{rh} \frac{\partial Q^h}{\partial w^r} \frac{dw^r}{dp_i} \right) \tag{9.A7}$$

$$= -N^r A z_i + (P - p) \left\{ \sum_h N^{rh} \left(-\frac{\partial x^{rh}}{\partial m^{rh}} \frac{\partial m^{rh}}{\partial p_i} + A^h \frac{\partial z}{\partial p_i} \right) \right.$$

$$\left. + \xi N^r A z_i \right\} \, . \tag{9.A8}$$

In obtaining (9.A8), we used the identity $Q^h = -x^{rh} + A^h z$ to separate out production goods and other goods (see n. 7). We also used (9.8), and defined the vector $\xi = \sum_h N^{rh} \frac{\partial Q^h}{\partial w^h} g / N^r A$. Substitution of (9.A4) and $N^r A = \sum_h N^{rh} A^h$ into (9.A8) yields

$$\frac{dI}{dp_i} = N^r A z_i \left[(P - p) \frac{\partial z}{\partial p_i} \frac{1}{z_i} + B \right] , \tag{9.A9}$$

where the scalar B is defined as

$$B = -1 + (P - p) \left(\xi - \sum_h N^{rh} \frac{\partial x^{rh}}{\partial m^{rh}} A^h / N^r A \right) \cdot \tag{9.A10}$$

Next,

$$(P - p) \frac{\partial z}{\partial p_i} \frac{1}{z_i} = \sum_j t_j \frac{\partial z_j p_j}{\partial p_i z_i} = \sum_h t_j \frac{\partial z_i}{\partial p_j} \frac{p_j}{z_i} = \sum_j t_j \varepsilon_{ij}^r \, .$$

Thus (9.A9) becomes $\dfrac{dI}{dp_i} = (c_i + B) N^r A z_i$, which is the same as (9.10).

It is obvious that expression (9.10) also applies to the special case in which there are no induced effects on the rural wage due to changes in the price of production goods. For this special case, we simply set $g = 0$, or equivalently $\xi = 0$, into (9.A10).

PART IV

The Urban Sector

This part of the book deals with a number of issues that we believe are fundamental to the analysis of taxation in the urban sector of LDCs. As emphasized in the introductory chapters, a satisfactory analysis of LDC taxation policies requires an assessment of their impact on such crucial endogenous variables as wages, the employment level and the magnitude of rural–urban migration. Chapter 10 presents a general model of urban wage and employment determination, and, taking these into account, it then analyses the nature of urban–rural prices (that is, the case in which sector-specific taxation policies are feasible) as well as the price scissors (that is, the case in which only economy-wide, rather than sector-specific, taxation policies are feasible). The underlying general model of urban wage and employment determination can accommodate many specific hypotheses. One such hypothesis that has been prominent in the literature is the wage–productivity hypothesis. Chapter 11 presents a treatment of this hypothesis. Our contribution here is to generalize this hypothesis to be able to deal with taxation issues and then to derive some of the relevant policy consequences of this hypothesis. Chapter 12 focuses on the taxation or subsidization of a multitude of goods in the urban sector. We develop and present the reasons for our conclusion that, regardless of one's concern for inequality, there should be a presumption against differential taxation or subsidization of goods in the urban sector of LDCs. Chapter 13 addresses the issue of migration in LDCs, and what this important aspect of modern-day LDC economies implies for taxation analysis. Chapter 14 is a brief overview of the approach we have developed for modelling the LDC urban sector. Chapter 15 is somewhat unrelated to the rest of the book, since it does not deal with taxation policies but with the calculation of the shadow cost of labour in LDCs. Our objective in this chapter is to illustrate how the models and approaches we have developed in this book can be used for purposes other than taxation analysis. Finally, Chapter 16 presents concluding remarks.

10

THE IMPACT OF URBAN WAGE AND EMPLOYMENT DETERMINATION ON TAXATION POLICIES

10.1 INTRODUCTION

In previous chapters, we assumed that the urban wage is fixed in terms of the numeraire good, and that it does not change as government tax policy changes.[1] While this assumption was only a means to simplify the analysis temporarily, it forms a bedrock of much of the literature on LDCs. In fact, a number of studies, while assuming that the government cannot reduce the urban money wage directly, assume that the government can indirectly reduce the real value of the urban wage by increasing the prices of various goods.

Such assumptions, we suspect, reflect a naïvety more on the part of the economist than on the part of the urban workers. The forces which limit the ability of the government to reduce wages directly should also limit its ability to reduce them indirectly. Thus, if it is the power of trade unions or the threat of political unrest which leads to high urban wages, then it is obvious that urban wages cannot be entirely insensitive to changes in prices and taxes (although there may be lags in adjustment).

Once it is recognized that urban wages may respond to government policies, then the analysis of the incidence of any policy change must take into account the indirect effects resulting from such wage changes. Thus, in the absence of an adjustment in urban wages, an increase in the urban food price might increase the investible surplus available to the government, but the investible surplus may actually decrease once the wage response is taken into account.

To examine how wages adjust in response to changes in tax policy, one needs to have a theory of wage-determination. One simple theory is provided by the conventional neoclassical model, where wages adjust to equate the demand and supply of labour. This is one of the theories used in Chapters 8 and 9 to examine rural wage-determination and its consequences for rural taxation policy. This theory, however, may have limited relevance for the

---

[1] Specifically, in chs. 4 and 5, we assumed that the urban wage is fixed in terms of the industrial good. In chs. 6 and 7, where we examined a closed socialist economy with the same set of prices in the two sectors, it was assumed that the government can adjust the urban wage. Note, however, that the rural wage was determined endogenously in chs. 8 and 9, where we examined a rural sector with a heterogeneous population.

urban sector of those LDCs which exhibit significant levels of urban unemployment. Instead, we need a theory of urban wage-determination which
is consistent with the possibility that the urban wage is set above the
market-clearing level. The wage–productivity hypothesis, discussed in some
detail in the next chapter, provides one such theory. It postulates that firms
set wages taking into account the effect of wages on productivity. Another
possible theory is one in which trade unions, firms, and the government
bargain over wage-setting. Such theories are also capable of answering the
question as to how urban wages are likely to change when urban prices
change.

In this chapter, rather than focusing on any particular theory of urban
wage-determination, we develop a general reduced-form formulation. This
formulation is consistent with a variety of wage-determination hypotheses,
including the case in which wages are fixed in terms of the industrial good,
the case in which wages are fixed in utility terms, and the case in which
wages are fixed in terms of the agricultural good. We use this general description of urban wage-determination to study the positive and normative
aspects of urban–rural pricing as well as the price scissors (that is, respectively, the cases in which the government can and cannot set different sets
of prices in the two sectors) in an open economy.

Our analysis of urban–rural pricing shows that in the central case in which
urban wages respond to price changes to keep workers' utility level unchanged, and in which workers' productivity depends on their utility level,
no commodity tax or subsidy should be imposed in the urban sector. The
intuition behind this result is straightforward. The government is constrained
to providing urban workers with a certain level of utility. It might as well
provide this utility efficiently. If relative prices of goods differ from the
corresponding international prices, then the utility is being provided ineffi-
ciently. This result needs to be modified if workers' productivity, at a given
level of utility, is a function of what they consume. Thus, if productivity is
particularly responsive to food consumption, food subsidies may well be desirable. Our analysis thus provides a perspective on certain types of pricing
policies which have been observed within LDCs, pricing policies which in
the past have been criticized on the grounds that they distort the economy.[2]

The above conclusions are predicated on the government being able to
maintain different prices in the urban and rural sectors. If this is not the
case (that is, when price scissors are the relevant instruments), and if urban
wages increase when prices increase, then there is some presumption that
agriculture will be taxed more heavily than it would have been in the absence
of the induced effect on urban wages. Lowering the prices received by
farmers now has the additional effect of inducing lower urban wages, and

[2] Chapter 12 shows how productivity effects alter the structure of taxes imposed on different
goods produced and consumed in the urban sector.

thus transferring resources from urban workers to the investible surplus. This transfer may be desirable in the early stages of development when investible surplus is viewed as more valuable, at the margin, than consumption.

To focus on one issue at a time, most of this chapter examines the determination of urban wages and its consequences, while abstracting from urban unemployment. This may appear inconsistent, since urban unemployment is a clear possibility if the urban wage is set above the market-clearing level. A general treatment of urban unemployment is, however, provided at the end of this chapter.

In the next section, we introduce some notation and discuss the main effects of the dependence of wages on prices. In Section 10.3 we analyse pricing and taxation when an urban–rural tax border exists. In Section 10.4, we consider the problem of the price scissors when wages are endogenous. Section 10.5 briefly describes the reasons why the assumption that the government can control urban wages (directly or indirectly) is not appropriate for today's LDCs, and, why one should instead focus on endogenous urban wage-determination mechanisms. Section 10.6 presents a brief note on the urban wage-determination mechanisms in which the utility level of urban workers is kept unaltered. Section 10.7 presents a general formulation of urban unemployment and analyses the consequences of the induced effects that taxation might have on urban unemployment.

10.2 A GENERAL FORMULATION OF URBAN WAGE-DETERMINATION

We begin with a general formulation which is consistent with several alternative hypotheses about how the urban wage is determined. This compact formulation has the advantage of identifying the central implications of the endogeneity of the urban wage. The urban wage-rate is represented in a reduced form as

$$w^u = w^u(p^u) . \tag{10.1}$$

We shall focus at present on the simple model in which each sector produces a single aggregate good. Thus, p^u in (10.1) is the urban price of the agricultural good in terms of the industrial good.

The effect of a change in prices on an urban worker's utility is:

$$\frac{dV^u}{dp^u} = \frac{\partial V^u}{\partial p^u} + \frac{\partial V^u}{\partial w^u} \frac{dw^u}{dp^u}$$

$$= \lambda^u \left(-x^u + L^u \frac{dw^u}{dp^u} \right)$$

$$= \lambda^u x^u \left(-1 + \frac{\varepsilon_{wp}^u}{\alpha^u} \right)$$

$$= \lambda^u x^u \, \rho, \tag{10.2}$$

where

$$\rho = -1 + \frac{\varepsilon_{wp}^u}{\alpha^u} \tag{10.3}$$

is a summary parameter to be used below,

$$\varepsilon_{wp}^u = \frac{d\ln w^u}{d\ln p^u}$$

is the elasticity of the urban wage with respect to price, and

$$\alpha^u = \frac{p^u \, x^u}{w^u \, L^u}$$

is the share of food in an urban worker's budget.

The parameter ρ provides a summary statistic of the nature of endogenous changes in the urban wage. It should be apparent that the motivation underlying the parameter ρ is quite different in the present formulation from that in the earlier model of price scissors in a closed economy (see Chapter 6, especially expression (6.6)). There, the urban wage was adjusted by the government in response to changes in price in order to maintain the demand–supply balance of the agricultural good. Here, on the other hand, employers (including public-sector firms) alter urban wages in response to a price change for endogenous reasons, such as trade-union pressure and productivity considerations.

Three Special Cases

Consider the following special cases of (10.3):

(a) The urban wage is fixed in terms of the industrial good. In this case, $\varepsilon_{wp}^u = 0$ and $\rho = -1$. From (10.2), thus, a price increase makes urban workers worse off. This was the case emphasized in Part II of this book.

(b) The urban wage is fixed in terms of the agricultural good. In this case, $\varepsilon_{wp}^u = 1$ and $\rho = -1 + 1/\alpha^u > 0$. From (10.2), thus, a price increase makes urban workers better off.

(c) The urban wage is fixed in terms of the utility level of urban workers. That is, w^u is set such that

$$V^u(p^u, w^u) = \bar{V}^u, \tag{10.4}$$

where the right-hand side is an exogenous parameter. In this case, from (10.2), ρ must equal zero. Hence, from (10.3),

$$\varepsilon_{wp}^{u} = \alpha^{u}. \tag{10.5}$$

Finally, note that the parameter ρ can also be viewed as a measure of money illusion in wage-setting. If there is no money illusion, that is, if wages are set to keep utility constant, then $\rho = 0$.

The Effects on Taxation Analysis

The presence of endogenous changes in the urban wage alters taxation analysis in three ways:

(*a*) If the urban wage increases in response to increased urban food prices, then the latter has a less deleterious effect on urban workers but a less beneficial effect on the investible surplus. The induced wage effect can thus be thought of as simply a transfer from investible surplus to urban workers. Such a transfer will decrease aggregate social welfare if the social weight on urban incomes, β^{u}, is smaller than the social weight on investment, δ.

(*b*) An increase in the urban wage, in response to an increase in the urban food price, leads to a smaller decrease in food consumption in the presence of an adjustment in the urban wage than that in the absence of the wage adjustment. As a result, the government's tax revenue is increased or decreased depending on whether the urban food price is higher or lower than the international food price.

(*c*) The endogeneity of wages alters the nature of productivity effects. When wages do not change, one might normally expect a price increase to reduce productivity. A higher wage, on the other hand, might raise productivity. In general, therefore, the overall effect is ambiguous.

Each of these three effects is seen clearly below, where we analyse pricing and taxation policies taking into account the endogeneity of urban wages. Throughout this analysis, it is assumed that the economy is open. In addition, both the rural and the urban sectors are described by representative individuals. As was shown in Chapters 8 and 9 (for the rural sector) and as will be shown in Chapter 12 (for the urban sector), one can easily incorporate intra-sectoral heterogeneity into the analysis.

10.3 URBAN–RURAL PRICES WITH AN ENDOGENOUS URBAN WAGE

Since the prices in the two sectors can be set independently of one another, and since the economy is open, the investible surplus is given by

$$I = N^u(Y - w^u L^u) + (P - p^r) N^r Q(p^r) + (p^u - P)N^u x^u(p^u, w^u) . \quad (10.6)$$

Profits of	Taxes on	Taxes on urban food
industry	rural surplus	consumption

To ascertain the effect of an increase in p^u on the investible surplus, we obtain

$$\frac{dI}{dp^u} = \frac{\partial I}{\partial p^u} + \frac{\partial I}{\partial w^u}\frac{dw^u}{dp^u} = N^u\left[\frac{\partial Y}{\partial p^u} + x^u + (p^u - P)\frac{\partial x^u}{\partial p^u}\right]$$

$$+ N^u\frac{dw^u}{dp^u}\left[\frac{\partial Y}{\partial w^u} - L^u + (p^u - P)\frac{\partial x^u}{\partial w^u}\right] . \quad (10.7)$$

On the right-hand side of the above expression, the first square bracket represents the direct effect of a price increase and the second square bracket represents the effect of the induced change in the urban wage. A rearrangement of (10.7) yields

$$\frac{dI}{dp^u} = N^u x^u\{t^u(e^u_{xp} - \rho\,\alpha^u\varepsilon^u_{xm}) - \rho - [\sigma_p - \alpha^u(1 + \rho)\sigma_w]/\alpha^u\gamma^u\} , \quad (10.8)$$

where it will be recalled that

$t^u \equiv \dfrac{P - p^u}{p^u}$ is the tax- or subsidy-rate on urban food consumption,[3]

$\sigma_p \equiv \dfrac{-\partial\ln Y}{\partial\ln p^u}$ is the elasticity of net industrial output with respect to the urban food price,

$\sigma_w \equiv \dfrac{\partial\ln Y}{\partial\ln w^u}$ is the elasticity of net industrial output with respect to the urban wage,

$\gamma^u \equiv \dfrac{w^u L^u}{Y}$ is the share of wage payments in industrial output,

$e^u_{xp} \equiv \varepsilon^u_{xp} - \alpha^u\varepsilon^u_{xm}$ is the compensated elasticity of urban food consumption with respect to the urban food price, and

$\varepsilon^u_{xm} \equiv \dfrac{\partial\ln x^u}{\partial\ln w^u}$ is the elasticity of urban food consumption with respect to the income of an industrial worker.

The elasticity ε^u_{xm} is positive because food is assumed to be a normal good. Also, to avoid trivial details, the elasticity e^u_{xp} is assumed to be strictly positive rather than non-negative, which it always is. Moreover, for later use,

---

[3] A positive t^u means a subsidy to, while a negative t^u means a tax on, urban food consumption.

recall from Chapter 6 (see expressions (6.8) and (6.9), in particular) the following two special cases of productivity effects:

$$\sigma_p - \alpha^u \sigma_w = 0 \quad \text{if productivity depends only on a worker's} \quad (10.9)$$
utility level.

$$\sigma_p - \alpha^u \sigma_w > 0 \quad \text{if productivity depends only on a worker's} \quad (10.10)$$
food consumption.

Now note from (10.2) that if $\rho > 0$ and $dI/dp^u \geq 0$, then an increase in the urban food price is Pareto-improving because it increases the investible surplus and urban workers' welfare, while leaving those in the agricultural sector unaffected. Likewise, if $\rho < 0$ and $dI/dp^u \leq 0$, then a decrease in the urban food price is Pareto-improving. It thus follows from (10.8) that: If $\rho \gtrless 0$, then the existing prices are Pareto-inefficient unless

$$t^u \lessgtr \frac{\rho + [\sigma_p - \alpha^u(1 + \rho)\sigma_w]/\alpha^u \gamma^u}{e^u_{xp} - \rho\alpha^u \varepsilon^u_{xm}} . \tag{10.11}$$

In the above expression, we assume that the denominator on the right-hand side, $e^u_{xp} - \rho\,\alpha^u \varepsilon^u_{xm}$, is positive. The underlying reason is explained in n. 4.

For any given theory of urban wage-determination, thus, the above result allows us to identify Pareto-inefficient price regimes. For instance, recall the earlier analysis in Chapter 4, where the urban wage was fixed in terms of the industrial good. In this special case, $\rho = -1$. Thus, it is straightforward to verify that (10.11) yields (4.24).

Another specialization of result (10.11), which has striking implications, is the case in which the real urban wage is fixed in terms of the utility level. That is, (10.5) holds and $\rho = 0$. Since, by assumption, the utility of urban workers is fixed and that of rural workers is unaffected by the price change, Pareto-efficiency requires that investment be maximized. That is, $dI/dp^u = 0$. By substituting $\rho = 0$ into (10.11), we obtain: The existing prices are Pareto-inefficient unless

$$t^u = \frac{P - p^u}{p^u} = \frac{(\sigma_p - \alpha^u \sigma_w)/\alpha^u \gamma^u}{e^u_{xp}} . \tag{10.12}$$

Using (10.9) and (10.10), two special cases of the above result are worth noting:

1. Any tax or subsidy on food in the urban sector is Pareto-inefficient if there are no productivity effects, or if productivity depends on the utility level of urban workers.
2. If productivity depends on food consumption, then Pareto-efficiency requires a subsidy on urban food consumption.

Optimal Prices

Recalling the Hamiltonian

$$H = N^r W(V^r) + N^u W(V^u) + \delta I ,$$ (10.13)

we observe that

$$\frac{\mathrm{d}H}{\mathrm{d}p^u} = N^u \frac{\partial W}{\partial V^u} \frac{\mathrm{d}V^u}{\mathrm{d}p^u} + \delta \frac{\mathrm{d}I}{\mathrm{d}p^u} .$$

Using (10.2) and (10.8), and setting $\mathrm{d}H/\mathrm{d}p^u = 0$, we obtain the following characterization of the optimum:

$$t^u = \frac{P - p^u}{p^u} = \frac{(1 - \beta^u/\delta)\rho + [\sigma_p - \alpha^u(1 + \rho)\sigma_w]/\alpha^u\gamma^u}{e_{xp}^u - \rho\alpha^u\varepsilon_{xm}^u} .$$ (10.14)

Alternatively, the optimal urban price is

$$p^u = P\mu^u ,$$ (10.15)

where

$$\mu^u = 1 \bigg/ \left\{ 1 + \frac{(1 - \beta^u/\delta)\rho + [\sigma_p - \alpha^u(1 + \rho)\sigma_w]/\alpha^u\gamma^u}{e_{xp}^u - \rho\alpha^u\varepsilon_{xm}^u} \right\} .$$ (10.16)

As one would expect, in the special case in which the urban wage is fixed in terms of the industrial good (that is, $\rho = -1$), it is straightforward to verify that the above result is the same as (4.10) and (4.18), or (4.18) and (4.26). Another special case is one in which the wage is set in terms of the utility level. That is, $\rho = 0$. Then, maximizing social welfare entails maximizing I. The optimal tax-rate in this case is again (10.12), which is just the special case of (10.14) with $\rho = 0$. In the more general case, there is an ambiguity concerning the desirability of a food tax versus a food subsidy in the urban sector. For instance, since $e_{xp}^u - \rho\alpha^u\varepsilon_{xm}^u$ is likely to be positive under plausible circumstances,[4] an implication of (10.14) is that: whether there should be a food tax or food subsidy in the urban sector depends on whether

$$\left[1 - \frac{\beta^u}{\delta} \right]\rho + \left\{ \frac{[\sigma_p - \alpha^u(1 + \rho)\,\sigma_w]}{\alpha^u\,\gamma^u} \right\}$$ (10.17)

Transfer	Productivity
effect	effect

---

[4] The required condition for this is $\rho < e_{xp}^u/\alpha^u\varepsilon_{xm}^u$, where the right-hand side of the preceding inequality is positive. This condition is obviously satisfied if the urban wage is fixed in terms of the industrial good (that is, $\rho = -1$) or in terms of the worker's utility level (that is, $\rho = 0$). It may be satisfied in other cases as well. For instance, if the urban wage is fixed in terms of the agricultural good (that is, $\rho = -1 + 1/\alpha^u$), then the required condition is satisfied if the price elasticity of urban food consumption exceeds its income elasticity; that is, if $\varepsilon_{xp}^u > \varepsilon_{xm}^u$.

is negative or positive. Thus, if wage changes do not fully offset the dele-terious welfare effects of price increases (that is, $\rho < 0$) and if the investible surplus is considered to be more valuable than the consumption of urban workers (that is, $\beta^u < \delta$), then the transfer effect (that is, the first term in (10.17)) calls for a food tax, whereas the productivity effect (that is, the second term in (10.17)) may call for a food subsidy.

10.4 PRICE SCISSORS WITH ENDOGENOUS WAGES

In an economy in which there is no urban–rural tax border (that is, different sets of prices cannot be maintained in the two sectors), we need to expand the preceding analysis to take account of the simultaneous effects of a price change on those in the rural sector. We continue to use the notation defined earlier, except that $p \equiv p^r = p^u$ now denotes the economy-wide price of the agricultural good in terms of the industrial good, and $t = (P - p)/p$ denotes the corresponding rate of taxation or subsidy.

The expression for the investible surplus, (10.6), is now simplified to

$$I = N^u(Y - w^u L^u) + (p - P)(N^u x^u - N^r Q) . \tag{10.18}$$

Let $\theta = (N^u x^u - N^r Q)/N^u x^u$ denote, once again, the net import of the agricultural good as a fraction of its urban consumption, where $1 > \theta$ because the rural surplus is always positive. The following, then, are the effects of a price increase on the investible surplus:

$\dfrac{dI}{dp} = -N^u x^u(\sigma_p - \alpha^u (1 + \rho) \sigma_w) /\alpha^u \gamma^u$ the total productivity effect in-cluding the effect of the induced change in the urban wage,

$-N^u x^u \rho$ the direct effect on government revenue due to the change in the urban price and the urban wage,

$+N^u x^u t(e^u_{xp} - \rho\alpha^u \varepsilon^u_{xm})$ the urban demand response in-cluding the effect of the induced change in the urban wage,

$+N^u x^u t(1 - \theta) \varepsilon^r_{Qp}$ the rural supply response,

$-N^u x^u(1 - \theta)$ the direct effect on government revenue due to the change in the rural price.   (10.19)

Note that the first three terms above are the same as those identified in (10.8). The last two terms arise because now a change in p affects the rural sector as well. A re-arrangement of the above yields

$$\frac{dI}{dp} = N^u x^u \{t[(1-\theta)\,\varepsilon^r_{Qp} + e^u_{xp} - \rho\alpha^u\varepsilon^u_{xm}]$$

$$- (1-\theta) - \frac{(\sigma_p - \alpha^u(1+\rho)\,\sigma_w)}{\alpha^u\gamma^u} - \rho\} \,. \tag{10.20}$$

Once again, a special case of the above formulation, examined in Chapter 5, is one in which the urban wage is fixed in terms of the industrial good; that is, $\rho = -1$. Making this substitution, it is straightforward to verify that expression (5.2) follows from (10.20). Another special case is one in which the rural surplus is small; that is, θ is close to one. In this case one can ignore the effects on the rural sector. Therefore, (10.20) approaches (10.8), as θ approaches one.

We focus here on the case in which the urban wage is set so as to keep the urban worker's utility level unchanged; that is, $\rho = 0$. Since an increase in the price of the agricultural good, p, increases the welfare of those in the agricultural sector,[5] and since the welfare of those in the urban sector is fixed, it follows that an increase in p is Pareto-improving so long as $dI/dp \ge 0$. Using (10.20) we conclude that: An increase in the price of the agricultural good is Pareto-improving if the following inequality is satisfied at the current prices:

$$t \ge \frac{(1-\theta) + (\sigma_p - \alpha^u\sigma_w)/\,\alpha^u\gamma^u}{(1-\theta)\,\varepsilon^r_{Qp} + e^u_{xp}} \,. \tag{10.21}$$

Note that the right-hand side of the above is positive if $(\sigma_p - \alpha^u\sigma_w)$ is non-negative,[6] and the latter is the case, for instance, if an urban worker's productivity depends on his utility level or on his food consumption. In either case, expression (10.21) allows us to identify the Pareto-inefficiency of a range of food prices for which t is positive (that is, the domestic food price is lower than the international food price).

Optimal Price Scissors

To examine the nature of optimal prices, we use (10.13) and (10.20), and set $dH/dp = 0$.[7] Upon re-arrangement, one obtains

$$t = \frac{P-p}{p} = \frac{(1-\theta)(1-\frac{\beta^r}{\delta}) + \rho(1-\frac{\beta^u}{\delta}) + \frac{\sigma_p - \alpha^u(1+\rho)\,\sigma_w}{\alpha^u\gamma^u}}{(1-\theta)\,\varepsilon^r_{Qp} + e^u_{xp} - \rho\alpha^u\varepsilon^u_{xm}} \,. \tag{10.22}$$

Now note that the denominator on the right-hand side of the above expression

[5] Here we abstract from the heterogeneity of rural individuals which was analysed in ch. 8. However, as was shown in that chapter, a higher price of the agricultural good can, under specific sets of circumstances, improve the welfare of each member of a heterogeneous rural population.

[6] This follows because, by definition, $1-\theta > 0$.

[7] Note that $\partial\{N^r W[V^r(p)]\}/\partial p = N^r Q\,\beta^r = N^u x^u(1-\theta)\beta^r$.

is positive in a range of plausible circumstances.[8] Focusing on the case in which productivity effects are negligible (that is, σ_p and σ_w are close to zero) and in which the social weight on the investible surplus exceeds the social weights on consumption (that is, δ is larger than β^r or β^u), it follows that: The domestic food price should be lower than the international food price provided the overall effect of a food price increase (that is, taking into account the induced wage changes) is not deleterious to urban workers' welfare (that is, provided $\rho \geq 0$).

Another special case worth noting is one in which $\beta^r \approx \beta^u \approx \delta$. In this case, society is unconcerned with distribution; it wishes only to maximize the net national product. Then the only effect that is relevant is the productivity effect. If the total productivity effect is positive (that is, an increase in food prices, taking into account the corresponding increases in wages, reduces net productivity), then $t > 0$ from (10.22). That is, food prices should be kept below international prices, regardless of whether the country is an exporter or an importer.

Finally, note that in the case in which the urban wage is fixed in utility terms (that is, $\rho = 0$), expression (10.22) for the optimum yields the same expression for the tax-rate as (6.25) (which was obtained for a socialist economy in which the government controls the urban wage and sets it at the socially optimal level).[9] A number of corresponding qualitative results concerning the nature of optimal prices and taxes, therefore, hold in the present context as well.

The reason why these two seemingly different models of the economy lead to the same set of conclusions is easy to understand. In the present model, the utility level of urban workers is being maintained at some exogenously specified level, and the qualitative results which we are focusing on here do not depend on what this utility level is. Not surprisingly then, these qualitative results hold also in the case in which the government's direct control over urban wages allows it to choose a particular (socially optimal) level of utility for urban workers.

10.5 ENDOGENOUS URBAN WAGE VERSUS GOVERNMENT-CONTROLLED URBAN WAGE: WHICH IS THE APPROPRIATE ASSUMPTION FOR LDCs?

Part I of the book emphasized the importance of the set of instruments which are available to the government, and illustrated how the analysis of taxation

[8] The denominator is positive under circumstances weaker than those described in n. 4.

[9] In ch. 6, it was also assumed that the economy is closed (at the margin) to external trade. But the qualitative properties of the optimal tax are unaffected whether the economy is closed or open. In the former case, the tax-rate is defined with respect to an endogenous shadow price of the agricultural good (in ch. 6, this price is represented as η/δ), whereas in the latter case it is defined with respect to the international price, P. This does not, however, affect expressions (6.25) or (10.22) for the optimum.

can change markedly depending upon what one assumes to be the set of instruments available to the government. A natural question that arises in the context of modern-day LDCs, then, is: should one assume that the government can control the urban wage, or should one assume that the urban wage is determined endogenously and that it may be influenced by the government's taxation policies? Throughout this book, we maintain the second assumption. An exception was Chapter 6, which dealt with a socialist economy, where we assumed that the government could control the urban wage.

We believe that the endogeneity of the urban wage, rather than the government's control of it, is the more appropriate assumption for modern-day LDCs. Even in those LDCs in which the government is the dominant urban employer, urban workers are a vocal and powerful political pressure group. For typical political economy reasons, therefore, it is impossible for the government to set the urban wage unilaterally. In most countries there are direct over-the-table negotiations between the government and trade unions representing the workers employed directly or indirectly by the government. In fact, there are not only negotiations on current wages but also on future allowances that would be paid to workers to compensate for the expected rate of price increase. If there are unexpectedly high price increases, then the pressure to renegotiate base wages builds up once again.

In those LDCs in which much of the urban employment is in the private sector, the ability of the government to control the wages that private firms pay to their workers is even more limited. If the government-mandated wage is higher than what private firms wish to pay (often based on an agreement with the local trade union), the government has no ability to enforce its policy. If the mandated wage is lower than what private firms wish to pay (which is virtually never the case), it is easily circumvented by declaring the workers to be more skilled than they actually are.

In fact, the ability of the government to influence the urban wage and employment indirectly, through a wage tax or subsidy, is also extremely limited. To see the importance of this point, suppose the government could institute an *ad valorem* as well as a specific wage tax (or subsidy).[10] Then, regardless of the mechanism employed by private firms to set the level of the wage (and the resulting level of employment), it will typically be possible for the government to manipulate the two taxes just noted such that the resulting urban wage and employment are at levels that the government considers optimal.[11]

However, there are serious problems in implementing such wage taxes. For example, a specific tax (subsidy) on each worker requires the government to monitor the number of workers. If there is a subsidy per worker, the employer has an incentive to claim that his labour-force is larger than

[10] Specific taxes and subsidies are levied as a fixed amount per worker, and *ad valorem* taxes and subsidies as a percentage of the wage bill.

[11] This is because there are two instruments to control two variables. To see how this can be done, see Stiglitz (1982c; 1987c).

it actually is. If there is a tax, underground transactions easily develop, and the tax becomes, in effect, a tax on employment in a few large firms, which the government can monitor. The resulting economic costs and distortions make such a tax undesirable. Taxes or subsidies based on wage-levels encounter all of these difficulties, plus two others: they require accurate reporting of wage-rates and, if enforced (which is typically not possible for the government), they distort the firm's choice of the labour-force (that is, the composition of skilled and unskilled workers). This issue is discussed further in Section 14.3.

10.6 NOTE ON THE URBAN WAGE FIXED IN TERMS OF THE UTILITY LEVEL

In this chapter, we have frequently analysed an urban wage-determination mechanism in which the urban wage changes in response to changes in prices such that the welfare of urban workers remains unaltered. This represents a central case in which private firms may set wages taking productivity effects into account. This wage-determination mechanism is also consistent with a setting in which the urban wage is determined through bargaining between the government and a trade union, and where the trade union does not suffer from money illusion. That is, the trade union understands how the welfare of its members is affected by wages and prices.

This wage-determination hypothesis greatly simplifies the analysis of pricing and taxation, for the following reasons:

(*a*) With the utility of urban workers fixed, government policies have two main effects—on the welfare of peasants and on the size of the investible surplus. Therefore, if there is a tax border between the two sectors, then urban price policies have only one effect—on the investible surplus. The social maximum is thus achieved by maximizing the investible surplus. In such cases, maximization of the investible surplus is a characteristic of Pareto-efficient tax structures; it holds regardless of the social welfare function.

(*b*) With the utility of the urban worker fixed, the relevant price response of urban consumption is the compensated price response. Thus, while there may be some ambiguity in the sign of the uncompensated price response,[12] the compensated response of demand with respect to price is always non-positive.

(*c*) If a worker's productivity depends simply on his utility level, then a price change (or any other policy change) has no effect on productivity. On the other hand, if productivity depends on food consumption, then an increase in the food price has the overall effect (after taking the wage changes into account) of lowering workers' productivity.

---

[12] Throughout this book, however, we have assumed downward-sloping demand curves.

(*d*) Accordingly if a worker's productivity depends simply on the utility level, then, as was shown in (10.12), Pareto-efficiency requires no tax or subsidy on urban food consumption, if there is an urban–rural tax border. With no urban–rural tax border, the optimal price scissors takes the simple form:

$$t = \frac{(1 - \theta)(1 - \beta'/\delta)}{(1 - \theta)\varepsilon^r_{Qp} + e^u_{Xp}}. \tag{10.23}$$

This expression follows by setting $\rho = 0$, and $\sigma_p - \alpha^u\sigma_w = 0$ in (10.22). It shows that the domestic food price should be lower than the international price if the social weight on the investible surplus is larger than that on rural income.

10.7 URBAN UNEMPLOYMENT

As was noted at the beginning of this chapter, if the urban wage is set above the market-clearing level, for any one of the reasons noted there, then there may be urban unemployment. Our objective in this section is not to discuss any specific model of urban unemployment, but to provide a general reduced-form treatment of urban unemployment, and to identify some of its consequences for taxation analysis. As we have seen earlier in the context of the urban wage, the taxation analysis becomes more tractable through the use of such reduced-form relationships.

A General Formulation

Two modifications need to be introduced in the previous analysis by the presence of urban unemployment. First, we write down a reduced-form relationship describing employment as a function of the urban wage; it will also be a function of urban prices, possibly of rural prices (the reasons for this are described later), and of the number of workers in the urban sector (which in this chapter we take as given, postponing until Chapter 13 a discussion of migration):

$$N^e = N^e(w^u, p^u, p^r, N^u) \leq N^u, \tag{10.24}$$

where N^e is urban employment and N^u is the number of workers in the urban sector. We define

$$N^n = N^u - N^e \tag{10.25}$$

as the number of unemployed individuals. The unemployment rate is thus N^n/N^u.

In the conventional neoclassical model, urban employment depends only on the urban wage. In this case (10.24) follows directly from the firm's setting the value of the marginal product equal to the wage, using a standard production function. Thus, N^e will not depend on p^r or p^u. In this case, the urban wage-rate, w^u, will adjust until an equality is achieved in the last part of (10.24). However, as previously argued, this is not the only, nor the most relevant, employment-determination mechanism. Among other relevant mechanisms are those in which trade unions play a role, and those in which firms set wages (and, hence, employment) based on productivity effects. In both of these cases, N^e will be affected by p^u.

Another modification that is required in the earlier analysis to accommodate urban unemployment is the distinction between the welfare of the urban employed and the urban unemployed. This is not as easy a task as it might seem, even if one employs an additive social welfare function of the form used in earlier chapters. In this case,

$$\psi = N^r W(V^r) + N^e W(V^u) + N^n W(V^n) \tag{10.26}$$

where V^u is the utility level of an employed urban individual and V^n is the utility level of an unemployed urban individual.

The utility level of the urban unemployed depends, however, on how they are supported. If the government provides a basic subsistence level of support to these individuals (for instance, through a free ration), then it is as if the government provides an income, m^n, out of the investible surplus, so that $V^n \equiv V^n(m^n, p^u)$. In this case, an amount $N^n m^n$ is deducted from the investible surplus I, defined in (10.6). Most LDC governments do not, however, provide subsistence support to the unemployed. The unemployed survive on the basis of transfers from the employed in the urban or rural sectors, from working in the informal market, or by using up previous savings. Each of these has different welfare consequences.

If there are transfers from those employed in the urban sector, the utility level of these individuals may be affected by the number of the unemployed.[13] We might then write the utility levels of an urban employed and an urban unemployed individual as

$$V^u = V^u(p^u, w^u; N^n), \text{ and} \tag{10.27}$$

$$V^n = V^n(p^u, w^u; N^n), \tag{10.28}$$

respectively. If there are inter-sectoral transfers (from the rural sector to those unemployed in the urban sector), then the amount of transfer received by an unemployed urban individual may be affected by the rural price, p^r. In turn, p^r will affect the incentive to remain unemployed versus employed and, accordingly, the number of the employed. This is one of the reasons (but not the only one as we shall see in later chapters) why p^r may affect N^e, as indicated in (10.24). Another effect of inter-sectoral transfers will be

---

[13] The presence of these transfers raises the possibility of an interdependent utility function. We ignore this, and evaluate each individual's welfare by his own consumption.

on food consumption in the rural sector, and hence on the rural surplus (at each value of p^r). This, in turn, will affect tax collections in the rural sector.[14] Further, if the marginal propensity to consume food differs between the urban unemployed and the urban employed, then the intra-sectoral redistribution will affect aggregate expenditures on food, and hence urban tax collections (or, if urban food is being subsidized, the aggregate value of food subsidies).

Informal Urban Employment. In many cases, the urban unemployed are engaged in subsistence employment (called the 'informal' or 'grey' sector), at tasks such as shining shoes, selling newspapers, or washing car windows, which have a small, but none the less positive, value. It is as if they produced a non-traded good which is consumed within the urban sector. Assume, for simplicity, that the output per person in the grey sector is fixed, and, choosing units appropriately, the total output (denoted by z) is just equal to N^n:

$$z = N^n . \tag{10.29}$$

We can solve for the demand for this good:

$$z^d = z^d (w^u, p^z, p^u), \tag{10.30}$$

where p^z is the price of the informal sector good. Setting demand equal to supply, we can solve for the price of the informal sector good, and hence for the income of those in the informal market:

$$m^n = p^z = p^z(N_i^n w^u, p^u) . \tag{10.31}$$

Thus, we can write

$$V^n = V^n[p^z(N^n, w^u, p^u), p^u] \tag{10.32}$$

to represent the utility of an unemployed urban person, as a function of his income and the urban price. We also need to modify the indirect utility function of the employed to reflect the price of the informal market goods. That is,

$$V^u \equiv V^u[w^u, p^u, p^z(N^n, w^u, p^u)] . \tag{10.33}$$

Finally, consider the case in which an unemployed urban individual derives support from his previous savings. If this were the only source of support, the number currently unemployed has no direct effect on the welfare of those currently employed in the urban or rural sectors. Further, if the consumption of the unemployed consists primarily of self-produced goods, then the current utility level of the unemployed could be assumed to be fixed. Though, for simplicity, we focus on this case in subsequent chapters, this

---

[14] If the transfers take the form of food, the rural surplus may be reduced, at each value of p^r.

case is not completely persuasive. If an individual expects a longer duration of unemployment, he will try to conserve his savings, and hence his consumption level and utility level will be lower. We assume that the consumption levels of the urban unemployed are sufficiently close to subsistence that these effects are negligible.

The Consequences of Tax-Induced Effects on Urban Unemployment

The presence of urban unemployment necessitates that in the analysis of the effects of taxation on individuals' welfare and on the investible surplus, one needs to include the induced effects on urban unemployment. As before, let $H = \psi + \delta I$ denote the Hamiltonian. Then, the change in this measure of overall social welfare, due to a change in the urban price, p^u, can be expressed as

$$\frac{dH}{dp^u} = \frac{\partial H}{\partial p^u} + \frac{\partial H}{\partial w^u}\frac{dw^u}{dp^u} + \frac{\partial H}{\partial N^n}\frac{dN^n}{dp^u} , \qquad (10.34)$$

and a similar relationship holds for a change in the rural price. The first term on the right-hand side of (10.34) abstracts from the induced effects on the urban wage as well as on urban unemployment. The second term represents the induced effect on the urban wage. This effect was emphasized in earlier parts of this chapter. The last term represents the induced effect on urban unemployment.

Suppose that the utility level and the consumption basket of an unemployed urban worker is not affected significantly by a change in the urban wage or price (the reasons for this simplification were given earlier). Then, recalling (10.25) and (10.26), the last term on the right-hand side of (10.34) becomes

$$\frac{\partial H}{\partial N^n}\frac{dN^n}{dp^u} = -[W(V^u) - W(V^n)]\frac{dN^n}{dp^u} . \qquad (10.35)$$

The interpretation of (10.35) is straightforward. The increase in urban unemployment due to a unit increase in p^u is dN^n/dp^u (which can be positive or negative). A previously employed person who becomes unemployed faces a utility loss from V^u to V^n. The corresponding loss in social welfare is $W(V^u) - W(V^n)$ Expression (10.35) thus represents the total change in the aggregate social welfare due to the induced effect of a price change on urban unemployment.

There are three circumstances in which the above induced effect can be ignored in taxation analysis. First, if urban employment is fixed. This is the simplification that was adopted in previous chapters. Second, if there is full employment. This will automatically be the case in the simple neoclassical model noted in the beginning of this section. A third circumstance in which the induced unemployment effect can be ignored for characterizing the optimal policy (but not for positive analysis or for reform analysis) is if the government can control the urban wage, w^u, as well as urban employment, N^e. If the latter control is set optimally, then $\partial H/\partial N^n = 0$. Thus, the last term on the right-hand side of (10.34) is zero. The same is true if the government does not directly control w^u and N^e, but can set these variables at any level it desires using indirect instruments such as an *ad valorem* tax and a direct-wage tax or subsidy (typically, two such instruments are required to be able to control w^u as well as N^e). However, for reasons outlined in Section 10.5, such an assumption is largely inappropriate for modern-day LDCs.

Finally, the reduced-form analysis of the induced effect on urban employment presented in this section can be specialized to a variety of alternative hypotheses. In turn, as we shall see in Chapters 12, 13, and 14, it becomes possible to do a more concrete taxation analysis under these alternative hypotheses.

11

SOME ASPECTS OF THE WAGE–PRODUCTIVITY HYPOTHESIS THAT ARE RELEVANT FOR TAXATION ANALYSIS

11.1 INTRODUCTION

In the previous chapter, we showed how taxation analysis can be extended in a straightforward way if urban wage and unemployment change as prices change. The formulations were general; they held no matter how wages were set, whether by unions, by government, by private firms, or through some form of bargaining among them. The formulations were also flexible; they could be specialized to the particular hypothesis appropriate to the economy under consideration.

In this chapter, we discuss an important sub-class of models in order to study how private firms might determine the urban wage and employment, and how these decisions might be affected by tax and price policy. Specifically, the present analysis is based on the hypothesis that the wage a firm pays or the prices which its workers face may have an important effect on the productivity of its labour-force. This theory is consistent with a wage-level in excess of the market-clearing level and with the presence of involuntary urban unemployment.

The above theory is referred to as the wage–productivity hypothesis. Though simple, it has important implications for the nature of market equilibrium and for the consequences of alternative government policies. It implies, in particular, that firms may not be price-takers in the labour-market, that they set their wage taking into account the effect that the wage has on the productivity of their labour-force. There may be competitive equilibria in which wages may not be cut in the face of an excess supply of labour. The traditional law of supply and demand is thus altered. It also implies that, since the wage–productivity relationship may differ for different jobs, equilibrium may be characterized by workers who are identical *ex ante facto* but who receive different wages *ex post facto*. Even with identical firms, equilibrium may be characterized by a wage distribution with the higher wages paid by some firms being exactly offset by the higher productivity. If the wage productivity curves characterizing different groups differ, there may be high rates of unemployment in some groups, while other groups may be fully employed. Moreover, reductions in the demand for labour (associated, say, with business cycles) may have their impact concentrated on particular groups, those for whom the ratio of productivity to wage is lower. Cyclical reductions in demand may be accompanied by lay-offs rather than work-sharing.

These explanations stand in marked contrast to the usual institutional ones that play a role in more traditional analyses. Institutional considerations are undoubtedly of importance; they may be particularly important in describing how (or more particularly, how fast) an economic system adapts to changes in the economic environment. However, invoking institutions too often provides an incomplete theory and an inadequate basis for policy prescriptions. For example, it would be unwise simply to assume that wage differentials would remain unchanged in the face of some government policy changes. Some economists have argued that if the government cannot lower urban wages, it should increase the prices urban workers have to pay, thus indirectly lowering their real wages. Such an approach is naïve because it ignores the reaction to price changes by those forces which determine urban wages and employment in the first place.

An extensive literature has developed during the last decade dealing with various aspects of the wage–productivity hypothesis, including its applications to both developed economies and to LDCs (see Yellen 1984 and Stiglitz 1987c for recent reviews). Rather than dealing with this literature, we focus in this chapter on those aspects of the wage–productivity hypothesis that are particularly relevant for taxation analysis. The existing literature on productivity effects has been limited to an environment where prices are fixed. Such formulations are obviously inadequate for the purpose of taxation analysis in which price changes are of fundamental importance. One of our contributions is to construct a class of models in which the prices faced by individuals are a generic part of the wage–productivity effects. We also establish some of the qualitative properties of such effects.

The central issue for taxation analysis is straightforward. Under the wage–productivity hypothesis, the wages paid and the number of workers hired are determined, in equilibrium, by each firm trading off the productivity gains from higher wages against the cost of higher wages. This equilibrium is altered by a change in prices and taxes. This chapter shows how these changes may be calculated for some special cases of the wage–productivity hypothesis. Recall that we discussed similar induced effects of taxation policy in the context of the rural sector in Section 8.4. There, the emphasis was on the endogeneity of the rural wage and employment, and also on the selectivity in employment that might result from wage–productivity effects. In this chapter, we apply the same approach, in somewhat greater detail, to the urban sector.

In Section 11.2 we briefly discuss alternative explanations of the dependence of productivity on prices and wages. In Section 11.3 we analyse market equilibrium wages and employment levels, and examine how these change when prices change. We conclude this chapter with a brief note on an aspect of welfare analysis that arises in a sub-class of models based on the wage–productivity hypothesis. Throughout the chapter we abstract from migration, a subject to which we turn in Chapters 13 and 14.

11.2 WHY DO WAGES AND PRICES AFFECT PRODUCTIVITY?

There are many reasons why a firm may expect that an increase in the wage it pays to workers, or the prices which workers face, may have an effect on the productivity of its labour-force.

(a) *The food–efficiency wage hypothesis.* This is the oldest explanation provided within the development literature.[1] When workers are close to subsistence level, increases in their nutritional level will lead to an increase in their productivity. An increase in wages is generally believed to result in an increase in nutrition and hence in productivity. We can represent the relationship between the wage paid by the i-th firm, w^{ui}, and the productivity of its labour-force, b^i, as

$$b^i = b^i(w^{ui}); \quad \partial b^i/\partial w^{ui} \geq 0 . \tag{11.1}$$

A particular case of the above relationship is depicted in Fig. 11.1. In this case, at low wages an increase in the wage leads to a more than proportionate increase in productivity. At wages higher than the threshold level, $\hat{w}^{ui}$, diminishing returns set in; that is, the increment in productivity from each successive increase in the wage becomes smaller. In this case

$$\partial^2 b^i/ \partial(w^{ui})^2 \gtrless 0 \text{ if } w^{ui} \lessgtr \hat{w}^{ui} . \tag{11.2}$$

When the effect of prices is taken into account (11.1) becomes

$$b^i = b^i(p^u, w^{ui}); \quad \partial b^i/\partial p^u \leq 0 . \tag{11.3}$$

Analogous generalizations to deal with changes in price regimes are relevant for other sources of productivity effects discussed below. The analysis of relationships such as (11.3) is presented in subsequent sections.

If an urban worker shares his earnings with family members living in the rural sector, then his productivity may also depend on variables such as the rural price, p^r. Also, the magnitude of the increase in productivity from a given change in the urban wage may be smaller if urban workers share their earnings with their family members in the rural sector. For this reason, firms may attempt to provide meals and health care to their workers, as well as to subsidize some other goods through company stores, in order to ensure

---

[1] See Leibenstein (1957). Some of the analytic implications have been explored by Mirrlees (1975) and Stiglitz (1969; 1976a). See Stiglitz 1987c for some historical antecedents.

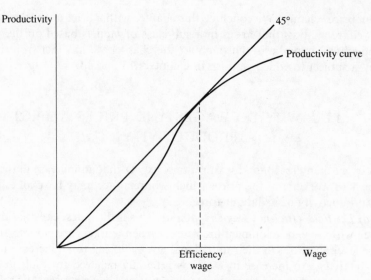

FIG. 11.1 THE WAGE-PRODUCTIVITY EFFECT

that a larger proportion of the wage is spent on productivity-enhancing expenditures.

Firms may also show a preference for hiring members of the same family
in an attempt to reduce the dissipation of the benefits of high wages through
sharing. If the worker shares his income with family members who are unemployed or who are employed elsewhere in the urban sector, then productivity may be positively related to the wages paid by other firms, (represented
by the vector $\underline{w}^u$, of which the j-th element is w^{uj}),[2] and negatively related to
the unemployment rate. That is

$$b^i = b^i(w^{ui}, \underline{w}^u, n); \quad \partial b^i/\partial w^{uj} > 0, \quad \text{and} \quad \partial b^i/\partial n < 0 , \qquad (11.4)$$

where n is the unemployment rate.

(*b*) *Labour turnover.* The productivity of firms may be affected by labour
turnover.[3] For most jobs, there are costs of hiring and training which are
specific to the firm. If individuals do not pay these costs fully at the moment
they are hired (recouping them later in the form of higher wages), then a
higher leaving rate increases the firm's training and hiring costs. Increasing
the wage-rate will then lead, in general, to a reduction in the leaving rate
and hence to an increase in the profits of the firm.

The leaving rate and turnover costs for a particular firm depend on the
relationship between the firm's wage and other firms' wages in the economy.

---

[2] In a symmetric equilibrium, all components of $\underline{w}^u$ would be identical.

[3] In the context of developed countries, this hypothesis has been explored by Arnott and
Stiglitz (1985), Hall (1975), Salop (1973), and Stiglitz (1986), among others. In the context of
LDCs, see Stiglitz (1974*a*).

Individuals receiving lower wages have a higher probability of finding a job at a higher wage, and thus of leaving their present job. Moreover, the greater the unemployment rate, the less likely it is that the worker will find a better-paying job. Thus, if g^i denotes the leaving rate for firm i, then under this hypothesis

$$b^i = b^i(w^{ui}, \underline{w}^u, n), \ \partial g^i/\partial w^{ui} < 0, \ \partial g^i/\partial w^{uj} > 0, \ \text{and} \ \partial g^i/\partial n < 0. \quad (11.5)$$

The effect of higher leaving rates is to decrease the 'net' productivity; that is, the value of output net of turnover costs. In response, therefore, firms may attempt to reduce turnover costs by forcing workers to sign binding contracts or by asking them to pay all of the training costs.

However, indentured servitude is illegal in most countries, and workers seldom pay the full turnover costs at the time they are hired. So long as workers are averse to risk-taking and there is some chance that they will leave the firm (because they are badly matched with the firm or because of some other exogenous reasons), the optimal contract between the firm and a worker will have the firm bearing some of the risks associated with the costs of labour turnover (see Arnott and Stiglitz 1985). Therefore turnover will be costly to the firm. There are additional reasons for workers not to bear the entire costs of training and hiring. Workers may have insufficient capital and the costs of training and hiring may not be verifiable. Were the workers to pay the full training and hiring costs, there might be an incentive for firms to exaggerate these costs and then to dismiss workers, and thus attempt to make a profit out of the difference between the payments and the true training costs.

(c) *Incentive effects.*[4] It is, in general, costly to monitor workers. If there were no unemployment and if all firms paid the market-clearing wage, then the threat of being dismissed would not lead individuals to reduce their shirking because they would know that they could quickly obtain another job. But if a firm pays a higher wage than that paid by other firms, or if there is unemployment (so that a dismissed worker must spend a period unemployed before he again obtains a job), then workers have less incentive to shirk because there is a real cost to being fired.[5] This again gives rise to a wage–productivity relationship of the form

$$b^i = b^i(w^{ui}, \underline{w}^u, n), \ \partial b^i/\partial w^{ui} > 0, \ \partial b^i/\partial w^{uj} < 0, \ \text{and} \ \partial b^i/\partial n > 0. \quad (11.6)$$

That is, an increase in other firms' wages reduces productivity, while an increase in unemployment increases productivity.

[4] The incentive effect of paying high wages, within the context of developed countries, has been analysed by Shapiro and Stiglitz (1984), Calvo (1979), and Calvo and Phelps (1977).

[5] A full analysis of this motive for paying higher wages again requires an investigation of alternative methods of providing incentives. One such method is the presence of a bond for a specific amount which the employee pays if he is detected to be shirking. The difficulties with this are similar to those discussed in the context of turnover costs above. Other alternative methods also face difficulties.

(*d*) *Morale effects.* It has been postulated that an individual's behaviour is affected by his views of how fairly he is being treated, or more generally, by how he sees himself being treated in relationship to others. Under this hypothesis, an individual's wage, relative to others' wages (in his firm as well as in other firms) enters into his utility function, and consequently affects his effort-supply function.[6]

(*e*) *Quality effects.* Changes in a firm's wage may affect the mix of applicants who apply to this firm. Thus, if the reservation wages are correlated with productivities on the job, then a firm can improve the quality of its labour-force by offering a higher wage. Consequently, the productivity of the workers in a firm is a function of the wage paid by this firm relative to the wages paid by other firms.[7]

(*f*) *Recruitment effects.* It is costly for firms to recruit workers, particularly to find workers who are well-matched with the firm. Even if searches were costless, a firm paying a higher wage would have a larger pool of applicants to choose from, and this would enable the firm to recruit a more productive labour-force.[8]

11.3 A MODEL OF WAGES, PRICES, PRODUCTIVITY, AND UNEMPLOYMENT

Regardless of the underlying hypothesis, the dependence of productivity on wages has the consequence that firms may not lower wages in the presence of an excess supply of labour. Such a determination of urban wages and the level of urban employment has implications for taxation analysis. We begin our analysis with a highly simplified model; more general approaches are considered later.

Consider expression (11.3). Assume that there are no inter-firm externalities, and that firms are symmetrical in their choices. Then, the aggregate output of firms can be expressed as

$$F = F[b(p^u, w^u) L^u N^e], \tag{11.7}$$

where N^e is the number of employed workers, and where we continue to assume that the number of hours worked by each worker, L^u, is fixed. We

---

[6] For a discussion of evidence for this effect in the psychology literature see Akerlof (1984).

[7] In the context of developed countries, this model has been explored by Stiglitz (1976*a*), Weiss (1980), and Nalebuff and Stiglitz (1983), and in the context of LDCs, by Stiglitz (1982*a*). The assumptions that firms can only imperfectly observe the inputs of individuals (as in the previous two explanations), and that they can only imperfectly screen individuals prior to hiring them, are critical for this hypothesis. This hypothesis also requires that individuals not be able to guarantee their future performance.

[8] In models with costly searches, it may take some time before a firm is successful in filling a vacancy. The expected length of time is dependent on the wages the firm pays. The effect of this is analogous to that of a direct increase in productivity resulting from a wage increase.

refer to (11.7) as the 'multiplicative productivity representation' because the productivity parameter multiplies the number of physical work hours to determine the hours in efficiency units.[9] The aggregate profit of firms is

$$\pi = F - N^e w^u L^u .$$ (11.8)

The firms maximize their profits with respect to w^u and N^e. The first-order conditions of optimality are

$$F_b b_w = 1 \quad \text{and}$$ (11.9)

$$F_b b = w^u ,$$ (11.10)

where $F_b = \partial F/\partial (bL^u N^e)$ and $b_w = \partial b/\partial w^u$. Dividing (11.9) by (11.10), we obtain

$$b_w = b/w^u .$$ (11.11)

The above expression simply says that firms choose a wage-rate to minimize the cost of their wages per efficiency unit of work. In other words (11.11) characterizes the solution to

$$\min_{w^u}: w^u/b(p^u, w^u) .$$ (11.12)

The solution to (11.11) is referred to as the 'efficiency wage', and it is depicted in Fig. 11.1 as the point of tangency of the line through the origin with the productivity curve. By inverting (11.10), the corresponding demand for labour is given by

$$N^e = \frac{F_b^{-1}(w^u/b)}{bL^u} .$$ (11.13)

This demand may be less than the supply, but firms will not be induced to lower their wages. A firm knows that an unemployed worker who offers to work for less than the efficiency wage will have a sufficiently lower productivity that its lower labour costs will not compensate for the correspondingly lower profits.

The above conclusion holds with equal force for any of the other hypotheses which were advanced earlier for the dependence of productivity on wages. At the same time, while each of the hypotheses can yield equilibrium unemployment, different hypotheses do differ in their welfare consequences and in their policy implications.

We next analyse the consequences of changes in prices or taxes on wages and employment in the simple model above. Differentiating (11.11) with respect to the urban price, p^u, we obtain

$$\frac{dw^u}{dp^u} = \frac{b_p - b_{wp}w^u}{w^u b_{ww}} ,$$ (11.14)

[9] To use the vocabulary of traditional growth theory, in formulation (11.7), increases in labour productivity are 'Harrod-neutral' or 'labour-augmenting'. A more general formulation would be $F = F(G^K(b)K, G^N(b) L^u N^e)$, where K is capital. Thus, if $\partial G^N(b)/\partial b = 0$, increases in productivity are purely capital-augmenting.

where the subscripts of b continue to represent its partial derivatives; that is, $b_{wp} = \partial b_w/\partial p^u$, and $b_{ww} = \partial b_w/\partial w^u$. In elasticity form (11.14) can be rewritten as

$$\varepsilon^u_{wp} = \frac{\mathrm{d}\ln w^u}{\mathrm{d}\ln p^u} = \frac{p^u(b_p - b_{wp}w^u)}{(w^u)^2 b_{ww}} . \tag{11.15}$$

Similarly, by perturbing (11.10) with respect to p^u, w^u, and N^e, we obtain the following expression for the change in the employment level due to a change in prices.

$$\frac{\mathrm{d}N^e}{\mathrm{d}p^u} = \left\{ [1 - b_w(F_b + F_{bb}bL^uN^e)] \frac{\mathrm{d}w^u}{\mathrm{d}p^u} \right.$$

$$\left. - b_p (F_b + F_{bb}bL^uN^e) \right\} / b^2 L^uF_{bb} , \tag{11.16}$$

where $\mathrm{d}w^u/\mathrm{d}p^u$ is given by (11.14).

Special Cases

(a) *Productivity depends on food consumption.* If a worker's productivity depends only on his food consumption, that is, $b = b[x^u(p^u, w^u)]$, then (11.11) implies

$$\varepsilon_{bx} \varepsilon^u_{xm} = 1, \tag{11.17}$$

where $\varepsilon_{bx} = \partial\ln b/\partial\ln x^u$ is the elasticity of productivity with respect to food consumption, and, as was defined in earlier chapters, ε^u_{xm} is the income elasticity of food consumption. In other words, any change in prices will lead to a change in the wage such that (11.17) is preserved. Now, assume further that the income elasticity of food consumption is a function of the quantity of food consumption alone (that is, ε^u_{xm} is a function of x^u alone). Then the left-hand side of (11.17) is a function of x^u alone. Expression (11.17) thus implies that wages adjust in response to a change in price to keep x^u unchanged. In other words,

$$\varepsilon^u_{wp} = \varepsilon^u_{xp}/\varepsilon^u_{xm} > 0. \tag{11.18}$$

Further, under the above assumptions a change in prices and the corresponding change in the wage does not affect b. Substituting $\mathrm{d}b/\mathrm{d}p^u = b_p + b_w(\mathrm{d}w^u/\mathrm{d}p^u) = 0$ into (11.16), we obtain

$$\frac{\mathrm{d}N^e}{\mathrm{d}p^u} = (1/b^2L^uF_{bb}) \frac{\mathrm{d}w^u}{\mathrm{d}p^u} < 0. \tag{11.19}$$

The above expression is negative because F_{bb} is negative and, from (11.18), $\mathrm{d}w^u/\mathrm{d}p^u$ is positive.

(b) *Productivity depends on utility.* The analysis of the case in which a worker's productivity depends on his utility level, that is, $b = b[V^u(p^u, w^u)]$, is similar to the previous special case. Analogous to (11.17), we now obtain

$$\varepsilon_{bV}\, \varepsilon^u_{Vm} = 1, \tag{11.20}$$

where $\varepsilon^u_{Vm} = \partial\ln V^u/\partial\ln m^u$ is the elasticity of the utility level with respect to income, and $\varepsilon_{bV} = \partial\ln b/\partial\ln V^u$ is the elasticity of productivity with respect to the utility level. Assume that ε^u_{Vm} is a function of the utility level alone. Then, it follows from (11.20) that the adjustment in wages will be such that the utility level of workers is kept unchanged. This in turn implies, as should be familiar by now,

$$\varepsilon^u_{wp} = \alpha^u > 0, \tag{11.21}$$

where it will be recalled that $\alpha^u = p^u x^u/w^u L^u$ is the urban worker's share of the budget spent on food. Furthermore, productivity is unaffected by a change in price and by the corresponding change in the wage. Thus, we obtain (11.19) once again.

A More General Model

The above analysis was based on several simplifications. In general, productivity effects need not interact with employment in the mutiplicative way represented by (11.7). The above analysis also abstracted from inter-firm externalities. A more general specification of the productivity trade-off facing the i-th firm is

$$b^i = b^i(w^{ui}, \underline{w}^u, p^u, n) \tag{11.22}$$

where w^{ui} is the wage paid by firm i, $\underline{w}^u$ is the vector of wages paid by other firms in the urban sector, and n is the urban unemployment rate. The output of firm i is represented as

$$F^i = F^i(b^i, N^{ei}), \tag{11.23}$$

where F^i denotes the net output of firm i, and N^{ei} is the number of workers it employs. Representing this firm's profit as $\pi^i = F^i - N^{ei}w^{ui}L^u$, profit-maximization entails the real wage equalling the value of the marginal product,

$$\frac{\partial F^i}{\partial N^{ei}} = w^{ui}L^u \tag{11.24}$$

and the wage-rate being chosen so that

$$\frac{\partial F^i}{\partial b^i}\,\frac{\partial b^i}{\partial w^{ui}} = N^{ei}L^u. \tag{11.25}$$

From (11.24) and (11.25), we obtain the 'generalized optimal productivity condition':

$$\frac{\partial \ln b^i}{\partial \ln w^{ui}} = \frac{\partial \ln F^i}{\partial \ln N^{ei}} \Big/ \frac{\partial \ln F^i}{\partial \ln b^i} . \qquad (11.26)$$

That is, the elasticity of productivity with respect to the wage should equal the ratio of the elasticity of output with respect to employment and the elasticity of output with respect to productivity.

Expression (11.26) is a generalization of (11.11). If we focus on a symmetric equilibrium across firms, in which all urban firms pay the same wage in the equilibrium, then an additional condition will be added to the characterization of equilibrium, (11.24) and (11.25), namely, that each element of the vector $\underline{w}^u$ has the same value. Denote this common value by w^u. That is,

$$w^{ui} = w^u \text{ and } \underline{w}^u = (w^u, \ldots, w^u). \qquad (11.27)$$

By differentiating the equilibrium (11.24), (11.25), and (11.27) with respect to w^u and p^u, we can calculate the impact that a change in p^u would have on w^u and N^e. These would be the generalizations of (11.15) and (11.16) respectively.

It should be apparent that the resulting expressions for dw^u/dp^u and dN^e/dp^u would not be simple; the presence of productivity effects introduces a complex set of trade-offs. For particular productivity hypotheses, however, it is possible to obtain more tractable expressions. For instance, as was shown earlier, if the productivity is multiplicative, and if productivity as well as the income elasticity of food consumption depend only on the level of food consumption, then the relevant expressions are (11.18) and (11.19). The corresponding expressions are (11.21) and (11.19) if a worker's productivity as well as the income elasticity of food consumption depends only on his utility level. In these special cases, increases in the price of food in the urban sector increase wages and decrease urban employment.

An Aspect of Taxation Analysis

A general formulation of how to incorporate the induced effects of taxes on urban wages and unemployment into taxation analysis was described in Chapter 10. The analysis presented there can obviously be specialized to the models based on the wage–productivity hypotheses discussed in this chapter. This involves using expressions such as (11.15) and (11.16), or its variants, to depict the effects of a price change on the urban wage and employment, respectively. As pointed out earlier, while the economic intuition underlying such expressions is straightforward, they are obtained in a simple form only under strong assumptions.

It is perhaps useful to note here an issue in taxation analysis that is specific to a sub-class of models based on productivity effects. Consider the effect of a change in the urban food price on the investible surplus

$$I = N^e(Y - w^u L^u) + (P - p^r)N^r Q + (p^u - P)N^e x^u, \qquad (11.28)$$

where it is assumed that the urban price can be changed independently of the rural price. Assume that private firms produce all the industrial output, and that there is a 100 per cent tax on the profits of these firms. Further, suppose that there are no inter-firm externalities. Then, the first term on the right-hand side of (11.28) is replaced by the aggregate firms' profit, denoted by $\pi(p^u, w^u, N^e)$. An example of the firms' profit was described in (11.8).

Now, since firms maximize their profit with respect to w^u and N^e, it follows that the only effect of a change in π that we need to deal with is the partial effect of p^u. This is simply an application of the envelope theorem. From the envelope theorem, $\partial\pi/\partial p^u$ denotes the price-induced change in profit and, hence, the corresponding change in government revenue. Exactly the same result will be obtained if the wage function, $w^u(p^u)$, and the employment function, $N^e(p^u)$, were solved from the firms' maximization, and the total derivative of the firms' profit, $d\pi(p^u, w^u(p^u), N^e(p^u))/dp^u$ were to be calculated.

For an illustration of this point, consider the multiplicative productivity described in (11.7) and (11.8). Then

$$\frac{d}{dp^u} N^e(Y - w^u L^u) = F_b b_p L^u N^e. \tag{11.29}$$

This expression is negative if productivity depends negatively on the prices that workers face.

12

TAXES AND SUBSIDIES ON DIFFERENT GOODS IN THE URBAN SECTOR

12.1 INTRODUCTION

The analysis of urban taxes presented in earlier chapters employed the simplification of two aggregate goods, an agricultural good and an industrial good. In this chapter, we deal with a multitude of goods. A similar disaggregated analysis for the rural sector was presented in Chapter 9. The critical question concerning the disaggregated structure of urban taxes is: Should some commodities be taxed or subsidized more heavily than others, and if so, according to what principles?

We will show that the answer depends critically on two factors: (*a*) how urban wages are set, and (*b*) the nature of the effect of wages and prices on urban employment and productivity. We show that if wages adjust to changes in prices to keep individuals at the same level of utility, then, in the absence of employment and productivity effects, there should be no urban commodity taxes or subsidies. If there are employment or productivity effects, then commodities which have a large positive effect on employment and productivity should be subsidized, while other commodities should be taxed. It should be apparent that the first result is a generalization, in a multi-good setting, of a result obtained in Chapter 10.

Our results differ markedly from the standard theory concerning the structure of taxes in the absence of lump-sum or income taxes. The latter (originally due to Ramsey and Pigou) emphasized that if the government wishes to raise a given amount of revenue with the least dead-weight loss, then it should tax less elastic commodities more heavily than more elastic commodities. More generally, it should set tax-rates in such a way that there is an equal proportional reduction of consumption (along the compensated demand curve) for all commodities.

These results, however, stood in contrast to standard practice in the design of commodity taxes. Governments typically tax luxuries and subsidize necessities, in part as an indirect attempt to make the rich bear a greater proportion of the costs of government. Since necessities tend to be price inelastic, and luxuries price elastic, this observed pattern of taxation is inconsistent with the kinds of taxation policies recommended by Ramsey and Pigou. In the subsequent literature (Atkinson and Stiglitz 1976; Diamond 1975), a unified model integrating both kinds of effects was developed. Whether necessities were taxed at higher or lower rates than luxuries depended, among other things, on distributional considerations.

Our results, derived below, seem more in accord with observed practice, not because of a greater concern for equality but because the conventional model is largely inappropriate for the analysis of taxation in LDCs. This is seen most forcefully by noting that the traditional analysis, focusing on dead-weight loss effects, can be interpreted as saying that one should tax commodities which are complements to leisure (which, we recall, is untaxed) while subsidizing the substitutes.[1] If labour supply were inelastic, no differential taxes would be imposed: uniformity is desirable. Differential commodity taxation can be seen as an attempt to reduce the disincentive effects on labour.

However, for most LDCs facing urban unemployment, the effects of tax changes on labour supply should not be viewed as first-order effects in determining policy. If anything, the government would like to reduce the amount of visible unemployment. Thus, policies which increase the labour supply may actually exacerbate the visibility of what the government sees as one of its central problems. We contend that the first-order effects, instead, are the effects of taxation and pricing policies on urban wages, employment, productivity, and migration. Price-induced changes in urban wages have an immediate effect on the investible surplus, on the welfare level, and on the consumption pattern of urban workers. Similarly, if productivity is particularly sensitive to the consumption of some commodity, it may be desirable to lower the price of that commodity. Likewise, it can be shown that if migration is particularly sensitive to the price of some commodities (like housing), it will have a significant effect on the analysis of taxation.

For simplicity, the present analysis of the disaggregated structure of urban taxation and pricing abstracts from migration, postponing its discussion until Chapter 13. We also assume that a tax border exists between the rural and urban sectors. We can therefore analyse the tax structure in the urban sector without considering its effects on the rural sector. In Section 12.2, we present a general model of taxation which permits any kind of endogeneity in urban wages and productivity. This general model is then specialized to the case in which the urban wage is fixed in terms of the numeraire good (the resulting optimal taxes are similar to those in the Ramsey case, with the difference that our analysis brings out the productivity effects), and to the case in which the urban wage changes to keep the workers' utility level unchanged. We conclude the chapter with a discussion of how our analysis can be extended to: (*a*) deal with the case in which the work hours of urban workers are not fixed, and are instead chosen by the workers themselves, and (*b*) incorporate the heterogeneity of urban individuals.

---

[1] These results were originally derived by Corlett and Hague (1953) and Meade (1955), for a model with two commodities and labour. Atkinson and Stiglitz (1972) extended the interpretation to many commodities. See Atkinson and Stiglitz (1980) for a review.

12.2 A GENERAL FORMULATION

We begin by generalizing our earlier notation to the present context where
there is a multitude of goods. Let the reduced-form dependence of the urban
wage on the vector of urban prices, p^u, be represented as

$$w^u = w^u(p^u) . \tag{12.1}$$

Let

$$\varepsilon^u_{wi} = \frac{\partial \ln w^u}{\partial \ln p^u_i} \tag{12.2}$$

denote the corresponding elasticity of the urban wage with respect to the
price of good i.

The effect of a change in the price of good i on the utility level of an urban
worker can be represented as

$$\frac{dV^u}{dp^u_i} = \frac{\partial V^u}{\partial p^u_i} + \frac{\partial V^u}{\partial w^u}\frac{dw^u}{dp^u_i} . \tag{12.3}$$

Using (12.2) and identities resulting from the envelope theorem,[2] (12.3) yields

$$\frac{dV^u}{dp^u_i} = \lambda^u x^u_i (-1 + \varepsilon^u_{wi}/\alpha^u_i) = \lambda^u x^u_i \rho_i , \tag{12.4}$$

where $\alpha^u_i = p^u_i x^u_i / w^u L^u$ is the share of a worker's budget spent on good i, and

$$\rho_i = -1 + \varepsilon^u_{wi}/\alpha^u_i \tag{12.5}$$

is a summary parameter to be used below. Note that the parameter ρ_i is a
generalization of the parameter ρ employed in Chapter 10.

It is apparent that if the urban wage is fixed in terms of the numeraire
good, then

$$\varepsilon^u_{wi} = 0 \quad \text{and} \quad \rho_i = -1. \tag{12.6}$$

On the other hand, if the urban wage adjusts to keep an urban worker's utility level unchanged, then

$$\varepsilon^u_{wi} = \alpha^u_i \quad \text{and} \quad \rho_i = 0. \tag{12.7}$$

Productivity Effects

Let

$$Y = Y(k, L^u, p^u, w^u) \tag{12.8}$$

---

[2] These identities are $\partial V^u/\partial p^u_i = -\lambda^u x^u_i$ and $\partial V^u/\partial w^u = \lambda^u L^u$, where it will be recalled that x^u_i is a worker's consumption of good i and L^u is the hours of work he supplies. L^u is assumed fixed at present.

denote the net industrial output per worker. Let

$$\sigma_i = -\frac{\partial \ln Y}{\partial \ln p_i^u} \quad \text{and} \quad \sigma_w = \frac{\partial \ln Y}{\partial \ln w^u} \tag{12.9}$$

denote respectively the elasticities of net output with respect to the price of good i and the urban wage. It is then straightforward to verify that the over-all impact of a price increase on productivity is

$$\frac{dY}{dp_i^u} = \frac{\partial Y}{\partial p_i^u} + \frac{\partial Y}{\partial w^u}\frac{dw^u}{dp_i^u} = \frac{-x_i^u}{\alpha_i^u \gamma^u}(\sigma_i - \varepsilon_{wi}^u \sigma_w) , \tag{12.10}$$

where $\gamma^u = w^u L^u / Y$ is the wage payment expressed as a fraction of the indus-trial output. Also, for later use, we note that in the special case in which a worker's productivity depends on his utility level, the following relationship holds:[3]

$$\sigma_i - \alpha_i^u \sigma_w = 0. \tag{12.11}$$

Characterization of the Optimum

For ease of exposition, we abstract at present from urban unemployment; however, as shown at the end of this section, it is straightforward to incor-porate this aspect.

The present value of the aggregate social welfare, including the value of the investible surplus, is given by the Hamiltonian

$$H = N^r W(V^r) + N^u W[V^u(p^u, w^u)] + \delta[N^u(Y - w^u L^u) \tag{12.12}$$

$$+ (P - p^r) N^r Q + (p^u - P) N^u x^u(p^u, w^u)] ,$$

where x^u, Q, p^u, p^r, and P are all vectors. In the Appendix to this chapter we show that the optimal structure of prices or taxes is given by the solution to

$$-\Sigma_j t_j^u e_{ij}^u = -\left[1 - \frac{\beta^u}{\delta} - (p^u - P)\frac{\partial x^u}{\partial m^u}\right]\rho_i - \left(\frac{\sigma_i - \varepsilon_{wi}^u \sigma_w}{\alpha_i^u \gamma^u}\right), \tag{12.13}$$

where

$t_j^u = (P_j - p_j^u)/p_j^u$ is the subsidy or tax rate on good j,

$$e_{ij}^u = -\frac{\partial \ln x_i}{\partial \ln p_j^u}\bigg|_{\text{utility}}$$

represents the compensated elasticities, and $\partial x^u / \partial m^u$ denotes the income re-sponses of the vector of consumption quantities. The left-hand side of (12.13), $-\Sigma_j t_j^u e_{ij}^u$, has a standard interpretation. It represents the proportional

[3] This can be derived using the identities in n. 2 for the case in which

$$Y = Y[k, L^u, V^u(p^u, w^u)] .$$

reduction in the compensated consumption of good i, as a consequence of any given set of taxes and subsidies.

Ramsey Case

First consider the case in which the urban wage is fixed in terms of the numeraire (that is, $\varepsilon^u_{wi} = 0$ and $\rho_i = -1$). Expression (12.13) then yields:

$$-\Sigma_j t^u_j e^u_{ij} = \left[1 - \frac{\beta^u}{\delta} - (p^u - P) \frac{\partial x^u}{\partial m^u} \right] - \frac{\sigma_i}{\alpha^u_i \gamma^u} . \tag{12.14}$$

Now recall the standard Ramsey result: The proportional reduction in the compensated consumption should be equal for all goods (see Atkinson and Stiglitz 1980, Chapter 12). For this result to hold, it is apparent from (12.14) that the urban wage responses need to be of a particular kind, (that is, the wage is fixed in terms of the numeraire) and also that productivity effects need to be negligible. Thus, even if the urban wage is fixed in terms of the numeraire, the Ramsey result need not hold in general because of the productivity effects (captured for good i by the last term on the right-hand side of (12.13)). For instance, if two goods have approximately the same share of a worker's budget, but a rise in the price of the first good decreases the productivity by a larger extent (that is, if $\sigma_1 > \sigma_2$ and $\alpha^u_1 \approx \alpha^u_2$), then it follows from (12.13) that the proportional reduction in the consumption of the first good should be smaller.

A special case of productivity effects for which the Ramsey result is restored is one in which a worker's productivity depends on his utility level. In this case, we note from (12.11) that σ_i / α^u_i is the same for all goods. Therefore, the right-hand side of (12.14) is the same for all goods.

Urban Wages Fixed in Terms of the Utility Level

A central example of urban wage-determination mechanisms is one in which the utility level of an urban worker remains unchanged in response to changes in the urban prices. In this case, $\varepsilon^u_{wi} = \alpha^u_i$, and $\rho_i = 0$. Substitution into (12.13) yields:

$$-\Sigma_j t^u_j e^u_{ij} = -\frac{\sigma_i - \alpha^u_i \sigma_w}{\alpha^u_i \gamma^u} . \tag{12.15}$$

Thus: Whether the compensated reduction should or should not be the same across goods and, indeed, whether there should be any taxation or subsidization at all, depends entirely on the nature of the productivity effects.

For instance, if the productivity effects are negligible (that is, if $\sigma_i = \sigma_w = 0$), then (12.9) yields that the proportional reduction should be zero for all goods. This, in turn, is possible only if there are no taxes or subsidies in the urban sector. Thus: There should be no taxation or subsidization in the urban sector if the urban wage adjusts to keep the workers' utility level unchanged and if price changes have negligible effects on productivity. The underlying reason is simple. The least costly method of providing a fixed level of utility (whatever that level might be) is to provide it using the international prices of goods. The distortion introduced by taxes and subsidies does not serve any useful purpose in this case.

The above result also holds if there are productivity effects but if a worker's productivity depends on his utility level. This is verified easily from (12.11) and (12.15). Once again the reason behind the result is straightforward. Since the utility level of workers is being kept unchanged through wage adjustments, it follows that productivity is also unchanged in this case.

For more general types of productivity effects, we note the following result from (12.10) and (12.15): If productivity increases (respectively, decreases) from the increase in the price of a good, taking into account the induced wage changes which keep the workers' utility level unchanged, then the proportional reduction in the consumption of this good should be positive (respectively, negative). Thus, for instance, the optimal taxation should increase the compensated food consumption, if a higher food price is likely to decrease productivity, and decrease compensated alcohol consumption, if an alcohol price rise is likely to increase productivity.

Unemployment Effects

The treatment of unemployment effects is similar to that of productivity effects, but somewhat more complicated. It involves calculating the effect on employment of any change in tax and the corresponding change in the urban wage. The change in employment, in turn, has direct welfare effects, because a person who becomes unemployed becomes significantly worse off. We discussed these effects in Section 10.7.

In addition, there are two important effects on the investible surplus. First, if urban employment decreases, then the aggregate profit from industrial production will decrease (assuming that the output of an employed worker exceeds his wage). The second effect is on the net tax paid or the net subsidy received by employed workers on their consumption basket. If an employed worker pays net taxes on his consumption basket, then a decrease in the number of employed individuals decreases the investible surplus. The opposite is the latter effect if there is a net subsidy on the consumption of an employed urban worker, as is the case in some LDCs.[4]

Consider the case in which an increase in the price of any good raises the urban wage, and the combined effect of these two changes is to lower urban

---

[4] These effects can be ascertained by noting that, instead of (12.12), the Hamiltonian is now
$H = N^r W(V^r) + N^e W(V^u) + (N^u - N^e)W(V^n) + \delta [N^e (Y - w^u L^u) + (P - p) N^r Q + (p - P) N^e x^u]$.
We assume here that the tax collected or the subsidy paid on the consumption of the urban

employment. Then, it follows from the above description that the aggregate welfare of urban individuals' declines. Assume further that an employed urban individual contributes positively to the investible surplus. Then, it is clear that the presence of unemployment effects makes it less attractive to raise taxes on different goods.

Finally, recall from the discussion in Chapter 10 that socially inefficient levels of urban wage and employment can arise in a market equilibrium (for example, if firms are setting wages and, hence, employment levels, based on productivity considerations), and that wage taxes or subsidies are typically infeasible in most LDCs. An added role of commodity taxation is thus to attempt to correct these inefficiencies. In the present model, there are many goods that can be independently taxed or subsidized. As a consequence, it might be possible to reduce significantly the inefficiencies just noted.

12.3 GENERALIZATIONS

We conclude this chapter with two generalizations. First, the analysis can be modified to the case in which urban workers choose their work hours rather than work for a pre-specified number of hours as assumed thus far. Second, the qualitative aspects of much of the analysis presented in this chapter extend to the more realistic case in which heterogeneity among employed individuals within the urban sector is explicitly taken into account.

Variable Hours of Work in the Urban Sector

Although it is reasonable to assume for most LDCs that the employed urban workers are constrained in the number of hours that they work, there are many dimensions of work decisions in which they are not so constrained, such as their level of effort. The wage may affect work effort and thus firms' profitability. To provide an illustration of how such interactions can be accounted for, we briefly discuss the case in which the number of hours of work an urban worker, L^u, is chosen by the worker and is thus not an exogenous parameter. We define the following:

$$\varepsilon_{Li}^u \equiv \partial \ln L^u / \partial \ln p_i \qquad = \qquad \text{elasticity of labour supply with respect to the price of good } i,$$

$$\varepsilon_{Lw}^u \equiv \partial \ln L^u / \partial \ln w^u \qquad = \qquad \text{the elasticity of labour supply with respect to the urban wage, and}$$

$$Y_L \equiv \partial Y / \partial L^u \qquad = \qquad \text{the value of marginal product of an extra work hour.}$$

---

unemployed is negligible, and that the utility level of an urban unemployed individual is not significantly affected by a change in taxes. See sect. 10.7 for additional discussion of these issues.

For brevity, we abstract, once again, from the effect of taxes on unemployment. Then it is straightforward to verify that expression (12.13) characterizing optimal taxation is now modified as

$$
-\Sigma_j t_j e_{ij}^u = -\left[1 - \frac{\beta^u}{\delta} - (p^u - P)\frac{\partial x^u}{\partial m^u} \right] \rho_i - \left(\frac{\sigma_i - \varepsilon_{wi}^u \sigma_w}{\alpha_i^u \gamma^u} \right)
$$

$$
+ \left(\frac{Y_L}{w^u} - 1 \right) \left(\frac{\varepsilon_{Li}^u + \varepsilon_{wi}^u \varepsilon_{Lw}^u}{\alpha_i^u} \right). \tag{12.16}
$$

We focus on the interpretation of the last term on the right-hand side of the above expression because this additional term captures the effects of changes in labour hours.

First note that expression (12.16) is the same as (12.13) if $Y_L = w^u$. This should not be surprising. If, at the optimum, the value of the marginal product of a labour hour exactly equals the wage-rate, then the optimum is unaffected by marginal changes in labour hours, no matter what the nature of these changes might be.

Next, suppose Y_L exceeds w^u; that is, an extra labour hour yields a net increase in industrial profit.[5] Note in (12.16) that $\varepsilon_{Li}^u + \varepsilon_{wi}^u \varepsilon_{Lw}^u$ is positive or negative depending on whether the overall impact of an increase in the price of good i is to increase or decrease the labour hours of urban workers. It thus follows from (12.16) that: The proportional reduction in the consumption quantity of good i due to taxation is larger (smaller) if a higher price of good i increases (decreases) the labour hours of urban workers.

Heterogeneity within the Urban Sector

The preceding analysis is easily generalized to incorporate heterogeneity of individuals in the industrial sector. The main implication of this extension is that, in general, various goods will differ not only in their employment and productivity effects, but also in their distributional effects. Goods such as food may have larger distributional effects (since the welfare of the poor is more sensitive to food prices) as well as larger productivity effects (due to the effect of food consumption on workers' health, for example). If this is the case, then the tax-induced proportional reduction in food consumption would be smaller than for other goods. This extension, however, does not alter our earlier results concerning the desirability or undesirability of urban commodity taxes and subsidies. For instance, when wages adjust to price changes to maintain the utility levels of different groups of workers, the direct distributional gains from any commodity subsidies are offset by changes in the wage structure. As a consequence, urban taxes or subsidies are once again undesirable unless they are designed to respond to particular kinds of

---

[5] The opposite case where $Y_L < w^u$ can be interpreted in an analogous manner.

unemployment or productivity effects, or unless the extent to which wage changes compensate price changes differs systematically across income levels.

APPENDIX

Derivation of Equation (12.13)

Expression (12.12) yields

$$\frac{1}{\delta}\frac{dH}{dp_i^u} = \frac{N^u}{\delta}\frac{\partial W}{\partial V^u}\frac{dV^u}{dp_i^u} + N^u\left(\frac{dY}{dp_i^u} - L^u\frac{dw^u}{dp_i}\right) + N^u x_i^u$$

$$+ N^u(p^u - P)\left(\frac{\partial x^u}{\partial p_i^u} + \frac{\partial x^u}{\partial m^u}L^u\frac{dw^u}{dp_i}\right). \tag{12.A1}$$

We substitute (12.2), (12.4), (12.10), and the definition of the social weight $\beta^u = \lambda^u \partial W/\partial V^u$ into (12.A1). This yields

$$\frac{1}{\delta}\frac{dH}{dp_i^u} = N^u x_i^u \frac{\beta^u}{\delta} \rho_i - N^u x_i^u \frac{(\sigma_i - \varepsilon_{wi}^u \sigma_w)}{\alpha_i^u \gamma^u} + N^u x_i^u \left(1 - \frac{\varepsilon_{wi}^u}{\alpha_i^u}\right)$$

$$+ N^u(p^u - P)\left(\frac{\partial x^u}{\partial p_i^u} + x_i^u\frac{\partial x^u}{\partial m^u}\right) + N^u x_i^u (p^u - P)\left(-1 + \frac{\varepsilon_{wi}^u}{\alpha_i^u}\right)\frac{\partial x^u}{\partial m^u}. \tag{12.A2}$$

Next, from the definition of compensated demand responses and the symmetry property of Slutsky terms,

$$(p^u - P)\left(\frac{\partial x^u}{\partial p_i^u} + x_i^u\frac{\partial x^u}{\partial m^u}\right) = (p^u - P)\left.\frac{\partial x^u}{\partial p_i^u}\right|_{\text{utility}}$$

$$= x_i^u \sum_j t_j^u e_{ij}^u, \tag{12.A3}$$

where $t_j^u = (P_j - p_j^u)/p_j^u$, and $e_{ij}^u = -\left.\frac{p_j^u}{x_i^u}\frac{\partial x_i^u}{\partial p_j^u}\right|_{\text{utility}}$.

Substitution of the above and of definition (12.5) allows (12.A2) to be rewritten as

$$\frac{1}{N^u x_i^u \delta}\frac{dH}{dp_i} = \sum_j t_j^u e_{ij}^u - \left[1 - \frac{\beta^u}{\delta} - (p^u - P)\frac{\partial x^u}{\partial m^u}\right]\rho_i - \frac{(\sigma_i - \varepsilon_{wi}^u \sigma_w)}{\alpha_i^u \gamma^u}. \tag{12.A4}$$

At an interior optimum, where $dH/dp_i = 0$, the above expression yields (12.13).

13

TAX POLICY IN THE PRESENCE OF MIGRATION AND URBAN UNEMPLOYMENT

13.1 INTRODUCTION

Two pervasive features of most LDCs are the presence of persistent urban unemployment and rural to urban migration. These phenomena are important for an analysis of taxes and prices. Any model which attempts to describe an LDC economy must at least be consistent with the presence of urban unemployment. Thus, the case is weak for an exclusive use of the neo-classical model—of the form typically exposited in public finance text-books—in which all markets clear and in which there is no unemployment.

Most models attempting to incorporate urban unemployment begin with the hypothesis that urban wages are higher than the market-clearing level. However, they do not explain why wages are high; they do not explain how wages are determined. In several earlier chapters, we described alternative mechanisms for urban wage and employment determination, and argued that taxation policies may well have an effect on wages and employment. We also illustrated how this effect, in turn, affects the analysis of taxation policies.

There is a further effect, which is a focus of concern in this and the following chapter: taxation policies may affect the nature of migration between the rural and the urban sectors. Therefore, a complete analysis of tax policy must take into account its induced effects on migration.

Taxation policies may affect migration because these policies affect the relative attractiveness of living in the rural sector versus living in the urban sector. This has immediate welfare consequences. The distribution of the population between urban and rural sectors, and between employed and unemployed urban individuals is altered by migration. Government tax revenue (or the investible surplus) is also altered because, for instance, migration affects output and consumption, and hence affects the taxes received from and subsidies paid out to workers in different groups.

The precise role that migration plays in taxation analysis obviously depends on other aspects of the economy, such as the mechanism determining wages and employment in each of the two sectors, and the nature of the productivity effects of prices and wages. Our framework is capable of accommodating a variety of hypotheses concerning each of these aspects. For brevity, however, we proceed in stages.

We begin, in Section 13.2, with a general migration equation, and then show that certain migration models which have been extensively studied in the literature can be viewed as special cases of this migration equation. For instance, various formulations of the Harris–Todaro hypothesis can be seen as special cases of our general equation. The standard neoclassical model is also a special case of our migration equation. Another advantage of this migration equation is that it allows a summary representation (in terms of certain reduced-form elasticities) of the aspects of migration which are relevant for taxation analysis.

In Section 13.3, we present an analysis of urban–rural pricing in an open economy, where we represent each sector's output as an aggregate good. This analysis can be viewed as a sequel to that in Chapter 4, where sectoral populations were assumed to be exogenously specified. For brevity, we assume in this section that urban employment is fixed, that urban wages are fixed in terms of the numeraire, and that productivity effects are negligible. Note, however, that although urban employment is assumed fixed here, the urban population (and, hence, urban unemployment) is endogenously determined.

This analysis yields a number of results. For instance, we show that, under plausible circumstances, the presence of migration is likely to increase the optimal food price in the rural as well as urban sector relative to what it would be in the absence of migration. The intuitive reasoning is as follows: A higher rural food price makes it more attractive to live in the rural sector, and a higher urban food price makes it less attractive to live in the urban sector. In either case, the net rural to urban migration is likely to decrease, and urban unemployment will be reduced. This, in turn, may increase the investible surplus because of the possibility of extracting a larger amount of tax from those who are employed than from those who are unemployed.

We conclude this chapter by providing an illustration, in Section 13.4, of how one can analyse the structure of taxation for a multitude of goods in the presence of migration. In this analysis, the urban wage and employment, as well as the urban population, are endogenously determined. We derive a condition for the Pareto-efficiency of the tax structure in the urban sector. What is noteworthy about this condition is that, though its form is similar to the Ramsey taxation formula, it is based on trade-offs which are quite different from those underlying the Ramsey-type analysis.

13.2 THE GENERAL MIGRATION RELATIONSHIP

The basic migration equation specifies how workers allocate themselves between the urban and rural sectors, depending on wages, prices, and employment opportunities in the two sectors. We write it as

$$N^r = \hat{N}^r(w^r, p^r, w^u, p^u, m^n, N^e) . \tag{13.1}$$

That is, the number of workers in the rural sector, N^r, is a function of the rural wage and prices, w^r and p^r, the urban wage and prices, w^u and p^u, the income of an unemployed urban worker, m^n, and the level of urban employment, N^e. Given any level of urban employment, N^e, and urban unemployment, N^n, and given the total population, N, the following identity holds:

$$N = N^r + N^e + N^n. \qquad (13.2)$$

It is obvious that the number of urban unemployed, N^n, can also be expressed as a function of the same set of variables as those which are the arguments on the right-hand side of (13.1).

One special case of (13.1) is that in which migration depends on the utility levels of workers in different groups. In this case, (13.1) can be restated as

$$N^r = \hat{N}^r(V^r(p^r, w^r), V^u(p^u, w^u), V^n(p^u, m^n), N^e), \qquad (13.3)$$

where V^r, V^u and V^n respectively denote the utility levels of a rural worker, an employed urban worker, and an unemployed urban worker. Another representation of (13.1), which is relevant when the rural sector consists of homogeneous self-employed farm households, is

$$N^r = \hat{N}^r(p^r, w^u, p^u, m^n, N^e). \qquad (13.4)$$

In this case the earnings and the utility level of a rural individual are determined by rural prices, p^r, and by the population of rural workers, N^r. The rural wage is suppressed because it does not play a role in a rural sector with homogeneous individuals. We will use different versions of (13.4) in the analysis below.

The Generalized Harris–Todaro Hypothesis

A formulation of the Harris–Todaro hypothesis, which, as we shall see, is more general than the conventional statement of that hypothesis, postulates that the expected utility of a potential migrant from the rural to urban sector should equal his utility in the rural sector. That is,

$$V^r(p^r, w^r) = \frac{N^e}{N - N^r} V^u(p^u, w^u) + \left(1 - \frac{N^e}{N - N^r}\right) V^n \qquad (13.5)$$

where $\dfrac{N^e}{N - N^r}$ is the probability of getting an urban job.[1]

The conventional special case. If it is assumed that prices in the two sectors are fixed and identical, that individuals exhibit risk-neutral behaviour (that is, utility is linear in income), that labour hours are fixed in each of the two sectors, and that there is no disutility from these hours of work,

---

[1] This formulation is consistent with either fixed or optimally chosen work hours in the urban sector.

then individuals' utility levels in (13.5) can be replaced by their respective earnings. Further, if it is assumed that an unemployed urban worker has zero earnings, then (13.5) becomes

$$\frac{N^e}{N - N^r} = \frac{m^r}{m^u},$$ (13.6)

where m^r and m^u denote, respectively, the income of a rural and an urban employed worker. According to (13.6), then, the urban employment rate (that is, one minus the urban unemployment rate) is the ratio of earnings of a rural worker to that of an employed urban worker. The special case (13.6) cannot be employed to asses the impact of changes in rural or urban prices on migration, because, by assumption, these prices are fixed and equal across sectors. However, model (13.6) has been extensively used in the literature. Its limitations have also been widely noted. For instance:

(*a*) If individuals can obtain urban jobs without migrating to the urban sector, then wage differences between the two sectors could be consistent with no urban unemployment.

(*b*) The risks associated with being unemployed for an extensive period may discourage many individuals from migrating. Model (13.6) assumes risk-neutrality, whereas the more general model (13.5) does not. Limitations on capital to finance travel and the initial periods of urban unemployment may also inhibit rural to urban migration.

(*c*) What is relevant for individuals' behaviour is real income, not the nominal wage. Since there are substantial inter-sectoral differences in the costs of living, these should be incorporated, as in (13.5). Account also needs to be taken of certain amenities which may be available only in the urban sector.

(*d*) An important reason why the Harris–Todaro model may overestimate urban unemployment is that it ignores the dynamic process of job acquisition. Most individuals are not hired on a daily basis. Rather, they enter the unemployment pool, remain unemployed for an extended period, and are then hired. What is relevant to a migrant, therefore, is the present discounted value of his expected future income. This depends on the number of job-seekers (new migrants) and vacancies, which in turn depends on the leaving rate and the rate of job creation.[2] Since the period of unemployment precedes the employment period, if discount rates are high, migration will appear less attractive than suggested by the Harris–Todaro formulation.

The Opportunity Cost of Urban Unemployment

One reason we are concerned with urban unemployment is the corresponding loss of production and welfare of these workers. Later analysis is based on an additive Bergson–Samuelson welfare function, defined over *ex post facto* utilities:

[2] For an analysis of models of job acquisition, and their implications for equilibrium migration, see Stiglitz (1974*a*).

$$\psi = N^r W(V^r) + N^e W(V^u) + (N - N^r - N^e) W(V^n) . \tag{13.7}$$

The social opportunity cost of urban unemployment is calculated as the aggregate social gain from a worker being in the rural sector rather than being in the pool of the urban unemployed. This gain is represented by

$$\Phi = \frac{\partial \psi}{\partial N^r} = W(V^r) - W(V^n) + N^r \frac{\partial W(V^r)}{\partial V^r} \frac{\partial V^r}{\partial N^r} . \tag{13.8}$$

In the above expression, $W(V^r) - W(V^n)$ denotes the direct welfare gain. The last term on the right-hand side of (13.8) represents the social value of the change in welfare (which we will show in this model to be negative) due to the 'congestion effect'; that is, the loss to those currently in the rural sector from there being one more worker in the rural sector.[3]

The nature of the congestion effect obviously depends on the nature of organization within the rural sector. Consider, for instance, the simple model of a rural sector consisting of self-employed homogeneous peasants in which the agricultural land released by a migrant is divided among those remaining in the rural sector. Expression (13.8), in this case, becomes

$$\Phi = W(V^r) - W(V^n) - \beta^r p^r X \varepsilon^r_{XA} , \tag{13.9}$$

where β^r is the social weight on the income in the rural sector and ε^r_{XA} is the elasticity of output with respect to per capita land.[4] Thus, the congestion effect is smaller—the opportunity cost of urban unemployment larger— the smaller is the elasticity of output with respect to land area per rural worker.

Another form of rural organization is the extended family. One model of extended families which has received attention in development economics posits that rural workers receive their average product, not their marginal product.[5] With a Cobb–Douglas production function, the ratio of the marginal to the average product is just the factor share of labour. If the share of labour is one-half, then the lost output from a migrant is only half of his

---

[3] It is assumed in (13.8), as well as in the rest of this chapter, that the utility of an unemployed urban worker is not affected by the changes under consideration. See sect. 10.7 for a discussion of this issue.

[4] Recall from (4.A2) the definition of the indirect utility level of a peasant:

$$V^r(p^r, N^r) = \max_{\{x^r, y^r, L^r\}} U^r + \lambda^r \{p^r [X(A, L^r) - x^r] - y^r\},$$

where A is the land area per rural worker. Thus, using the envelope theorem:

$$\frac{\partial V^r}{\partial N^r} = \lambda^r p^r \frac{\partial X}{\partial A} \frac{\partial A}{\partial N^r} = -\lambda^r p^r \frac{\partial X}{\partial A} \frac{A}{N^r} = -\lambda^r p^r X \varepsilon^r_{XA} / N^r,$$

where $\varepsilon^r_{XA} = \partial \ln X / \partial \ln A$. Expression (13.9) follows by substituting $\beta^r = \lambda^r \partial W(V^r)/\partial V^r$.

[5] As discussed earlier, even though there are some circumstances in which this model may be appropriate, it implies a particular set of property rights and social institutions (see sect. 8.3).

earnings. The relevant issue for determining the equivalent of expression (13.9) in this case is the nature of a migrant's property right; for example, whether a migrant to the urban sector continues receiving some support from his family. This would be the case if there is joint family decision concerning migration and the sharing of family income including the income of the migrant when he finds an urban job (see Stiglitz 1969).

Next, note that when the heterogeneity of rural workers is taken into account, the opportunity cost for the marginal migrant will, in general, exceed the opportunity cost of the average migrant. What is relevant, of course, for the migration equilibrium is the behaviour of the marginal migrant.

Finally, if individuals migrate to the urban sector during slack periods in the rural sector and return to the rural sector during harvesting and planting periods, then the social cost of observed urban unemployment may be relatively low.

13.3 RURAL–URBAN PRICES

Perhaps the easiest way to see the implications of migration on the analysis of taxation is to consider an open economy in which the output of each sector is represented as an aggregate good, and in which there is a tax border between the two sectors (that is, the government can set different prices in the two sectors). To simplify the analysis of rural–urban prices further, we assume that urban employment (but not the urban population or urban unemployment) is fixed, that the urban wage is fixed in terms of the industrial good, and that price changes do not have a significant effect on the productivity of industrial workers. The model under consideration is therefore similar to that of Chapter 4 except that now there is an explicit recognition of migration and urban unemployment.

Since there is unemployment, the social welfare function must take into account the three distinct groups in the population: those in the rural sector, the urban employed, and the urban unemployed. We thus write the social welfare function as (13.7), and the Hamiltonian as

$$H = \psi + \delta I. \tag{13.10}$$

The investible surplus is given by

$$I = N^e(Y - w^u L^u) + (P - p^r)N^r Q + (p^u - P)N^e_x x^u, \tag{13.11}$$

where it is assumed that the net tax revenue collected (or the subsidy spent) on the consumption of the urban unemployed is a negligible part of the investible surplus.

Rural Prices

The derivative of (13.7) and (13.11) with respect to p^r can be written as[6]

$$\frac{d\psi}{dp^r} = \beta^r N^r Q + \frac{1}{p^r} N^r \varepsilon^r_{Np} \Phi \quad \text{and} \tag{13.12}$$

$$\frac{dI}{dp^r} = -N^r Q + N^r Q t^r \hat{\varepsilon}^r_{Qp}, \tag{13.13}$$

where

$$t^r = (P - p^r)/p^r$$

is the tax-rate on the output of the rural sector,

$$\varepsilon^r_{Np} = \frac{\partial \ln N^r}{\partial \ln p^r}$$

is the elasticity of the rural workforce with respect to the price in the rural sector,

$$\hat{\varepsilon}^r_{Qp} = \varepsilon^r_{Qp} + (1 - \varepsilon^r_{QA}) \, \varepsilon^r_{Np} \tag{13.14}$$

is the total elasticity of the rural surplus with respect to price (taking into account the induced migration),[7]

$$\varepsilon^r_{QA} = \partial \ln Q / \partial \ln A$$

is the elasticity of per capita rural surplus with respect to the land per rural worker, and Φ is defined in (13.9).

Recall from (13.8) that Φ has the interpretation of the net gain in welfare if one unemployed individual leaves the urban sector and becomes a part of the rural sector. The effect of an increase in the rural price on the aggregate individual welfare thus consists of two parts, as shown on the right-hand side of (13.12). The first part is the direct gain to those who are already in the rural sector, and the second part is the welfare gain or loss due to migration. In the interpretations below, we shall assume that

$$\Phi > 0 \quad \text{and} \quad \varepsilon^r_{Np} > 0. \tag{13.15}$$

That is, there is a net social welfare gain if an urban unemployed migrates to the rural sector; and a higher rural food price increases the population of rural workers.[8] It then follows from (13.12) that the social welfare gain from

---

[6] A brief derivation of (13.12) and (13.13) is presented in the Appendix to this chapter. The derivation of expressions (13.20) and (13.21) below is analogous.

[7] It is straightforward to confirm that $\hat{\varepsilon}^r_{Qp} \equiv \partial \ln N^r Q(p^r, N^r)/\partial \ln p^r = \varepsilon^r_{Qp} + (1 - \varepsilon^r_{QA}) \, \varepsilon^r_{Np}$.

[8] $\Phi > 0$ follows from the assumptions that: (a) $V^u > V^r > V^n$, that is, an employed urban worker is better off than a peasant, who in turn is better off than an unemployed urban worker, and (b) ε^r_{XA} is not too large; that is, agricultural land is not too scarce. The assumption that

a rise in rural food price is larger than it would have been in the absence of migration, because this price rise leads to lower urban unemployment.

Next, note from (13.13) that for calculating the effect of a rural price change on the investible surplus, the relevant elasticity is now the price elasticity of the total agricultural surplus, $\hat{\varepsilon}^r_{Qp}$, rather than the price elasticity of the per capita agricultural surplus, ε^r_{Qp}, which was relevant for the analysis in earlier chapters. This is how it should be, because now the rural population is itself potentially sensitive to price changes. For brevity, we assume below that

$$\varepsilon^r_{QA} < 1. \tag{13.16}$$

This would be the case, for instance, if the agricultural land were not too scarce. From (13.14), (13.15), and (13.16), then, the price elasticity of the total agricultural surplus is larger than that of the per capita agricultural surplus.

Optimal Policy. Using (13.10), (13.12), and (13.13), and setting $dH/dp^r = 0$, the first-order condition for optimality with respect to rural prices is:

$$t^r = \frac{P - p^r}{p^r} = \left(1 - \frac{\beta^r}{\delta} - \frac{\Phi}{\delta}\frac{\varepsilon^r_{Np}}{p^r Q}\right)\frac{1}{\hat{\varepsilon}^r_{Qp}}. \tag{13.17}$$

Now, consider the special case in which there is no migration or, more generally, the sensitivity of migration to rural price changes is negligible. Substitution of $\varepsilon^r_{Np} = 0$ into (13.14) and (13.17) yields, as one would expect, the results of Chapter 4 (see expression (4.20)) where we abstracted from migration.

Next, we compare the optimal rural tax in the presence and absence of migration. That is, we contrast two sub-cases of expression (13.17): one in which $\varepsilon^r_{Np} > 0$ and the other in which $\varepsilon^r_{Np} = 0$. It is straightforward to verify that the effect of migration is to decrease the right-hand side of (13.17). Heuristically, this implies that: Migration decreases the level of optimal tax on the rural surplus. By paying a higher price to peasants for their surplus, the government can reduce the pressure of migration to cities and hence reduce the resulting urban unemployment which otherwise would lower society's welfare. This insight appears to be particularly relevant in the context of many LDC cities, such as Bangkok, Cairo, and Mexico City where the in-migration from the rural sector has led to serious social degradation.

$\varepsilon^r_{Np} > 0$ is automatically satisfied under many migration hypotheses including, as we shall see later, the Harris–Todaro hypothesis.

The Harris–Todaro Migration Hypothesis

A special case of the above formulation is the Harris–Todaro hypothesis discussed earlier. In this case, migration continues to the point where the expected utility of the marginal migrant (taking into account the probability of being unemployed) is equal in the two sectors. A perturbation of (13.5) with respect to N^r and p^r yields,[9] as shown in the Appendix,

$$\varepsilon^r_{Np} = \frac{(N - N^r)\,\lambda^r p^r Q}{N^r\,[V^r - V^n + \lambda^r p^r X \varepsilon^r_{XA}\,(N - N^r)/N^r]}.\qquad(13.18)$$

Substitution of (13.18) into (13.17) yields the corresponding optimal tax.

Another, perhaps more useful, way to look at the Harris–Todaro special case is as follows. Assume for simplicity that the social welfare function is utilitarian, that is $W(V) \equiv V$, and $\beta^i = \lambda^i$. From (13.5) and (13.7), then, the main implication of the Harris–Todaro hypothesis is that

$$\psi = NV^r.\qquad(13.19)$$

That is, social welfare maximization in this case is equivalent to maximizing the welfare of a rural worker. Thus, the corresponding results also hold for any other migration mechanism, and in all circumstances in which the government is concerned solely with the rural welfare.

If we further assume that the scarcity of agricultural land is not significant (that is, $\varepsilon^r_{XA} \approx 0$), then the substitution of (13.18) into (13.17) yields:

$$t^r = \left(1 - \frac{N\lambda^r}{N^r\delta}\right)\frac{1}{\hat{\varepsilon}^r_{Qp}}.$$

This expression has an interesting implication. In the early stages of development, when the relative social weight on investment, δ/λ^r, is expected to be large and when the fraction of the population in the agricultural sector is expected to be large, there should be a tax on the rural surplus. The price paid to peasants should be less than the international price. However, as the economy develops, the price paid to peasants should increase, and it is quite possible that it should even exceed the international price.[10]

Urban Prices

The derivatives of (13.7) and (13.11) with respect to p^u are:

$$\frac{d\psi}{dp^u} = -\beta^u N^e x^u + \frac{1}{p^u}\,N^r \varepsilon^u_{Np}\,\Phi \quad \text{and}\qquad(13.20)$$

[9] As we noted in establishing the sign of Φ in (13.15), ε^r_{Np} is positive under the Harris–Todaro hypothesis.

[10] Note also that the rules of price reform derived earlier, in ch. 4, apply with some modifications to the present case as well. The primary modification is that the relevant elasticity is now $\hat{\varepsilon}^r_{Qp}$ and not ε^r_{Qp}.

$$\frac{dI}{dp^u} = N^e x^u + N^e x^u t^u \varepsilon^u_{xp} + (P - p^r)(1 - \varepsilon^r_{QA}) \frac{N^r Q}{p^u} \varepsilon^u_{Np}, \qquad (13.21)$$

where

$$t^u = (P - p^u)/p^u \quad \text{and} \quad \varepsilon^u_{Np} = \frac{\partial \ln N^r}{\partial \ln p^r}.$$

For brevity in interpretation we assume that

$$\varepsilon^u_{Np} > 0; \qquad (13.22)$$

that is, the rural population increases if urban prices have increased and hence living in the urban sector has become relatively less attractive.[11] It is clear from the right-hand side of (13.20) that, as in models without migration, an urban food price rise lowers the welfare of those in the urban sector. In addition, however, there is a welfare gain because of the migration of some of the urban unemployed to the rural sector. The latter effect of migration is captured in the last term on the right-hand side of (13.20).

Next we consider the response of the investible surplus to an increase in the urban food price. The effect of migration in this case is captured by the last term on the right-hand side of (13.21). In the presence of migration, an increase in the urban food price leads to an increase in the investible surplus if the rural food surplus is being taxed; that is, if the rural food price is lower than the international food price.[12] This is because migrants to the rural sector increase the rural output and hence the tax revenue derived from the rural sector.

Optimal Policy. Using (13.10), (13.20), and (13.21), and setting $dH/dp^u = 0$, we obtain the following characterization of the optimal urban tax-rate:

$$t^u = \frac{P - p^u}{p^u}$$

$$= -\left[\left(1 - \frac{\beta^u}{\delta}\right) + \left(\frac{\Phi}{\delta} + (P - p^r)(1 - \varepsilon^r_{QA})Q\right)\frac{N^r}{N^e p^u x^u} \varepsilon^u_{Np}\right]\frac{1}{\varepsilon^u_{xp}}. \qquad (13.23)$$

Note that when migration effects are negligible (that is, when ε^u_{Np} is close to zero) then, as one would expect, the above expression reduces to the familiar case of no migration, i.e. to expression (4.20′) in Chapter 4.

Next assume that the social weight on the investible surplus is no smaller than the social weights on consumption, that is, $\delta \geq \beta^r$ and $\delta \geq \beta^u$. Then under a set of plausible assumptions, we showed earlier that the likely effect

---

[11] This assumption is automatically satisfied under the Harris–Todaro hypothesis, as can be verified from (13.5).
[12] Here we are assuming that $\varepsilon^r_{QA} < 1$, as was assumed in (13.16).

of migration would be to raise the optimal food price in the rural sector. Under the same assumptions it can be established[13] that

$$\frac{\Phi}{\delta} + (P - p^r)(1 - \varepsilon^r_{QA})Q > 0. \tag{13.24}$$

From (13.23), therefore: (*a*) The likely effect of migration is to increase the optimal food price in the urban sector, and (*b*) the optimal food price in the urban sector exceeds the international food price, regardless of whether migration is or is not significant.

Related Issues

We rewrite the Hamiltonian (13.10) as a function of urban and rural prices, and of the number of individuals in the rural sector:

$$H = H(p^r, p^u; N^r). \tag{13.25}$$

For simplicity, we continue with the assumption that urban employment is fixed and that the urban wage is fixed in terms of the industrial good. Then

$$\frac{\mathrm{d}H}{\mathrm{d}p^i} = \frac{\partial H}{\partial p^i} + \frac{\partial H}{\partial N^r}\frac{\partial N^r}{\partial p^i}, \quad \text{for} \quad i = r \text{ and } i = u. \tag{13.26}$$

Obviously, migration has no effect on the optimal value of p^i if prices have no effect on migration.

It is clear from our migration equation that prices will in general have an effect on migration: an increase in the urban or the rural price typically reduces migration from the rural to the urban sector. Expression (13.5) provides a concrete example of such price effects. For instance, (13.18) is the percentage change in the rural population due to a percentage change in the rural price, if migration hypothesis (13.5) holds.

One might argue that migration effects can be ignored in taxation analysis because, at the margin, an individual fully internalizes all the costs and benefits of migration. To look at this issue, we can use (13.10) and (13.11) to calculate the effect of migration on social welfare:

$$\frac{\mathrm{d}H}{\mathrm{d}N^r} = \Phi + \delta (P - p^r)Q(1 - \varepsilon^r_{QA}). \tag{13.27}$$

It is clear that, in making migration decisions, individuals ignore the effect of those decisions on tax revenue; that is, the second term on the right-hand side of (13.27).

However, even in the absence of taxes, Φ will not, in general, be zero. First, even if families make migration decisions collectively, the family welfare function need not coincide with the social welfare function. Second,

---

[13] The inequality in (13.24) can be established by substituting (13.17) into the left-hand side of (13.24), and then using (13.15), (13.16), and the assumption $\delta \geq \beta^r$.

even if the two did coincide, each family would ignore the effect that its decisions had on the likelihood of members of other families obtaining a job. This is a standard search externality. Third, in many situations, migration decisions are not made by the family collectively, but by individuals. They are likely to ignore the congestion effect (that, as they leave, those remaining in the rural sector may become better off). Moreover, in many societies, those who leave the rural sector lose their claims on rents within the rural sector. On the other hand, in societies where the marginal migrant is a landless worker, and in which the congestion effect is small, the search externality is likely to be important. In each case, therefore, the effects represented by expressions such as (13.27) cannot be ignored in taxation analysis.

13.4 PARETO-EFFICIENT URBAN TAXES ON DIFFERENT GOODS

It is conceptually straightforward to study the implications of migration on the analysis of taxation in models which are more disaggregated than those discussed above. We therefore conclude this chapter with an illustration of how one can analyse the urban structure of taxation of a multitude of goods (instead of the two aggregate goods represented in the preceding model) in the presence of migration. At the same time, we show how one can easily incorporate the induced effects on urban wage and employment. We consider a special case, but a central one, in which the utility level of urban workers is fixed. The focus here is on deriving a set of criteria which urban taxes must satisfy if they are to be Pareto-efficient.

The analysis below can be seen as an extension of Chapter 12 to the case in which the size of the urban population is endogenous. We again obtain a Ramsey-like formula, but it is based on principles quite different from those employed in the conventional analysis. We begin by abstracting from productivity effects, but they are incorporated later.

Urban wage-determination. We assume that the urban wage adjusts to keep the utility level of urban workers fixed. That is, an increase in the urban price of good i leads to a wage change according to

$$\frac{\mathrm{d}w^u}{\mathrm{d}p_i^u} = \frac{x_i^u}{L^u}. \tag{13.28}$$

Migration. We assume that migration depends on the number of urban jobs and on the individuals' utility levels in the two sectors.[14] That is

$$N^r = N^r [V^r(p^r, N^r), V^u(p^u, w^u), N^e]. \tag{13.29}$$

---

[14] We maintain the assumption that the utility level of an unemployed urban worker is not significantly sensitive to the perturbations under consideration.

This representation of migration is not particularly restrictive. The Harris–Todaro hypothesis, (13.5), can be shown to be a special case of expression (13.29).

Urban employment. We posit that the level of urban employment is potentially sensitive to the urban wage. That is

$$N^e = N^e(w^u), \quad \frac{\partial N^e}{\partial w^u} \leq 0. \tag{13.30}$$

Expression (13.30) is consistent with the case in which profit-maximizing private firms (which reinvest all profits) bargain with trade unions who require that the utility level of an employed urban worker be kept unchanged if there is a change in prices. This formulation is also consistent with the case in which public-sector managers are instructed to be sensitive to the wage-level when setting the level of public-sector employment. From (13.28), (13.29), and (13.30), therefore, the level of the urban wage as well as employment is endogenously determined.

Pareto-efficient taxes. Now, suppose the urban price of good i is increased by Δp_i^u, and that of good j is increased by Δp_j^u, such that the overall effect of these two perturbations leaves the urban wage unchanged. Recalling the wage-determination rule (13.28), it follows that

$$\Delta p_i^u / \Delta p_j^u = -x_j^u / x_i^u. \tag{13.31}$$

Next, since the urban wage is unchanged, expression (13.30) implies that the level of urban employment is unchanged. This, in turn, means from (13.29) that population levels in the two sectors as well as utility levels of workers in the two sectors remain unaltered by a perturbation satisfying (13.31). Thus, the economy is unambiguously worse off if the investible surplus, I, is not maximized with respect to all perturbations satisfying (13.31). Using expression (13.11) for the investible surplus, it is easy to verify that such a maximization yields:

$$\sum_j t_j^u \, e_{ij}^u \text{ is the same for all } i. \tag{13.32}$$

In (13.32), $t_j^u = (P_j - p_j^u)/p_j^u$ denotes the rates of subsidy or taxes, and

$$e_{ij}^u = - \left. \frac{\partial \ln x_i^u}{\partial \ln p_j^u} \right|_{\text{utility}} \tag{13.33}$$

denotes the compensated price elasticities (see the Appendix for a derivation of (13.32) and of (13.34) presented below).

As discussed in Chapter 12, $-\sum_j t_j \, e_{ij}^u$ represents the proportional change (due to taxes and subsidies) in the compensated demand of good i. Thus, according to (13.32), this proportional change should be the same for all commodities. This result represents a condition for Pareto-efficiency. It is obviously based on considerations altogether different from those emphasized in the traditional literature (these considerations were noted in Chapter 12).

Productivity effects. In deriving (13.32) we abstracted from productivity effects but these effects are easily incorporated. In particular, expression (13.32) continues to hold if productivity depends on the utility level of urban workers. In the more general case of productivity effects (13.32) is modified to:

$$-\sum_j t_j^u e_{ij}^u + \frac{\sigma_i - \alpha_i^u \sigma_w}{\alpha_i^u \gamma^u} \quad \text{is the same for all } i. \tag{13.34}$$

The additional term in the above expression represents the productivity effects.

Finally, consider a special case in which the level of urban employment is not sensitive to the urban wage. It is clear then that a change in urban prices affects neither the welfare levels nor the numbers of workers in different groups. The analysis of urban taxation is therefore the same as that in the part of Section 12.2, where we abstracted from migration effects and assumed that the urban wage is fixed in terms of the utility level. In this case, in the absence of productivity effects, the most desirable way to provide any given level of utility to urban workers, is to do so at international prices. Correspondingly, taxation or subsidization of goods in the urban sector is undesirable.

13.5 CONCLUDING REMARKS

This chapter's analysis has shown how tax and pricing policies affect migration, and how migration affects the level of welfare of those remaining in the rural sector, and the urban wage and employment rate. It has also shown how our earlier analyses of taxation can easily be modified to take into account migration and its consequences.

We described how the reduced-form elasticities (for instance of the rural surplus to the rural price), which are critical for taxation analysis, are easily modified to take account of the induced migration. The rural surplus elasticity, for instance, is likely to be higher because of migration. Higher rural prices not only increase the surplus per rural worker, but also increase the number of rural workers.

In many LDCs high urban unemployment remains an important problem. Tax policy therefore may need to reflect the role that these instruments can play in reducing rural–urban migration. Higher rural and urban prices can typically serve to reduce urban unemployment. We have shown how to incorporate these effects into taxation analysis.

Governments are concerned about unemployment, both because of the opportunity cost of the labour (the forgone output) and because of the political unrest to which unemployment often gives rise. Our analysis has focused only on the former. If the government has a further, direct reason for avoiding urban unemployment, it may wish to set both rural and urban prices higher than our analysis has suggested.

Finally, we have undertaken a disaggregated analysis of urban taxation of various goods. We obtained some criteria that urban taxes or subsidies need to satisfy if they are to be Pareto-efficient. This result takes into account the induced effects of taxes on migration, the urban wage, and urban employment. It appears similar to the multi-good Ramsey tax result, but is based on considerations altogether different from those of Ramsey-type analyses.

APPENDIX

Derivation of (13.12)

The derivative of (13.7) with respect to p^r is

$$\frac{d\psi}{dp^r} = N^r \frac{\partial W(V^r)}{\partial V^r} \frac{\partial V^r}{\partial p^r} + \frac{\partial N^r}{\partial p^r} \frac{\partial \psi}{\partial N^r}. \tag{13.A1}$$

Recall that $\partial V^r/\partial p^r = \lambda^r Q$ and $\beta^r = \lambda^r \partial W(V^r)/\partial V^r$. Thus, substituting (13.8) and (13.9) into (13.A1), we obtain (13.12).

Derivation of (13.13)

The derivative of (13.11) with respect to p^r, keeping N^e unchanged, is

$$\frac{dI}{dp^r} = -N^r Q + (P - p^r) \left[N^r \frac{\partial Q}{\partial p^r} + \left(Q + N^r \frac{\partial Q}{\partial A} \frac{\partial A}{\partial N^r} \right) \frac{\partial N^r}{\partial p^r} \right]$$

$$= -N^r Q + \frac{(P - p^r)}{p^r} N^r Q \left\{ \frac{\partial \ln Q}{\partial \ln p^r} + \left(1 - \frac{\partial \ln Q}{\partial \ln A} \right) \frac{d \ln N^r}{d \ln p^r} \right\}. \tag{13.A2}$$

We have substituted $\partial A/\partial N^r = -A/N^r$ in deriving the last step of (13.A2). Now, a substitution of (13.14) and of the definitions of t^r and the elasticities into (13.A2) yields (13.13).

Derivation of (13.18)

Multiply both sides of (13.5) by $(N - N^r)$. The derivative of the resulting expression with respect to p^r is

$$-(V^r - V^n) \frac{dN^r}{dp^r} + (N - N^r) \frac{\partial V^r}{\partial N^r} \frac{dN^r}{dp^r} + (N - N^r) \frac{\partial V^r}{\partial p^r} = 0. \tag{13.A3}$$

From n. 4, $\partial V^r/\partial N^r = -\lambda^r p^r X \varepsilon^r_{XA}/N^r$. Substituting this into (13.A3), we obtain

$$\frac{dN^r}{dp^r} = \frac{(N - N^r) \lambda^r Q}{[V^r - V^n + \lambda^r p^r X \varepsilon^r_{XA}(N - N^r)/N^r]}. \tag{13.A4}$$

(13.18) follows from (13.*A*4) and the definition $\varepsilon^r_{Np} = \partial \ln N^r / \partial \ln p^r$.

Derivation of (13.32) and (13.34)

Taking productivity effects into account, the derivative of (13.11) with respect to p^u_i is

$$\frac{dI}{dp^u_i} = N^e\left[\frac{\partial Y}{\partial p^u_i} + \frac{\partial Y}{\partial w^u}\frac{dw^u}{dp^u_i} - L^u\frac{dw^u}{dp^u_i} - (P - p^u)\frac{\partial x^u}{\partial p^u_i}\bigg|_{\text{utility}} + x^u_i\right]. \quad (13.A5)$$

Note that the derivative of x^u on the right-hand side of (13.*A*5) is at a fixed utility level because a price change leaves an urban worker's utility unchanged. Using the Slutsky symmetry property,

$$(P - p^u)\frac{\partial x^u}{\partial p^u_i}\bigg|_{\text{utility}} = \Sigma_j \frac{(P_j - p^u_j)}{p^u_j} p^u_j \frac{\partial x^u_j}{\partial p^u_i}\bigg|_{\text{utility}} = \Sigma_j t^u_j p^u_j \frac{\partial x^u_i}{\partial p^u_j}\bigg|_{\text{utility}}$$

$$= -x^u_i \Sigma_j t^u_j e^u_{ij}.$$

Recall the notation $\sigma_i = -\partial \ln Y / \partial p^u_i$, $\sigma_w = \partial \ln Y / \partial \ln w^u$, $\alpha^u_i = p^u_i x^u_i / w^u L^u$, $\gamma^u = w^u L^u / Y$. Substituting these and (13.28) into (13.*A*5) we obtain

$$\frac{dI}{dp^u_i} = -N^e x^u_i\left[-\Sigma_j t_j e^u_{ij} + \frac{(\sigma_i - \alpha^u_i \sigma_w)}{\alpha^u_i \gamma^u}\right]. \quad (13.A6)$$

Now, recall that the individual's welfare remains unchanged if p^u_i and p^u_j are changed according to (13.31). The maximization of H thus requires that dI/dp^u_i be proportional to x^u_i for all i. From (13.*A*6) therefore, the expression in the square bracket on the right-hand side of (13.*A*6) should be the same for all i. This yields (13.34). A special case of this, when productivity effects are negligible (that is, $\sigma_i \approx 0$ and $\sigma_w \approx 0$), is (13.32).

14

TAXATION IN THE URBAN SECTOR: SOME ASPECTS OF THE UNDERLYING MODEL

14.1 INTRODUCTION

A basic difference between this book and much of the earlier public finance literature is that the latter typically focuses on analysing public finance policies using conventional neoclassical models, whereas our task has been two-fold: to develop a class of analytical models for LDCs; and using these models as the settings, to analyse the positive and normative aspects of taxation and pricing policies.

The reason behind this approach is quite simple. LDCs display a wide variety of economic characteristics. Thus, even if it were the case that a particular LDC approximated to the conventional neoclassical model (which we seriously doubt), this model could not be a good approximation of other LDCs with widely different characteristics. In addition, the conventional neo-classical model is inconsistent with some of the stylized facts of most LDCs, such as urban unemployment. Moreover, the conventional neoclassical paradigm cannot explain or deal with a variety of economic organizations which are observed in practice, particularly in the rural sectors of LDCs.

Our approach to developing models of LDCs has been to begin with simpler models, and then gradually to introduce features (often, but not always, one at a time) which impart greater richness and realism. For instance, in Part II of the book we abstracted from the effects of taxes on rural and urban wages (it was assumed that wages were fixed in terms of the numeraire good), on the employment levels in the two sectors, and on migration between the two sectors (however, we did show, in the last part of Chapter 4, how to take account of productivity effects). In Part III the focus was on the structure of rural taxes on different (disaggregated) goods and on the role of individuals' heterogeneity and inequality within the rural sector (including alternative forms of rural organizations). Here we also developed and incorporated a model of rural wage-determination. Part IV examined some of the crucial features of the urban sector of modern-day LDCs; namely, urban unemployment, rural to urban migration, and the sensitivity of the urban wage to prices. Our earlier analysis assumed fixed wages, fixed employment, and a fixed urban population. These assumptions were removed in Chapters 10, 12, and 13. Chapter 12 demonstrated further how the analysis could be extended to study the structure of taxes and subsidies on a multitude of goods.

There are three reasons why we have followed the approach of constructing successively more complicated models, rather than the opposite approach in which one begins with a very general model and then presents a number of special cases. First, we believe our approach is more intuitive because basic economic considerations (such as the role of individuals' responses, the role of demand and supply responses, the role of social weights on different individuals' incomes, and the consequences of the government's ability or inability to tax different sectors differently) are best understood in the simplest possible models. Second, each extension focuses on a specific phenomenon (e.g. urban wage-determination, rural or urban employment determination, and the inter-sectoral migration of workers) while keeping the background model simple. It therefore becomes possible to isolate the effects (as well as to evaluate the importance) of the particular phenomenon on the positive and normative analysis of taxation policies. Subsequently, when different phenomena are studied together, it becomes possible to identify easily their individual effects as well as the effects which arise from interactions among them. Third, a task of the present book has been to deal with the wide variety of economic characteristics observed across LDCs. This was done by emphasizing different aspects in different sub-classes of models. For example, the simple models of Chapters 6 and 7 were meant to capture the central aspects of the Soviet industrialization debate, whereas Chapter 8 was aimed at analysing controversial issues facing today's non-socialist LDCs, such as the effect of taxation policies on rural income distribution.

In this chapter, we discuss some aspects of modelling the urban sector of today's LDCs, aspects that are central for taxation analysis. These aspects have typically been underemphasized in development economics. We consider an economy in which private firms make the decisions concerning the urban wage and employment, and individuals migrate from one sector to another. The objective here is not to derive results concerning taxation but instead to highlight briefly some issues that need to be taken into account in taxation analysis for the urban sector of LDCs.

The model is presented in the next section. In Section 14.3, we describe the inefficiencies which arise in the market equilibrium, and the role of taxes in partially correcting these inefficiencies. The chapter concludes with a brief discussion of the relationship between the urban demand and supply of labour; this relationship is different from that in the conventional neoclassical model.

14.2 A GENERAL MODEL OF THE URBAN SECTOR

The following three equations are central in determining the equilibrium in the urban sector:

$$w^u = \hat{w}^u \ (N^u, N^e, p^r, p^u):$$ the wage determination equation, $\qquad$ (14.1)

$$N^u = \hat{N}^u \ (w^u, N^e, p^r, p^u):$$ the migration equation, $\qquad$ (14.2)

$$N^e = \hat{N}^e \ (w^u, N^u, p^r, p^u):$$ the employment equation. $\qquad$ (14.3)

As before, w^u denotes the urban wage, N^e is urban employment and N^u is urban population. Thus, $N^n = N^u - N^e$ is the population of the urban unemployed and $n = N^n/N^u$ is the urban unemployment rate. These equations hold, and the equilibrium can be solved for, at any given set of prices, p^r and p^u. When prices change, say as a result of taxation policy, these equations determine the relevant changes in urban wages and in urban employment and unemployment. Incorporating these effects of taxation has been one of the tasks of the preceding chapters.

The following features of this set of equations are perhaps worth noting. First, we have not introduced the rural wage, w^r, as an argument of the functions on the right-hand side of (14.1) to (14.3). The underlying model of the rural sector here is a simple one; namely, a rural sector consisting of homogeneous land-owning farmers. If other models of the rural sector (analysed in Chapters 6, 8, and 9) were used, then we would need to include the rural wage and rural employment in equations (14.1) to (14.3). Further, in such models the rural wage cannot be treated as an exogenous parameter; we need to specify the rural wage-determination mechanism. In general, we expect the rural wage to depend on the number of rural workers (this number is $N^r = N - N^e - N^n$, where N is the total working population in the economy), and the rural price, p^r. This aspect of the dependence of the rural wage on N^r and p^r is thus accounted for in equations (14.1) to (14.3). In addition, the rural wage (or, what is more relevant for migration, the real income of the marginal migrant if he stayed in the rural sector) will depend on the distribution of rural land, and on other features of the rural sector such as the mix of organizational forms (e.g. extended family, share-cropping, etc.). These aspects are taken as given.

Second, equations (14.1) to (14.3) are in reduced form. For instance, the wage equation (14.1), partly discussed in Chapter 10, asserts that the equilibrium urban wage is a function of the number of workers in the urban sector and the number of employed individuals in the urban sector. The wage may, in addition, be a function of the unemployment rate, n, but this is a function, in turn, of N^e and N^u. Similarly, the urban labour population, N^u, may be a function of the level of utilities in the urban and rural sectors as well as the probability of getting an urban job. Each of these is, in turn, determined by variables w^u, N^e, and N^u.[1] Likewise, urban employment may be determined by urban wages and productivity. These, in turn, can be related to the wage and unemployment rates and, hence, to w^u, N^e, and N^u.

---

[1] The migration equation is discussed more fully in ch. 13.

Third, equations (14.1) to (14.3) are consistent with a variety of alternative hypotheses concerning the behaviour of economic agents. For example, the wage equation and employment equation, (14.1) and (14.3) respectively, may arise as a result of firms' setting wages taking into account the wage–productivity effects (these were analysed in Chapter 11). Alternatively, wages (and hence, the number of urban employed) may be determined through bargaining between firms and worker unions. Similarly, the migration equation, (14.2), can be specialized to a Harris–Todaro model in which the marginal migrant compares his expected utility in the two sectors.

Fourth, the equation system (14.1) to (14.3) is, in general, a sub-system of a more complete description of the economy. For instance, the market-clearing equations for non-traded goods will involve variables such as w^u, N^u, and N^e. In turn, the prices of non-traded goods will appear as arguments of the equation system under consideration. These interrelations were discussed in earlier chapters (for instance, in Chapter 6). At present, we abstract from them.

Finally, the equation system (14.1) to (14.3) can easily be generalized to different categories of urban workers (e.g. skilled and unskilled), each with different levels of unemployment. Moreover, workers who belong to the same category in one sector may belong to different categories in another sector (for example, small differences in education may be much more important for workers' earnings in the urban sector than in the rural sector). In such cases, it is the behaviour of different types of marginal migrants which will be depicted by the corresponding migration equations.

Solving the reduced-form wage, migration, and employment equations, (14.1) to (14.3), we obtain expressions for wages, employment, and migration as functions of urban and rural prices:

$$w^u = w^u(p^r, p^u) \tag{14.4}$$
$$N^u = N^u(p^r, p^u) \tag{14.5}$$
$$N^e = N^e(p^r, p^u). \tag{14.6}$$

The Analysis of Taxation

As shown in previous chapters, for a rural sector consisting of homogeneous land-owning peasants, we can write the welfare of a rural individual as a function of the rural price and the number of rural workers:

$$V^r = V^r(p^r, N^r). \tag{14.7}$$

Similarly, the welfare of the representative employed worker in the urban sector is a function of the urban wage and the urban price:

$$V^u = V^u(p^u, w^u). \tag{14.8}$$

The above specifications, (14.7) and (14.8), also allow us to calculate the impact of tax changes on the consumption of a rural worker and an employed urban worker. These calculations are important in ascertaining the impact of tax changes on the investible surplus. The tax revenue received by the government, or the subsidy it pays, depends on the consumption basket of the individuals in the economy.

As discussed in Chapter 10, the description of the utility level of an unemployed urban individual is not easy, because it depends critically on the nature of private transfers to the urban unemployed from those employed in the rural and urban sectors. As a first approximation, however, we assume that this utility level is unaffected by the changes in tax policy under consideration. That is,

$$\frac{\partial V^n}{\partial p^i} \approx 0, \text{ for } i = r \text{ and } i = u. \tag{14.9}$$

Correspondingly, we assume that the tax paid by an unemployed urban individual, or the subsidy received, is unaffected by the tax changes under consideration.

The investible surplus is a function of the rural price, the urban price, the number of individuals in the rural sector, the level of urban employment, and the urban wage:

$$I = I(p^u, p^r; w^u, N^r, N^e). \tag{14.10}$$

Expressions (14.4) to (14.10) form a basis for positive analysis; that is, for examining the qualitative nature of changes in V^r, V^u and I when p^r and p^u change. These expressions also form a basis for identifying Pareto-improving tax reforms; that is, tax reforms which do not lower V^r, V^u, or I, and increase at least one of these variables. As a corollary to this reform analysis, we derive properties of Pareto-efficient taxation; that is, the properties that a set of taxes must satisfy if there are no available Pareto-improving reforms in taxes.

Finally, the social welfare function provides a method for aggregating the welfare of different sets of individuals. This aggregated welfare plus the social value of the investible surplus is represented by the Hamiltonian

$$H = H(p^u, p^r; w^u, N^r, N^e). \tag{14.11}$$

Substituting (14.4) to (14.6) into (14.11), we can express social welfare as a function of urban and rural prices. By differentiating with respect to the prices, we obtain the conditions for the optimality of taxes, taking into account the effect of price changes on urban wages, employment, and migration. They are the solutions to the pair of equations

$$\frac{dH}{dp^i} = \frac{\partial H}{\partial p^i} + \frac{\partial H}{\partial N^e} \frac{\partial N^e}{\partial p^i} + \frac{\partial H}{\partial w^u} \frac{\partial w^u}{\partial p^i} + \frac{\partial H}{\partial N^u} \frac{\partial N^u}{\partial p^i} = 0,$$

$$i = r \text{ and } i = u. \tag{14.12}$$

It should be apparent that qualitative insights are unlikely to be obtained, for either positive or normative taxation analysis, at the level of generality at which expressions (14.4) to (14.11) are written. It becomes useful, therefore, to specify particular salient features of the rural and urban sectors, and particular hypotheses concerning migration and concerning the determination of urban wages and employment. We have used a variety of such specifications in previous chapters to obtain many insights.

14.3 INEFFICIENCY OF MARKET EQUILIBRIUM

As we highlighted in several of the previous chapters, there are a number of reasons why inefficiencies may exist in the market equilibrium that arises in typical LDCs. The simplest and perhaps the most common case is one in which, though the economy is otherwise mostly competitive, firms set the urban wage through a process of bargaining with a trade union. In this case, wages are set by the firms without taking into account the externality for the rest of the economy, in particular, for unemployed workers.

Similarly, externalities arise if, for wage–productivity reasons, firms set the urban wage at a level higher than the market-clearing level. For instance, in making employment decisions, private firms may fail to take into account the induced changes in migration and, hence, in urban unemployment. On the other hand, they may also fail to take into account the effect of increased unemployment on the productivity of workers.

Moreover, inefficiencies arise in firms' employment and wage decisions not only because the wage incorrectly measures the opportunity cost of labour, but also because firms fail to take into account a broad range of pecuniary externalities which their employment and wage decisions have on other firms. For example, in paying higher wages, firms often see themselves as recruiting more able workers away from other firms. These gains may not, however, be social gains. Efficient labour allocation would allocate workers to jobs at which they have a comparative advantage. The wage-setting policies of private firms do not necessarily ensure this. For example, those with a comparative advantage in agriculture are not necessarily sorted to remain in the rural sector. Similarly, paying higher wages may have deleterious effects on other firms' labour turnover and the efforts exerted by workers in other firms. The worker's cost of being dismissed by another firm may be reduced if his opportunities have been improved. This may lead firms to pay too high a wage.

Finally, note that these are not the only sources of inefficiency in a market economy. As discussed in Part II of the book, a variety of organizational forms exist (such as the extended family, share-cropping, and property rights that someone who has migrated to the urban sector has on a part of his family's income in the rural sector), which entail inefficiencies. Obviously, the fact that the market equilibrium is inefficient in some ways does not mean that such organizational forms and institutional arrangements do not have some economic rationale.

One role that taxes and subsidies play in such environments is partially to correct such inefficiencies. Our earlier analysis attempted to identify this role in different circumstances. In Chapter 8, for instance, we showed the extra considerations that arise in taxation analysis due to the disincentives that are a part of the share-cropping arrangement. Similarly, in Chapters 10, 12, and 13, we noted the productivity effects that need to be taken into account in taxation analysis when these effects are not fully internalized by firms.

These inefficiencies would not be an issue in taxation analysis if the government possessed instruments which could directly eliminate them. This, however, is not an appropriate assumption in the context of LDCs. An example is the inefficiency that might arise in the wage and employment decisions of firms. In this case, there are two choices that firms make—concerning the wages they pay and the number of workers they hire. If the government can implement two wage taxes (an *ad valorem* as well as a specific wage tax or subsidy), then it can alter the wages that are relevant for the firms' two decisions. The government may attempt therefore to remove the corresponding inefficiencies which would otherwise arise. However, for reasons described in Section 10.5, such wage taxes are unlikely to be available in LDCs.

Furthermore, our analysis has assumed that all labour is identical, or that, if there are differences, firms cannot identify who is more able, who is less able, other than by their willingness to work at a given wage. In reality, there is a wide variety of categories of workers. Corrective wage taxation requires two wage taxes for each category of workers. If the government does not differentiate the treatment of workers of different types, wage taxes and subsidies will distort the mix of workers hired by firms. For example, a specific wage subsidy may encourage hiring more low-quality workers, substituting quantity for quality. Thus, heterogeneity further reduces the government's ability to implement fully corrective taxes and subsidies.

14.4 INTERDEPENDENCE OF DEMAND AND SUPPLY OF URBAN LABOUR

Finally, we describe an aspect of our model of the urban sector which is particularly different from the conventional neoclassical model. Though this aspect is incorporated in the analysis of taxation presented in Chapter 13, we discuss it here because it may not be fully apparent.

In the conventional neoclassical model, a firm takes the wage as parametrically specified, and chooses its level of labour demand. In the present set-up, on the other hand, a firm chooses the wage-level as well as the labour demand. Moreover, it is apparent from (14.3) that even when the urban wage is fixed, urban employment may depend on the number of individuals in the urban sector (that is, on the urban labour supply). On the other hand, from (14.2), the urban population may depend on the level of urban employment. It should also be apparent that (14.2) may be viewed as an 'urban labour supply equation' and (14.3) as an 'urban labour demand equation'.

To see the resulting implication for the relationship between the demand and supply of labour, we consider the case in which the urban wage, w^u, and the urban and rural prices, p^u and p^r, are fixed. The issue emphasized here, however, is general, and it remains present even when the urban wage is endogenous, or when prices are changed as a part of the taxation policy. Figure 14.1 shows the case in which urban labour demand, N^e, does not depend on the urban population, N^u. This is the case, for instance, if the urban wage is set by nutritional considerations, and if there are no transfer payments from the employed to the unemployed (because, then, productivity does not depend on the employment level). The demand curve for labour, accordingly, does not depend on the supply of labour. It is a horizontal line (shown as the solid horizontal line in Fig. 14.1). The supply (from the migration equation (14.2)), on the other hand, is an increasing function of demand (shown as the solid curved line). The equilibrium is at the intersection of the two curves. The horizontal gap between the 45° line and the point of intersection between the demand and supply curves represents the level of unemployment.

The same outcome occurs in the following situation. Suppose an increase in the urban labour supply leads to an increase in productivity (for example, because the unemployment rate rises and the increase in the perceived loss from unemployment lowers turnover rates and shirking) and a decrease in the cost of an efficiency unit of labour. This will cause an increase in the demand for efficiency units of labour. Whether this leads to an increase or a decrease in the number of workers demanded depends on the elasticity of demand for labour in efficiency units with respect to the cost of such labour. If this elasticity is unitary, a lowering of the cost of labour per efficiency unit by 1 per cent increases the demand for labour, in efficiency units, by 1 per cent. Thus the number of workers demanded is unchanged.

In Fig. 14.2, the cost elasticity of the demand for labour in efficiency units is less than unitary. Thus, the greater productivity resulting from increased unemployment actually results in a lower level of employment. Such would be the case, for instance, if there were no substitutability between capital and efficiency-labour units (L-shaped isoquants); with a given capital capacity, an increase in productivity would (in the short run) simply lead to a proportionate decrease in employment.

In Fig. 14.3, the relevant demand elasticity is greater than unitary. The greater productivity resulting from increased unemployment results in a

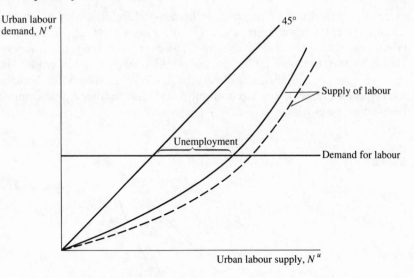

FIG. 14.1 URBAN LABOUR DEMAND AND SUPPLY.
The case in which the demand does not depend on the urban population.

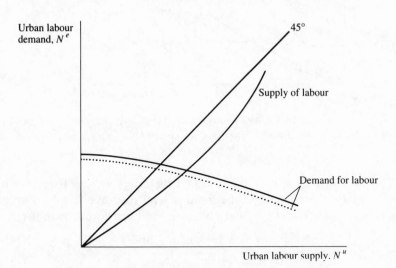

FIG. 14.2 URBAN LABOUR DEMAND AND SUPPLY.
The case in which the cost elasticity of labour demand in efficiency units is less than one.

more than proportionate increase in the demand for efficiency units; as the unemployment rate increases, the demand for labour actually increases (the labour turnover model described in Chapter 11 can have this property). Hence, as the supply of labour increases, the demand may increase. There may be multiple equilibria, as illustrated in Fig. 14.3. There can be a low-level equilibrium, with low urban employment, and another equilibrium with high urban employment.

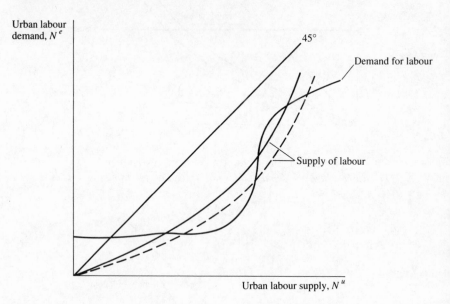

FIG. 14.3 URBAN LABOUR DEMAND AND SUPPLY.
The case in which the cost elasticity of labour demand in efficiency units is more than one.

The preceding discussion assumed that the urban wage is fixed, but it is easy to adapt the analysis to the more general case. We simply substitute (14.1) into (14.2) and (14.3), and obtain two reduced-form equations,

$$N^u = \tilde{N}^u(N^e; p^r, p^u) \quad \text{and} \tag{14.13}$$

$$N^e = \tilde{N}^e(N^u; p^r, p^u), \tag{14.14}$$

which, respectively, are pseudo-supply and pseudo-demand equations for urban labour. These equations incorporate the effects of endogenously determined wages within them. Now, an increase in labour supply may (by increasing the unemployment rate) lead to lower wages, which, if the wage elasticity of labour demand is high, may lead to an even greater increase in the demand for labour than in the case in which wages are fixed.

Thus, in the present model, the supply of labour in the urban sector is a function of the demand; and the demand for labour is a function of the unemployment rate, and hence, of labour supply. Consequently, there is no simple dichotomy between supply and demand that characterizes conventional neoclassical models.

Effects of Price Changes

Recall the simple model of the rural sector described in Section 14.2. A decrease in the rural price will increase the rural to urban migration. This will shift the labour supply curve downwards; that is, there will be a larger supply for a given level of urban labour demand (see the broken line in Figs. 14.1 and 14.3). In Fig. 14.1, unemployment increases but employment remains unchanged. In Fig. 14.3, the increased migration has an additional effect. It leads to more unemployment, which leads to greater productivity, which leads to more employment. Hence, corresponding to each of the stable equilibria in the initial situation, there will exist a new equilibrium with a different level of employment.

Changes in urban prices may have effects on both the supply and demand curves. The effects depend partly on how wages adjust. In the central case in which wages adjust to keep the utility of the employed unchanged, the supply curve does not shift, only the demand curve shifts up or down. If the demand curve shifts down due to a change in urban prices (as shown by the dotted line in Fig. 14.2), then there will be lower urban unemployment and lower employment.

14.5 CONCLUDING REMARKS

The objective of this chapter has been to discuss some of the critical components of modelling the urban sector of many modern-day LDCs in which the bulk of employment and wage decisions are made by private-sector firms, and where there is urban unemployment. We have argued why the conventional neoclassical model is inadequate for describing such an urban sector. We have also pointed out a variety of reasons why the market equilibrium will, in general, be inefficient. Though such inefficiencies can be fully corrected in principle, the policy instruments which are required (for example, *ad valorem* as well as specific wage taxes and subsidies for different categories of workers) are infeasible in most LDCs. It is easily possible, however, to take account of these inefficiencies, along with other relevant effects, in the analysis of taxation and pricing, as we have done in preceding chapters. Finally, this chapter highlighted some new types of relationships between urban labour demand and urban labour supply which arise as a result of firms choosing not only the level of employment (as they do in conventional neoclassical models) but also the wage-level.

15

THE SOCIAL COST OF LABOUR

15.1 INTRODUCTION

During the past two decades, there has been growing consensus on the use-fulness as well as the limitations of social cost–benefit analysis for project and expenditure evaluation in developing economies, and on the general pro-cedures for determining shadow prices for such analyses. If a new project is viewed as a perturbation in the economy, then its consequences (and hence the shadow prices) depend critically on the salient features of the economy. For instance, if the economy is open to foreign trade and there are tariffs, then the induced changes in domestic demand and supply of goods affect the public revenue from tariffs. If, on the other hand, the economy is closed, then there are general equilibrium changes in domestic prices which, in turn, affect the welfare of various individuals in the economy. For an analysis of shadow prices, therefore, it is important to identify the relevant structure of the economy.

The fact that we are interested in social cost–benefit analysis indicates that market prices may not always reflect social costs; that is, there are some im-portant distortions in the economy which need to be explicitly identified. More-over, reasonable individuals may differ over the appropriate social weights to be employed in aggregating the full consequences of a project (that is, over the appropriate social weights to be associated with the gains and losses to different individuals and to the government). Therefore, the role of social weights in determining shadow prices needs to be clearly distinguished from the role of the specification of the structural features of the economy.

The problem of determining the appropriate shadow prices for cost–benefit analysis is closely related to the problem of ascertaining the overall social consequences of particular taxation policies. While in the latter case (which has formed the focus of the book) we considered perturbations of prices and taxes from various bench-mark levels, in cost–benefit analysis we are concerned with perturbations generated by the undertaking of a public project. In this chapter we show how the general methodology developed in earlier chapters can be modified to calculate the shadow wage; that is, to evaluate the full consequences of the government's hiring of an additional worker.[1]

All the various features of the economy emphasized in our earlier

---

[1] It might be useful here to clarify our usage of the term 'shadow wage'. The shadow wage is a summary statistic which sums up all the changes in the economy due to the creation of industrial employment, multiplied by the social marginal valuation of each of these changes.

discussion are central to the determination of shadow wages. The purpose of this chapter is to illustrate the usefulness of our methodology, rather than to deal with the most comprehensive model. We therefore focus on the case of an open economy facing fixed international prices, in which the government cannot (or does not) set different prices in the two sectors and in which tariffs are fixed.[2]

15.2 THE MODEL

The investible surplus, I, is given by[3]

$$I = N^e(-w^u L^u) + (p - P)(N^e x^u - N^r Q), \qquad (15.1)$$

and the aggregate social welfare is given by the Hamiltonian

$$H = N^r W(V^r) + N^e W(V^u) + N^n W(V^n) + \delta I. \qquad (15.2)$$

As in previous chapters, the numbers N^r, N^e, and N^n respectively denote the rural population, urban employment, and urban unemployment. V^r, V^u, and V^n respectively denote the utility levels of a rural worker, an employed urban worker, and an unemployed urban worker. w^u is the urban wage rate, L^u is the fixed number of hours worked by employed urban workers, Y is urban output per employed worker, x^u is urban food consumption per employed worker, Q is food surplus per rural worker, p is the domestic price of food, and P is the international price. If N denotes the total population in the economy, then

$$N = N^r + N^e + N^n. \qquad (15.3)$$

The equilibrium in the economy is represented, as in earlier chapters, by a set of reduced-form equations. The wage determination equation is

---

The shadow wage excludes the value of the direct output contributed by the newly employed workers. As we shall see later, this statistic is more general than another summary statistic, the opportunity cost of labour, often employed in the literature, which calculates the net change in the aggregate output (exclusive of the value of the direct output contributed by the newly employed workers) due to employment creation.

[2] Implicit here is the assumption that the post-perturbation equilibrium in the economy is achieved through changes in traded quantities while the domestic prices remain unaltered. Note, however, that this is only one of many possible equilibrating mechanisms and that the calculation of shadow prices and wages can be sensitive to what the relevant equilibrating mechanism is. For an analysis of alternative equilibrating mechanisms, see Sah and Stiglitz (1985). It is also worth emphasizing that the term 'equilibrium' does not necessarily imply a conventional Walrasian equilibrium; it may also denote temporary equilibria of the kind investigated by Solow and Stiglitz (1968), Benassy (1975), and Malinvaud (1977), among others.

[3] Recalling our notation that N^e is the number of employed urban workers and x^u is the food consumption of an employed urban worker, it is apparent that (15.1) abstracts from the net tax revenue collected from the food consumption of the urban unemployed. In fact, in the analysis below, we assume that the utility of an unemployed urban worker, V^n, does not change due to the perturbation under consideration.

$$w^u = w^u(p, N^e) \,. \tag{15.4}$$

The urban wage depends on prices and urban employment (see Chapters 10 and 11 for a fuller discussion of this equation). The migration equilibrium condition is

$$N^r = N^r(p, N^e) \,. \tag{15.5}$$

Migration depends on prices and urban employment (see Chapters 13 and 14 for a fuller discussion of this equation).[4] Finally, we write the per capita industrial output as

$$Y = Y(k, L^u; p, N^e) \,, \tag{15.6}$$

where the first two arguments of the function Y continue to represent the conventional capital and labour inputs, while the last two arguments reflect all the indirect productivity effects.[5]

If the shadow wage rate is denoted by s, then[6]

$$sL^u = -\frac{1}{\delta}\frac{dH}{dN^e} + \frac{\partial(N^e Y)}{\partial N^e} \,. \tag{15.7}$$

The first term on the right-hand side of the above expression is the net social gain from employment creation. The second term represents the direct contribution of the newly employed worker. This contribution is excluded from the calculation of the shadow wage because the fruits of employment creation should not be counted while computing its cost.[7] The industrial good is the numeraire throughout.

The Shadow Wage

Using (15.1), (15.2), and (15.7), an explicit expression for the shadow wage is obtained as

[4] The sense in which the above expressions are reduced-form representations should be apparent from discussions in earlier chapters. For instance, the urban wage may also depend on the number of urban unemployed, but since the latter depends, in turn, on (p, N^e) using (15.3) and (15.5) we can represent the urban wage as (15.4).

[5] The dependence of industrial productivity on other variables in the economy is implicit in (15.6): productivity may, for instance, depend on urban wages, but urban wages depend on p and N^e. Note also that (15.6) is an aggregation over firms' production functions, each of which can be written (in a symmetric equilibrium) as $Y^i = Y^i(k^i, p, N^{ei})$ where the superscript i denotes a firm, and k^i is a firm's capital per worker. In a more general model, Y^i may also be a function of the entire distribution of industrial wages.

[6] This formulation assumes that the government directly controls N^e. If the government controls only a proportion of N^e, then increased urban government employment may, through wage effects, partially displace urban private employment. Also, our analysis focuses on evaluating projects which are of sufficiently small size that δ can be taken as fixed.

[7] We exclude only the direct contribution, however. Thus, if industrial employment creation has indirect repercussions on industrial output (for example, because of a change in workers' productivity) then these indirect effects are not excluded.

$$sL^u = w^u L^u + (P - p) Z - \frac{1}{\delta} (W^u - W^n) + \frac{\Phi\Omega}{\delta}$$

$$+ \left(1 - \frac{\beta^u}{\delta} \right) w^u L^u \varepsilon^u_{wN} - Y\sigma_N , \qquad (15.8)$$

where the notations used are as follows:

$$W^i = W (V^i)$$

denotes the social welfare corresponding to an individual's utility level V^i.

$$\beta^i = \lambda^i \, \partial W^i / \partial V^i$$

denotes the social weights on different individuals' incomes.

$$\varepsilon^u_{wN} = \partial \ln w^u / \partial \ln N^e$$

is, from (15.4), the elasticity of the urban wage with respect to urban employment.

$$\varepsilon^u_{xm} = \partial \ln x^u / \partial \ln w^u$$

is the income elasticity of an urban employed worker's consumption of the rural good.

$$\sigma_N = \partial \ln Y / \partial \ln N^e$$

is, from (15.6), the elasticity of the urban output per worker with respect to urban employment.

$$\Omega = - dN^r / dN^e \qquad (15.9)$$

is the number of rural workers who migrate out of the agricultural sector if one industrial job is created.

$$\Phi = W^r - W^n - \beta^r p X \varepsilon^r_{XA} \qquad (15.10)$$

represents the net welfare loss when one worker leaves the rural sector and joins the pool of urban unemployed (we had calculated this loss in expressions (13.8) and (13.9) in Chapter 13).

$$\varepsilon^r_{XA} = \partial \ln X / \partial \ln A > 0$$

is the elasticity of the agricultural output per rural worker with respect to the land area per rural worker. Note that $W^r - W^n$ is the direct welfare loss due to the above movement of a worker, whereas $\beta^r p X \varepsilon^u_{XA}$ represents the gain to those remaining in the rural sector from the reduced congestion on agricultural land.

$$Z = Q (1 - \varepsilon^r_{QA}) \Omega + x^u (1 + \varepsilon^u_{xm} \varepsilon^u_{wN}) \qquad (15.11)$$

is the net decrease in the supply of the agricultural good from the creation of one industrial job.

$$\varepsilon^r_{QA} = \partial \ln Q / \partial \ln A$$

is the elasticity of the agricultural surplus per rural worker with respect to the land area per rural worker. ε^r_{XA} and ε^r_{QA} depend on the scarcity of agricultural land. If land is not scarce, then $\varepsilon^r_{XA} = \varepsilon^r_{QA} = 0$. To understand (15.11), note that $Q (1 - \varepsilon^r_{QA})$ is the decrease in the surplus supplied if there is one less agricultural worker. Recalling (15.9), then, it follows that the first term on the right-hand side of (15.11) is the reduction in the agricultural surplus when one industrial job is created, while the second term represents the increase in the urban demand of the agricultural good. This is because x^u is the direct increase in demand, whereas $x^u \varepsilon^u_{xm} \varepsilon^u_{wN}$ is the indirect increase due to the change in the urban wage.

For brevity in interpreting our results, we assume that $1 > \varepsilon^r_{QA}$ (that is, if an increase in land size per person increases the per person agricultural surplus then this increase is not too large) and that $\varepsilon^u_{wN} \geq 0$ (that is, larger urban employment does not reduce the urban wage). Under these assumptions and the natural assumption that Ω in (15.9) is non-negative, it follows from (15.11) that $Z > 0$. That is: Industrial employment creation decreases net domestic agricultural surplus. Thus, if the country is currently exporting food, exports are reduced.

Interpretation of the Shadow Wage

Each of the terms in the expression for the shadow wage (15.8) represents a distinct social effect of industrial employment creation. The first term is the direct cost of the wage payment to the newly employed industrial worker. Naturally, a larger market wage implies a larger shadow wage. The meaning of the second term should be apparent by recalling from (15.11) that Z is the net decrease in the domestic supply of the agricultural good from the creation of one industrial job. This term, therefore, is the corresponding change in government revenue. Moreover, since Z is positive, it follows that this change in government revenue decreases or increases the shadow wage depending on whether the current domestic price of the agricultural good is higher or lower than the international price.

The third term is the welfare gain from hiring an unemployed worker. The next term in (15.8) represents the effect of employment creation on labour mobility. Ω migrants from the agricultural sector join the pool of the unemployed, and Φ is the net loss in welfare for each such worker, as explained in (15.10). The total welfare loss from this is $\Phi\Omega/\delta$.

The effect of employment creation on the industrial wage is felt through ε^u_{wN}. If, for example, the industrial wage increases with industrial employment, then the new project will increase the wage payment to infra-marginal industrial workers. This, in turn, makes them better off, but at the expense of public revenue. The net of these two effects is represented in the fifth term in (15.8). (The induced change in the industrial wage also affects the net shortfall in the agricultural good, as seen in expression (15.11), an effect we have already taken into account.) Finally, the loss or gain due to indirect effects on industrial productivity is represented by the last term on the right-hand side of (15.8).

Most of the effects identified above have been ignored in the literature on shadow wages. For instance, the general-equilibrium effect of industrial employment creation on public revenue has typically been ignored by assuming that there is no price distortion; that is, $p = P$. Not only is this assumption incorrect but, in fact, the price distortions in many developing economies are often very large (see, for example, Peterson 1979 and Bale and Lutz 1979). Moreover, even if the government was to set domestic prices at their socially optimal levels, as we have seen in earlier chapters, the optimal prices would generally entail deviations from the international price.

A simple example might help in understanding the practical consequences of price distortions. Suppose the domestic price of food is twice the international price, and workers spend roughly half their income on food. Assume that investment is extremely scarce (that is, δ is very large), that neither the urban wage nor productivity is sensitive to the size of urban employment (that is, $\varepsilon^u_{wN} = \sigma_N = 0$), that agricultural land is not scarce (that is, $\varepsilon^r_{XA} = \varepsilon^r_{QA} = 0$), that $\Omega = 1$ (so the number of unemployed remains unchanged), and that a worker's earnings in both sectors are roughly equal. Then, we find from (15.8) that the shadow wage is half the market wage.[8] Under the same assumptions, the shadow wage is twice the market wage if the domestic food price is half the international price. In contrast, the shadow wage equals the market wage if one ignores the general-equilibrium effects under consideration. Quite plausible parameters therefore show that the magnitude of the shadow wage will be substantially erroneous if general-equilibrium effects are not correctly taken into account.

15.3 SPECIAL CASES

A key advantage of the analysis presented above is that much of the earlier literature on the shadow wage can be viewed as special cases of our general model. We now examine several of these cases. Throughout the rest of the chapter we assume that industrial employment creation has negligible effects on the urban wage and on industrial productivity (that is, ε^u_{wN} and σ_N are close to zero). Our analysis is divided into two parts: in the first part migration from the rural sector is assumed just to equal the number of

---

[8] This is because in this case (15.8) and (15.11) yield $sL^u = w^u L^u + (P - p)(Q + x^u)$. We assume that $pX = w^u L^u$, and $px^u = px^r = w^u L^u /2$. Thus, $pQ = w^u L^u/2$ and $sL^u = w^u L^u P/p$. Therefore, $sL^u = w^u L^u/2$ if $p = 2P$.

jobs created;[9] in the second part migration may differ from employment creation.

Migration Equals Employment Creation

If the number of workers migrating from the rural to the urban sector equals the number of industrial jobs created, then from (15.9), $\Omega = 1$. Substituting this, and using the assumptions that ε^u_{wN} and σ_N are close to zero, we obtain the following from (15.8) and (15.10):

$$sL^u = w^u L^u + (P - p) Z - \frac{1}{\delta} (W^u - W^r) - \frac{\beta^r}{\delta} pX\varepsilon^r_{XA}. \qquad (15.12)$$

We now look at some special cases of (15.12).

(a) *Highly Scarce Capital.* In this case, δ is very large, and

$$sL^u = w^u L^u + (P - p) Z . \qquad (15.13)$$

If capital is highly scarce, then the shadow wage is higher (lower) than the market wage if the domestic price of the agricultural good is lower (higher) than its international price. Obviously, the shadow wage equals the market wage if there are no price distortions.

(b) *No Price Distortions.* A direct implication of (15.12) is that: In the absence of price distortions, the shadow wage is less than the market wage, so long as industrial workers are better off than agricultural workers. Other special cases considered below also employ this assumption of no price distortions.

(c) *Utilitarianism.* Utilitarianism implies that $W^i = V^i$ and $\beta^i = \lambda^i$. We denote the value of the marginal product of an agricultural worker by g. The marginal value product of an agricultural worker is the number of hours a worker works times the marginal value product of one working hour. Thus, $g = pL^r \, \partial X/\partial L^r$, where L^r is the hours worked by one rural worker. Constant returns to scale in agricultural production implies $pX = g + pA \, \partial X/\partial A$. Hence, $pX\varepsilon^r_{XA} = pX - g$ is the difference between the value of the average and marginal product of the rural worker. Then (15.12) can be rewritten as

$$sL^u = w^u L^u - \frac{1}{\delta} (V^u - V^r) - \frac{\lambda^r}{\delta} (p X - g). \qquad (15.14)$$

This corresponds to a result obtained by Little and Mirrlees (1969), Stern (1972), and Newbery (1972).

(d) *Fixed Labour Hours in the Agricultural Sector.* In addition to utilitarianism, assume that the labour hours supplied by an agricultural worker

[9] The implicit assumption here is that: (a) urban unemployment is negligible, or (b) the government can control migration. These assumptions were extensively employed in the earlier literature on shadow wages. They are, however, far less plausible for most LDCs than the view (adopted in the second set of special cases examined below) that migration is endogenously determined.

are fixed and equal to the hours supplied by an industrial worker. Then the utility of an individual can be expressed as a function of his income and the price he faces, that is: $V^r = V(p, pX)$ and $V^u = V(p, w^u L^u)$. Moreover, it is reasonable to assume that V is concave in a worker's income.[10] Expression (15.14) then yields

$$sL^u \geq \left(1 - \frac{\lambda^r}{\delta}\right) w^u L^u + \frac{\lambda^r}{\delta} g.$$

Thus, the shadow wage is not smaller than a weighted average of the market wage and the marginal product of an agricultural worker.

(*e*) *Output-Maximizing Society.* Assume that for a rural worker and for an employed urban worker, the hours of work are the same and fixed. Assume that there is no disutility from work up to this fixed level, and beyond it disutility is infinite. Assume that individuals are risk-neutral, and that the society not only is utilitarian (that is, $\beta^i = \lambda^i$) but also does not differentiate between investment and consumption. With these assumptions our model will yield the same results as those for the special case of an output-maximizing society. The corresponding results can be obtained by using

$$V^r = pX, \quad V^u = w^u L^u, \quad \text{and} \quad \lambda^i = \delta = 1. \tag{15.15}$$

Substitution of (15.15) into (15.14) yields

$$sL^u = g.$$

That is, the shadow wage equals the value of the marginal product of an agricultural worker. Under this set of assumptions, the opportunity cost of labour equals the shadow wage. This was one of the earliest views on the magnitude of the shadow wage. It implies a zero shadow wage if the marginal product of agricultural labour is zero.

Endogenous Migration: The Harris–Todaro Migration Hypothesis

A special case of the general model of labour mobility described earlier is the Harris–Todaro hypothesis, according to which a migrant from the agricultural sector has probability $N^e/(N - N^r)$ of finding an industrial job, and otherwise becomes unemployed.[11] Migration continues until the expected utility level of a potential migrant equals the utility level of an agricultural worker. This hypothesis is therefore a special case of (15.5) in which

$$NV^r(p, N^r) = N^r V^r(p, N^r) + N^e V^u(p, w^u) + (N - N^r - N^e)V^n. \tag{15.16}$$

For simplicity we assume here that the social welfare function is utilitarian,

---

[10] That is, the marginal utility of income is non-increasing in income. This implies $V^u - V^r \leq \lambda^r(w^u L^u - pX)$.

[11] See Harris and Todaro (1970) for an early statement. Our generalized description of this hypothesis was presented in ch. 13.

that is $W(V) = V$ and $\beta^i = \lambda^i$. While a more general approach is easily possible, as we shall see below, this assumption enables us to ignore the issue of defining social welfare over the *ex ante facto* versus the *ex post facto* utilities of workers. We also assume that $V^u > V^r > V^n$ (otherwise, urban unemployment, N^n, will not be positive).

Perturbing (15.16) we obtain:

$$\Omega = \frac{(V^u - V^n) + \lambda^u w^u L^u \varepsilon^u_{wN}}{(V^r - V^n) + \lambda^r p X \varepsilon^r_{XA} (N - N^r) / N^r} . \tag{15.17}$$

Substitution of the above, along with the assumption that ε^u_{wN} and σ_N are close to zero, into (15.8) yields

$$s L^u = w^u L^u + (P - p) Z - \frac{N \lambda^r}{N^r \delta} p X \varepsilon^r_{XA} \Omega . \tag{15.18}$$

We now look at two special cases of (15.18).[12] In both cases, it is assumed that there is no price distortion; that is, $p = P$.

(a) *No Congestion on Agricultural Land.* Substituting $\varepsilon^r_{XA} = 0$ and $p = P$ into (15.18), we find: The shadow wage equals the market wage regardless of society's valuation of investment versus consumption. This result reverses the presumption of the earlier literature (see Harberger 1971, Heady 1981, and Stiglitz 1974*a*, among others) that the shadow wage is smaller than the market wage, that its value is critically dependent on society's inter-temporal valuation, and that it approaches the market wage only when the social value of investment (relative to consumption) is very high.

The basic reason for this result is that migration in the present special case does not change the aggregate level of utility in the economy and, hence, the only effect of employment creation is on investment. The utility level of an agricultural worker is fixed since $\varepsilon^r_{XA} = 0$. Average utility is fixed in the urban sector since the expected utility of a migrant equals the utility of a rural worker, which is fixed. Since the only effect of creating an industrial job is on investment, which is reduced by the market wage, it follows that the shadow wage equals the market wage.

These results are particularly transparent for the special case of an output-maximizing society. Assume further that an urban unemployed person has zero income (that is $V^n = 0$). Then, the substitution of (15.15) into (15.16) yields

$$p X = \frac{N^e}{N - N^r} w^u L^u. \tag{15.19}$$

---

[12] Note that the Hamiltonian can be rewritten, using (15.16), as $NV^r + \delta I$. Expression (15.18) for the shadow wage, based on the Harris–Todaro hypothesis, and those to be derived later are thus more general than they appear. This is because the only property of the migration hypothesis which has actually been used here is that current social welfare can be represented by NV^r. The resulting expressions for the shadow wage therefore hold under any migration mechanism, provided society focuses its attention only on the welfare of agricultural workers.

Note that N^e is the number of jobs, $N - N^r$ is the number of job-seekers, and $N^e / (N - N^r)$ is the probability of getting an urban job. (15.19) thus implies that the expected income in the urban sector must equal the rural income. Since the rural income is assumed to be fixed (because there is no land congestion), (15.19) yields

$$- \frac{dN^r}{dN^e} = \frac{w^u L^u}{pX} \, .$$

Since a rural worker's income is pX, the opportunity cost of creating one urban job is

$$pX \left(- \frac{dN^r}{dN^e} \right) = w^u L^u.$$

Under the special assumptions employed in the present case, the impact on the aggregate output of creating an industrial job is the output (or income) of one agricultural worker times the number of such workers who migrate. Under the simplified version of the Harris–Todaro hypothesis relevant for the present case (in which the expected wage in the two sectors is the same), this product is just equal to the industrial wage.[13]

(*b*) *Output-Maximizing Society with Agricultural Land Congestion.* Substitution of (15.15) into (15.18) yields

$$sL^u = w^u L^u N^r (1 - \varepsilon^r_{XA}) / [N \varepsilon^r_{XA} + N^r (1 - \varepsilon^r_{XA})] \, .$$

Thus, $s < w^u L^u$, since $\varepsilon^r_{XA} < 1$ from the standard properties of the production function. This result shows that the effect of land congestion is to reduce the shadow wage (see Stiglitz 1982*a* for a parallel result).

15.4 CONCLUDING REMARKS

In this chapter we have shown how the general framework developed in this book can be used to analyse policy issues other than taxation. We have focused on the derivation of shadow wages because, though the importance of using shadow prices and wages in the evaluation of public expenditure and projects has been widely recognized in LDCs, the correct magnitude of the shadow wage—and its relationship to the market wage—have remained controversial.

Our analysis of the shadow wage has dealt explicitly with many salient features of LDCs which are important but have not received the attention they deserve. These include: (*a*) the differences between domestic and international prices (*b*) the mechanisms which determine earnings in agricultural

---

[13] For a discussion of this simple case, see Harberger (1971) and Stiglitz (1974*a*). Our analysis in this chapter is, of course, much more general and does not depend on these restrictive assumptions.

and industrial sectors (*c*) the consequences of industrial employment creation
on migration and on the welfare of those who remain in the agricultural sector (for example, through what we identify as congestion effects), and (*d*)
the effects of industrial employment creation on the productivity of the
current industrial labour-force.[14] Many of these aspects have first-order
effects on the magnitude of the shadow wage; to ignore them may lead to
misleading results. Thus, for instance, in many LDCs, induced migration
appears to be significant and the domestic prices of agricultural goods appear to be lower than the international prices. In such cases, it is appropriate
to use a shadow wage which is considerably in excess of the market wage.
The argument for a high shadow wage is further strengthened if increased
industrial employment leads to a higher urban market wage.

An important feature of this analysis is that we have identified those
reduced-form relationships for describing the economy which are central to
the determination of the shadow wage. The same reduced-form relationships
(and hence the same formulae for the shadow wage) can be specialized to
different technological assumptions (e.g. the nature of production relationships in the agricultural and industrial sectors) and institutional settings, as
well as to different behavioural hypotheses. For example, our formulae for
the shadow wage contain certain critical elasticities which can be specialized
to alternative migration hypotheses (including the Harris–Todaro case) and
to alternative hypotheses concerning wage-determination. This method has
the virtue of analytical simplicity because it provides an integrated view of
the critical determinants of the shadow wage. We have thus been able to
derive earlier results on shadow wages as special cases of our formulae, and
have also identified a number of new qualitative results concerning the relationship between the shadow wage and the market wage.

---

[14] Elsewhere (see Sah and Stiglitz 1985) we have further extended this analysis not only to
alternative equilibrating mechanisms (see n. 2) but also to alternative distributional structures
within the agricultural sector, to alternative mechanisms of urban wage-determination, and to
those cases in which domestic prices are set at socially optimal levels.

16

CONCLUDING REMARKS

16.1 SOME KEY ISSUES

This book has attempted to develop a general framework for analysing taxation policies within the context of the development process. A basic feature of this framework is its emphasis on identifying the important consequences of any given set of policies. This includes the direct effects on different individuals and on government revenue as well as the indirect effects that arise due to changes in wages, productivity, migration, and other endogenous features of the economy. With this framework, it becomes possible to isolate the efficiency consequences, and the distributional consequences of alternative policies. Among the distributional consequences are those within the rural and urban sectors, between the two sectors, and between consumption (the welfare of the current generation) and investment (the welfare of future generations). In turn, this analysis helps us to assess the relative desirability of alternative policies.

There are different concepts which one might use as a basis for identifying desirable policies. Our methodology first allows for the identification of those reforms which are Pareto-improvements. These could be viewed to be desirable regardless of one's attitudes towards inequality.[1] It then allows us to identify policies and reforms which would be desirable based on quite weak value-judgements; for example, if one viewed inequality to be undesirable (but did not hold any further opinion on the value of an increase in one person's income compared to another's), and if one treated those in the urban and rural sectors symmetrically. The identification of other types of desirable policies and reforms may depend quite sensitively on precisely how one values increases in the incomes of different individuals (for example, increases in the incomes of those in the rural sector relative to those in the urban sector, increases in the income of the rich relative to the poor, and increases in the income of the current generation relative to future generations). The last kind of analysis allows us to describe, in simple terms, properties of the optimal set of taxes and subsidies. That is, policies which, given the set of instruments available to the government, and given a social welfare function, are most desirable. An advantage of this type of analysis is that it enables the discussion of alternative policies to be conducted in a way which separates controversies over value-judgements from controversies over the consequences of the given policy.

---

[1] There is, of course, no universal agreement on this issue. Some might claim that a reform which increased everyone's income, but at the same time increased inequality, is undesirable.

Our approach thus provides a methodology for the assessment of various policies, both minor reforms and major new programmes. It explicitly incorporates:

(*a*) the range of economic features (including rigidities and organizational forms) of LDCs;

(*b*) the limitations on the set of instruments available in LDCs; and

(*c*) the limitations of data and the knowledge of the values of parameters for the policy analysis of LDCs.

We have shown that it is possible to make qualitative statements about the desirability of certain kinds of policy, simply on the basis of qualitative data. This is important because, even though it may in principle be possible to obtain much of the required data (although this is rarely the case in practice), some critical pieces may be missing. Two such examples of qualitative results are recounted below, chosen, in particular, because of the controversies among both policy-makers and economists which have surrounded these issues.

First, we have shown that, regardless of one's attitude towards inequality, there should be a presumption against policies which entail the simultaneous subsidization of some cash-crops and the taxation of other cash-crops. Similarly, there should be a presumption against the taxation of some manufactured inputs to agriculture (e.g. fertilizers, pesticides, etc.) and the subsidization of other manufactured inputs. Certainly, there are particular circumstances, noted in Chapter 9, in which such policies may be justified. However, there is no more than a loose connection between these circumstances and those under which such policies have, in fact, existed. Thus, the burden of proof should be shifted to those who advocate such policies to show that, for instance, a policy of subsidizing fertilizer while taxing a cash-crop has a desirable distributive effect, compared to the situation in which both the tax and the subsidy are eliminated, or to show that such policies do indeed induce peasants to adopt new technologies in a more equitable and efficient manner than, say, the provision of agricultural extension services.

Second, we have shown that there should also be a presumption against the imposition of differential taxes and subsidies in the urban sector. The elasticity of labour supply (on which the literature on optimal taxation has focused) is not a central problem in the urban sector of LDCs. The more important issue in LDCs is high urban wages and the resulting urban unemployment. A related issue is how urban wages change in response to changes in taxes and prices. To see the consequences, consider the simple case in which, for one reason or another, the urban wages of different groups of workers change in response to changes in taxes and prices, so that the pre-change utility levels are approximately restored. In this case, it follows that subsidization or taxation of goods in the urban sector has no useful role. This is because if the urban workers are going to end up with the same given levels of utilities, then it is more efficient to provide these utility levels at undistorted prices.

Consider now some specific settings. Urban wages may be high because by paying higher wages, workers can be made more productive; this is what is referred to as the wage–productivity hypothesis. In that case, there may be an argument for food subsidies, if the consumption of food is more closely linked to productivity than is the consumption of other commodities. But if productivity is related to the general level of consumption, food subsidies are not desirable, nor is differential subsidization or taxation of other goods.

Another possible explanation for high urban wages is union pressure and the government's need for political stability. Focusing on such explanations, many economists in the past have advised LDC governments, almost always without success, that they should lower urban wages. Some economists have gone even further; they have predicated their subsequent policy advice concerning tax policy on the assumption that the governments have already followed their earlier advice concerning wage policy. To us, this approach seems unproductive.

Other economists have suggested that in the face of high rigid urban wages, taxes can be imposed on the goods which the workers purchase, and that the real wage received by the workers can thereby be lowered. We suspect that the possibility of such indirect reductions in the real wage involves a greater naïvety on the part of the economists than on the part of the workers in the LDCs. The workers will know that their standard of living has been cut. They will respond with whatever pressures they can bring to bear on their union leaders or political representatives. If these are the pressures which sustained the high urban wage in the first place, the same pressures will lead to an increase in the nominal wage. Even with political explanations for high urban wages (such as union pressure), our presumption in favour of no taxation or subsidization in the urban sector remains valid so long as the forces that determine urban wages are based approximately on the levels of utility of workers in the urban sector.

A theme that recurs throughout the book is that tax policies have important consequences for a variety of economic variables; for prices of non-tradables, for migration, for urban wages, and for employment. To analyse the consequences of any tax policy, one must consider its ramifications, or as public-finance economists put it, the full incidence of the tax policy. This full-incidence analysis requires theories of how wage and employment decisions are made and what determines migration from the rural to the urban sector. It requires, in other words, a model of the LDC that deals with these aspects. Previous analyses have failed on this count, or have made the unrealistic assumption that tax policies have no effect on wages, employment, or migration.

An aspect of LDCs that we have emphasized is the observed variety of institutional forms and patterns of behaviour. A good model must be rich enough to accommodate this wide variety. On the other hand, there is a paucity of data in most LDCs, and so reliable estimates of critical behavioural parameters are generally unavailable. Fortunately, we have been able to address both these concerns at the same time by constructing models in which the central reduced-form relationships are identified. In this way, we have managed to reduce the number of parameters for which estimates are required to implement the model, and we have developed a theory which can easily be specialized to the particular circumstances of individual LDCs (reflecting, for instance, that there is share-cropping or that there are family farms in the rural sector).

An issue which has long been controversial is the taxation of imports and exports. Farmers do not need sophisticated analysis to realize that taxes on the exports of agricultural goods will adversely affect their interests. Such taxes can have a substantial effect on the distribution of income between town and country. It is thus not surprising that, in the late eighteenth century, the framers of the US Constitution banned export taxes. At that time, the major exports of the United States consisted of agricultural goods. Thus, this Constitutional ban was, in effect, an attempt to ensure against the efforts of the towns to redistribute income in their favour.

But the general-equilibrium effects of taxes and subsidies are not always so transparent. For instance, it would have been impossible for the framers of the US Constitution to see that other policies could have the same effect as export taxes. For instance, when the industrial North imposed a tariff on manufactured goods, the effect was similar to export taxes; namely, it redistributed income from the country (the agricultural South) to the towns of the industrial North. In most LDCs today, the workers in the rural sector are poorer than those in the urban sector. While redistribution from the country to the towns is sometimes said to contribute to political stability, it cannot easily be justified on egalitarian grounds. In many LDCs, a possible justification for the imposition of trade taxes with the foregoing effects has been that the administrative costs of doing so are less than those associated with raising revenues in other ways. But the distributive implications need also to be considered when determining the levels at which taxes should be imposed.

Though this book is primarily a contribution to economic methodology, one of the uses to which our models and analysis can be put is to examine some of the important historical controversies concerning the conflict between town and country. An example of such a controversy is the conflict, noted earlier, between the industrial North and the agricultural South in the United States. Another example is the debate in England in the early nineteenth century over the repeal of the Corn Laws. Yet another example, for which we have shown in some detail how our approach provides a new understanding, is the Soviet industrialization debate of the 1920s, which preceded the collectivization of agriculture of the Soviet Union.

Similar debates concerning the conflict between town and country have taken place, using different terminology and emphases, in a number of LDCs during the last three decades. In fact, this conflict has taken on increasing urgency as countries have attempted to raise the funds required to finance the process of development. Often what is considered to be at stake is more than just a matter of economics, or the distribution of income. What is called into question concerns more fundamental values, the nature of social institutions and styles of life. This is because the process of urbanization and industrialization changes many aspects of human relations. The risks which individuals face as a result of the process of development are more than economic risks.[2]

16.2 POLITICAL ECONOMY CONSIDERATIONS

Most LDC governments employ a range of taxes and subsidies of such complexity that it is difficult to tell who, in the end, is subsidized and who is taxed. They may appear to provide subsidies to all, but it is a truism that not everyone can be subsidized. Governments may pursue these policies out of naïvety, or as an attempt to fool each group into believing that it is being subsidized. To us, 'truth in government' is a central aspect of public policy in a democratic society. With this perspective, policies whose consequences (e.g. the final incidence) can be clearly ascertained have a distinct advantage.

This book has emphasized the central role of constraints on the set of policies available to the government. Consider for instance the constraints on the government's ability to change urban wages. Where do these constraints come from? Who imposes them? How do we know that they really are constraints? We are particularly uneasy with arbitrary constraints (e.g. the government cannot lower nominal wages directly, but can lower real wages indirectly by increasing prices). Such constraints should, as far as possible, be derived, rather than assumed. Thus, among the models we have constructed are those in which real wages are set above market-clearing levels not because of political economy constraints, but because it is in the interests of firms as well as public employers to do so. Likewise, we have argued that governments do not impose income taxes because the costs of monitoring income make such taxes administratively infeasible. Changes in economic circumstances may thus change the set of admissible taxes as well as the constraints faced by the government.

Good economic theory does not, however, entail deriving everything from first principles. Some intermediate theorizing is inevitable, and desirable. But

---

[2] For example, those brought up in an environment of continuing change may come to value change as a virtue in its own right, while those brought up in more stable environments may value stability as a virtue in its own right. See Scitovsky (1976) for a discussion of such aspects of human behaviour.

care must be exercised. Thus, the wages may be above market-clearing levels for reasons other than the efficiency-wage model. However, wages may still change when taxes change, and it is imperative to develop a theory which takes that into account, as we have done here.

16.3 THE POLICY PREDICAMENT

Finally, we discuss a central predicament facing all those economists who are involved in policy analysis and policy comparisons. What assumptions should they make about government behaviour? At one extreme, there are those who hold that all analyses of desirable policies and reforms are irrelevant. Governments are actors, just as firms and individuals are. Economists can only describe how governments behave. They can attempt to predict what governments will do. But it makes no more sense to ask what the government should do, than to ask whether a consumer should spend a dollar on food or on clothing. At the other extreme, there are those who prescribe policies as if the government will follow all of their dictates, in spite of the ample evidence that governments are selective listeners. Thus, the policy adviser may say that differential taxation of goods is desirable, and then describe precisely how to determine which goods should be subsidized or taxed and at what rates. However, the government may only listen to the first part of the advice, and then set differential subsidy- or tax-rates at levels quite different from those prescribed by the adviser. In the past, differential taxation has been used by one region or group to discriminate against another. In some cases, discrimination has been the consequence, even if it was not the objective, of differential taxation. Should the policy adviser take such experiences into account? Should they make him or her wary about recommending differential taxation?

While both of these views are important, the present book is based on a third view which is orthogonal to them. The view here is that one of the determinants of the set of policies that are implemented in a country is the knowledge base that currently exists for examining the consequences of various policies and for identifying (from different points of view, some of which may be hypothetical) the nature of desirable policies. Such a knowledge base has the potential of informing and clarifying the debates on policies which are a part of the policy formulation process in most democratic societies. The presence of such a knowledge base seldom guarantees that good policies will be chosen, but its absence is likely to lead to bad policies. This book can be viewed as an attempt to add, from the side of the economic discipline, to the knowledge base concerning taxation policies in LDCs.

REFERENCES

AKERLOF, G. (1984) 'Gift Exchange and Efficiency Wage Theory: Four Views', *American Economic Review Papers and Proceedings* 74: 79–83.

ALLEN, F. (1982) 'Optimal Linear Income Taxation with General Equilibrium Effects on Wages', *Journal of Public Economics* 17: 135–43.

—— (1985) 'On the Fixed Nature of Sharecropping Contracts', *Economic Journal* 95: 30–48.

ARNOTT, R. and STIGLITZ, J. E. (1985) 'Labor Turnover, Wage Structures, and Moral Hazard', *Journal of Labor Economics* 3: 434–62.

ARROW, K. J. and KURZ, M. (1970) *Public Investment, the Rate of Return, and Optimal Fiscal Policy*, Johns Hopkins University Press, Baltimore.

ATKINSON, A. B. and STIGLITZ, J. E. (1972) 'The Structure of Indirect Taxation and Economic Efficiency', *Journal of Public Economics* 1: 97–119.

—— and——(1976) 'The Design of Tax Structure: Direct versus Indirect Taxation', *Journal of Public Economics* 6: 55–75.

—— and——(1980) *Lectures on Public Economics*, McGraw-Hill, New York.

BALAND, J.-M. (1989) 'The Economics of Price Scissors: A Note', Working Paper, University of Namur, Namur Belgium.

BALE, M. D. and LUTZ, E. (1979) 'Price Distortions in Agriculture and their Effects: An International Comparison', Staff Working Paper 359, The World Bank, Washington, DC.

BARDHAN, P. K. (1970) *Economic Growth, Development, and Foreign Trade*, Wiley, New York.

BARKER, R. and HAYAMI, Y. (1976) 'Price Support versus Input Subsidy for Food Self-sufficiency in Developing Countries', *American Journal of Agricultural Economics* 58: 617–28.

BARNUM, H. N. and SQUIRE, L. (1979) *A Model of an Agricultural Household*, Johns Hopkins University Press, Baltimore.

BAUMOL, W. J. and BRADFORD, D. F. (1970) 'Optimal Departures from Marginal Cost Pricing', *American Economic Review* 60: 265–83.

BEHRMAN, J. R. (1968) *Supply Response in Underdeveloped Agriculture: A Case Study of Four Major Annual Crops in Thailand, 1937–1963*, North-Holland, Amsterdam.

BENASSY, J. P. (1975) 'Neo-Keynesian Disequilibrium Theory in a Monetary Economy', *Review of Economic Studies* 42: 503–23.

BERTRAND, T. (1980) 'Thailand: Case Study of Agricultural Input and Output Pricing', Staff Working Paper No. 385, The World Bank, Washington, DC.

BLISS, C. and STERN, N. (1978) 'Productivity, Wages and Nutrition', *Journal of Development Economics* 5: 331–98.

BLITZER, C., DASGUPTA, P., and STIGLITZ, J. E. (1981) 'Project Appraisal and Foreign Exchange Constraints', *Economic Journal* 91: 58–74.

BLOMQVIST, A. (1986) 'The Economics of Price Scissors: Comment', *American Economic Review* 76: 1188–91.

BOITEUX, M. (1956) 'Sur la gestion des monopoles publics astreints à l'équilibre budgétaire', *Econometrica* 24: 22–40.

BREWER, A. (1988) 'The Dynamic Economics of Price Scissors', Working Paper, University of Bristol, Bristol, UK.

BUKHARIN, N. I. (1920) *Economics of the Transformation Period*, Bergman Publishers, New York, 1971.

CALVO, G. (1979) 'Quasi-Walrasian Theories of Unemployment', *American Economic Review* 69: 102–7.

—— and PHELPS, E. (1977) 'Indexation Issues: Appendix: Employment Contingent Wage Contracts', *Journal of Monetary Economics* 5, Supplement, 160–8.

CARTER, M. (1986) 'The Economics of Price Scissors: Comment', *American Economic Review* 76: 1192–4.

CORLETT, W. J. and HAGUE, D. C. (1953) 'Complementarity and the Excess Burden of Taxation', *Review of Economic Studies* 21: 21–30.

DALTON, H. (1954) *Principles of Public Finance*, Routledge and Kegan Paul, London.

DASGUPTA, P. and RAY, D. (1986) 'Inequality as a Determinant of Malnutrition and Unemployment: Theory', *Economic Journal* 96: 1011–34.

—— and —— (1987) 'Inequality as a Determinant of Malnutrition and Unemployment: Policy', *Economic Journal* 97: 177–88.

DEATON, A. (1981) 'Optimal Taxes and the Structure of Preferences', *Econometrica* 49: 1245–60.

DIAMOND, P. A. (1975) 'A Many-Person Ramsey Tax Rule', *Journal of Public Economics* 4: 335–42.

—— and MIRRLEES, J. A. (1971) 'Optimal Taxation and Public Production I: Production Efficiency' and 'Optimal Taxation and Public Production II: Tax Rules', *American Economic Review* 61: 8–27 and 261–78.

DIXIT, A. K. (1968) 'Optimal Development in the Labour-Surplus Economy', *Review of Economic Studies* 35: 23–34.

—— (1969) 'Marketable Surplus and Dual Development', *Journal of Economic Theory* 1: 203–19.

—— (1971) 'Short-run Equilibrium and Shadow Prices in the Dual Economy', *Oxford Economic Papers* 23: 384–400.

—— (1973) 'Models of Dual Economies', in J. A. Mirrlees and N. H. Stern (eds.) *Models of Economic Growth*, Wiley, New York, 325–52.

—— and STERN, N. H. (1974) 'Determinants of Shadow Prices in Open Dual Economies', *Oxford Economic Papers* 26: 42–53.

DOBB, M. H. (1966) *Soviet Economic Development since 1917*, Routledge and Kegan Paul, London.

DORFMAN, R. (1989) 'Thomas Robert Malthus and David Ricardo', *Journal of Economic Perspectives* 3: 153–64.

EATON, J. and GERSOVITZ, M. (1981) 'Debt with Potential Repudiation: Theoretical and Empirical Analysis', *Review of Economic Studies* 48: 289–309.

——, ——, and STIGLITZ, J. E. (1986) 'The Pure Theory of Country Risk', *European Economic Review* 30: 481–513.

THE ECONOMIST (1991) ' A Map Up Here, in the Mind', June 29, London, 16.

EDGEWORTH, F. Y. (1897) 'The Pure Theory of Taxation', *Economic Journal* 7: 46–70, 226–38, and 550–71.

ELLMAN, M. J. (1975) 'Did the Agricultural Surplus Provide the Resources for the Increase in Investment in the USSR during the First Five Year Plan?' *Economic Journal* 85: 844–63.

ELLMAN, M. J. (1979) *Socialist Planning*, Cambridge University Press, Cambridge.

—— (1987) 'Collectivisation and Soviet Investment in 1928–32 Revisited', Working Paper, University of Amsterdam, Amsterdam.

ERLICH, A. (1960) *The Soviet Industrialization Debate*, Harvard University Press, Cambridge, MA.

EVENSON, R. E. (1986) 'The Production and Transfer of Technology', Working Paper, Yale University, New Haven, CT.

FEI, J.C. and RANIS, G. (1964) *Development of the Labor Surplus Economy: Theory and Policy*, Irwin, Homewood, IL.

FELDSTEIN, M. S. (1972) 'Distributional Equity and the Optimal Tax Structure of Public Prices', *American Economic Review* 62: 32–6.

FIELDS, G. (1987) 'Public Policy and the Labour Market in Developing Countries', in D. M. G. NEWBERY and N. H. STERN (eds.) *The Theory of Taxation for Developing Countries*, Oxford University Press, Oxford, 264–77.

FILTZER, D. (1979) (ed.) *The Crisis of Soviet Industrialization: Selected Essays*, M. E. Sharpe, White Plains, NY.

FRIEDMAN, M. (1952) 'The "Welfare" Effects of an Income Tax and an Excise Tax', *Journal of Political Economy* 60: 25–33.

GRAAFF, J. de V. (1957) *Theoretical Welfare Economics*, Cambridge University Press, London.

GREGORY, P. and ANTEL, J. (1991) 'Agricultural Surplus Models and Peasant Behavior: Soviet Agriculture in the 1920's', Working Paper, University of Houston, Houston, TX.

GREGORY, P. and STUART, R. C. (1981) *Soviet Economic Structure and Performance*, Harper and Row, New York.

HALL, R. (1975) 'The Rigidity of Wages and the Persistence of Unemployment', *Brookings Papers on Economic Activities*: 301–35.

HARBERGER, A. (1962) 'The Incidence of the Corporation Income Tax', *Journal of Political Economy* 70: 215–40.

—— (1971) 'On Measuring the Social Opportunity Cost of Labor', *International Labor Review* 103: 559–79.

HARRIS, J. R. and TODARO, M. P. (1970) 'Migration, Unemployment, and Development: A Two-Sector Analysis', *American Economic Review* 60: 126–42.

HEADY, C. J. (1981) 'Shadow Wages and Induced Migration', *Oxford Economic Papers* 33: 108–21.

HOFF, K. and STIGLITZ, J. E. (1990) 'Imperfect Information and Rural Credit Markets—Puzzles and Policy Perspectives', *World Bank Economic Review* 4: 235–50.

HORNBY, J. M. (1968) 'Investment and Trade Policy in the Dual Economy', *Economic Journal* 78: 96–107.

JANVRY, A. de and SUBBARAO, K. (1986) *Agricultural Price Policy and Income Distribution in India*, Oxford University Press, New Delhi.

KALHON, A. S. and TYAGI, D. S. (1980) 'Inter-Sector Terms of Trade', *Economic and Political Weekly* 15: *A*173–84, Bombay.

KASER, M. (1969) 'A Volume Index of Soviet Foreign Trade', *Soviet Studies* 20: 523–6.

KATZ, M. L. (1984) 'Nonuniform Pricing With Unobservable Numbers of Purchases', *Review of Economic Studies* 51: 461–70.

KHAN, M. A. (1980) 'The Harris–Todaro Hypothesis and the Heckscher–Ohlin–Samuelson Trade Model', *Journal of International Economics* 10: 527–47.

—— and CHAUDHURI, T. D. (1985) 'Development Policies in LDC's with Several Ethnic Groups: A Theoretical Analysis', *Zeitschrift für Nationalökonomie* 45: 1–19.

KRUEGER, A. O. (1990) 'The Political Economy of Agricultural Pricing Policies', Working Paper, Duke University, Durham, NC.

LAU, L. J. (1978) 'Some Applications of Profit Functions', in M. Fuss and D. McFadden (eds.) *Production Economics: A Dual Approach to Theory and Applications*, vol. 1, North-Holland, Amsterdam, 133–216.

——, LIN W. L., and YOTOPOULOS, P. A. (1978) 'The Linear Logarithmic Expenditure System: *An Application to Consumption–Leisure Choice*', Econometrica 46: 843–68.

LAZEAR, E. P. and ROSEN, S. (1981) 'Rank-Order Tournaments as Optimum Labor Contracts', *Journal of Political Economy* 89: 841–64.

LEIBENSTEIN, H. (1957) *Economic Backwardness and Economic Growth*, Wiley, New York.

LENIN, V. I. (1919) 'Economics and Politics in the Era of the Dictatorship of the Proletariat', in *Selected Works,* vol. 3, International Publishers, New York, 1967, 274–82.

—— (1921) 'The Tax in Kind', in *Selected Works*, vol. 3, International Publishers, New York, 1967, 583–614.

LI, D. and TSUI, K. Y. (1987) 'The Generalized Efficiency Wage Hypothesis and the Scissors Problem', Working Paper, University of Guelph, Guelph, Canada.

LIPSEY, R. G. and LANCASTER, K. (1956–7) 'The General Theory of Second Best', *Review of Economic Studies* 24: 11–32.

LIPTON, M. (1977) *Why Poor People Stay Poor*, Harvard University Press, Cambridge, MA.

—— (1984) 'Urban Bias Revisited', *Journal of Development Studies* 20: 139–66.

LITTLE, I. M. D. (1950) A *Critique of Welfare Economics,* Clarendon Press, Oxford.

—— and MIRRLEES, J. A. (1969) *Manual of Industrial Project Analysis in Developing Countries*, vol. 2, Development Centre of the Organization for Economic Co-operation and Development, Paris.

MCLURE, C. E., JR. (1971) 'The Theory of Tax Incidence with Imperfect Factor Mobility', *Finanzarchiv* 30: 27–48.

—— (1974) 'A Diagrammatic Exposition of the Harberger Model with One Immobile Factor', *Journal of Political Economy* 82: 56–82.

MALINVAUD, E. (1977) *The Theory of Unemployment Reconsidered*, Blackwells, Oxford.

MARCHAND, M., MINTZ, J., and PESTIEAU, P. (1983) 'Public Production and Shadow Pricing in a Model of Disequilibrium in Labor and Capital Markets', Centre for Operations Research and Econometrics Discussion Paper No. 8315, Louvain-la-Neuve, Belgium.

MARX, K. (1867) *Capital*, vol. 1, International Publishers, New York, 1967.

—— and ENGELS, F. (1848) 'Manifesto of the Communist Party' in *Karl Marx and Friedrich Engels, Collected Works*, vol. 6, International Publishers, New York, 1961, 477–519.

MEADE, J. E. (1955) *Trade and Welfare: Mathematical Supplement*, Oxford University Press, Oxford.

MIRRLEES, J. A. (1971) 'An Exploration in the Theory of Optimum Income Taxation', *Review of Economic Studies* 38: 175–208.

MIRRLEES, J. A. (1975) 'A Pure Theory of Underdeveloped Economies', in L. G. Reynolds (ed.) *Agriculture in Development Theory*, Yale University Press, New Haven, CT, 84–106.

—— (1983) 'Market Prices and Shadow Prices', mimeo, Nuffield College, Oxford.

MITRA, A. (1977) *The Terms of Trade and Class Relations*, Frank Cass, London.

MODY, A. (1981) 'Financing of Modern Economic Growth: The Historical Role of Agricultural Resources', Working Paper No. 121, Centre for Development Studies, Trivandrum, Kerala, India.

NALEBUFF, B. J. and STIGLITZ, J. E. (1983) 'Prizes and Incentives: Towards a General Theory of Compensation and Competition', *Bell Journal of Economics* 14: 21–43.

NEWBERY, D. M. G. (1972) 'Public Policy in the Dual Economy', *Economic Journal* 82: 567–90.

—— (1974) 'The Robustness of Equilibrium Analysis in the Dual Economy', *Oxford Economic Papers* 26: 32–41.

—— and STIGLITZ, J. E. (1981) *The Theory of Commodity Price Stabilization*, Oxford University Press, Oxford.

NOVE, A. (1965) 'Introduction', in E. Preobrazhensky, *The New Economics*, Clarendon Press, Oxford.

OSBAND, K. (1985) 'Taxing the Peasants: Soviet Public Finance and the End of NEP', Working Paper, Russian Research Center, Harvard University, Cambridge, MA.

PETERSON, W. L. (1979) 'International Farm Prices and the Social Cost of Cheap Food Policies', *American Journal of Agricultural Economics* 61: 12–21.

PREOBRAZHENSKY, E. (1921) 'The Outlook for the New Economic Policy', in D. Filtzer (ed.) *The Crisis of Soviet Industrialization: Selected Essays*, M. E. Sharpe, White Plains, NY, 1979, 3–19.

—— (1926) *The New Economics*, Clarendon Press, Oxford, 1965.

RAMSEY, F. P. (1927) 'A Contribution to the Theory of Taxation', *Economic Journal* 37: 47–61.

ROBERTS, K. (1982) 'Desirable Fiscal Policies under Keynesian Unemployment', *Oxford Economic Papers* 34: 1–22.

SAH, R. K. (1978) 'Egalitarian Commodity Taxes', Working Paper, Economic Research Unit, University of Pennsylvania, Philadelphia.

—— (1982) 'A Welfare-based Determination of Urban–Rural Prices', paper presented at the World Bank Conference on Public Economics, Washington, DC.

—— (1983a) 'Analysis of Intra-Household Consumption Patterns: A Methodology and its Implementation', Center for Analysis of Developing Economies Research Paper, University of Pennsylvania, Philadelphia.

—— (1983b) 'How Much Redistribution is Possible Through Commodity Taxes?' *Journal of Public Economics* 20: 89–101.

—— (1987) 'Queues, Rations and Market: Comparisons of Outcomes for the Poor and the Rich', *American Economic Review* 77: 69–77.

—— and SRINIVASAN, T. N. (1988) 'Distributional Consequences of Rural Food Levy and Subsidized Urban Rations', *European Economic Review* 32: 141–59.

—— and STIGLITZ, J. E. (1984) 'The Economics of Price Scissors', *American Economic Review* 74: 125–38.

—— and —— (1985) 'The Social Cost of Labor and Project Evaluation: A General Approach', *Journal of Public Economics* 28: 135–63.

SAH, R. K. and STIGLITZ, J. E. (1986) 'The Economics of Price Scissors: Reply', *American Economic Review* 76: 1195–9.

—— and —— (1987a) 'Price Scissors and the Structure of the Economy', *Quarterly Journal of Economics* 102: 109–34.

—— and —— (1987b) 'The Taxation and Pricing of Agricultural and Industrial Goods in Developing Economies', in D. M. G. Newbery and N. H. Stern (eds.) *The Theory of Taxation for Developing Countries*, Oxford University Press, Oxford, 426–61.

—— and WEITZMAN, M. L. (1991) 'A Proposal for Using Incentive Pre-commitments in Public Enterprise Funding', *World Development* 19: 595–605.

SALOP, S. C. (1973) 'Wage Differentials in a Dynamic Theory of the Firm', *Journal of Economic Theory* 6: 321–44.

SCHULTZ, T. W. (1978) *Distortions of Agricultural Incentives*, Indiana University Press, Bloomington, IN.

—— (1987) 'A Long View of the Economic Value of Agricultural Research', Working Paper, University of Chicago, Chicago.

SCITOVSKY, T. (1945) 'Some Consequences of the Habit of Judging Quality by Price', *Review of Economic Studies* 12: 100–5.

—— (1976) *The Joyless Economy*, Oxford University Press, Oxford.

SEN, A. K. (1968) *Choice of Techniques*, Blackwells, Oxford.

—— (1972) 'Control Areas and Accounting Prices: An Approach to Economic Evaluation', *Economic Journal* 82: 486–501.

SHAPIRO, C. and STIGLITZ, J. E. (1984) 'Equilibrium Unemployment as a Worker Discipline Device', *American Economic Review* 74: 433–44.

SELDEN, T. M. (1989) 'The Optimal Design of Famine Relief in a Dual Economy', Working Paper, Syracuse University, Syracuse, NY.

SINGH, I., SQUIRE, L., and STRAUSS, J. (1986) 'A Survey of Agricultural Household Models: Recent Findings and Policy Implications', *World Bank Economic Review* 1: 149–80.

SOLOW, R. M. and STIGLITZ, J. E. (1968) 'Output, Employment, and Wages in the Short Run', *Quarterly Journal of Economics* 82: 537–60.

SPULBER, N. (1964) *Foundations of Soviet Strategy for Economic Growth*, Indiana University Press, Bloomington, IN.

STALIN, J. (1926) *Problems of Leninism*, Progress Publishers, Moscow, 1954.

STERN, N. H. (1972) 'Optimum Development in a Dual Economy', *Review of Economic Studies* 39: 171–84.

—— (1982) 'Optimum Taxation with Errors in Administration', *Journal of Public Economics* 17: 181–211.

STIGLITZ, J. E. (1969) 'Rural–Urban Migration, Surplus Labor and the Relationship Between Urban and Rural Wages', *East African Economic Review* 1–2: 1–27.

—— (1974a) 'Alternative Theories of Wage Determination and Unemployment in LDCs—I: The Labor Turnover Model', *Quarterly Journal of Economics* 88: 194–227.

—— (1974b) 'Incentives and Risk Sharing in Sharecropping', *Review of Economic Studies* 41: 219–56.

—— (1976a) 'The Efficiency Wage Hypothesis, Surplus Labour, and the Distribution of Income in LDCs', *Oxford Economic Papers* 28: 185–207.

STIGLITZ, J. E. (1976*b*) 'Prices and Queues as Screening Devices in Competitive Markets', IMSSS Technical Report No. 212, Stanford University, Stanford, CA.

—— (1982*a*) 'Alternative Theories of Wage Determination and Unemployment: The Efficiency Wage Model', in M. Gersovitz *et al.* (eds.) *The Theory and Practice of Development*, Allen and Unwin, London, 78–106.

—— (1982*b*) 'Self-Selection and Pareto Efficient Taxation', *Journal of Public Economics* 17: 213–40.

—— (1982*c*) 'The Structure of Labor Markets and Shadow Prices in LDCs', in R. H. Sabot (ed.) *Migration and the Labor Market in Developing Countries*, Westview Press, Boulder, CO, 13–63.

—— (1985) 'Equilibrium Wage Distributions', *Economic Journal* 95: 595–618.

—— (1986) 'Theories of Wage Rigidities', in J. L. Butkiewicz *et al.* (eds.) *Keynes' Economic Legacy: Contemporary Economic Theories*, Praeger, New York, 153–206.

—— (1987*a*) 'Pareto Efficient and Optimal Taxation and the New New Welfare Economics', in A. Auerbach and M. Feldstein (eds.) *Handbook of Public Economics*, North-Holland, Amsterdam, 991–1042.

—— (1987*b*) 'Technical Change and Taxation', prepared for the conference on Tax Policy in the Twenty-First Century, Washington, DC.

—— (1987*c*) 'The Wage–Productivity Hypothesis: Its Economic Consequences and Policy Implications', in M. Boskin (ed.) *Modern Developments in Public Finance: Essays in Honor of Arnold Harberger*, Blackwells, Oxford (forthcoming).

—— (1987*d*) 'The Causes and Consequences of the Dependence of Quality on Prices', *Journal of Economic Literature* 25: 1–48.

—— (1988) *Economics of the Public Sector*, 2nd. edn., W. W. Norton & Co., New York.

—— (1990) 'Peer Monitoring and Credit Markets', *World Bank Economic Review* 4: 351–66.

—— and DASGUPTA, P. S. (1971) 'Differential Taxation, Public Goods and Economic Efficiency', *Review of Economic Studies* 38: 151–74.

—— and WEISS, A. (1981) 'Credit Rationing in Markets With Imperfect Information', *American Economic Review* 71: 393–410.

—— and —— (1986) 'Credit Rationing and Collateral', in J. Edwards *et al.* (eds.) *Recent Developments in Corporate Finance*, Cambridge University Press, New York, 101–35.

STRAUSS, J. (1986) 'Does Better Nutrition Raise Farm Productivity?' *Journal of Political Economy* 94: 297–320.

SWARUP, R. (1954) *Communism and Peasantry*, Prachi Prakashan, Calcutta.

TOLLEY, G. S., THOMAS, V., and WONG, C. M. (1982) *Agricultural Price Policies and the Developing Countries*, Johns Hopkins University Press, Baltimore.

TROTSKY, L. (1909) *1905*, Random House, New York, 1971.

VANDERBILT, J. (1734) *Money Answers All Things*, London.

WEISS, A. (1980) 'Job Queues and Layoffs in Labor Markets with Flexible Wages', *Journal of Political Economy* 88: 526–38.

YELLEN, J. L. (1984) 'Efficiency Wage Models of Unemployment', *American Economic Review Papers and Proceedings* 74: 200–5.

YOTOPOULOS, P. A. and NUGENT, J. B. (1976) *Economics of Development*, Harper and Row, New York.

INDEX